Childrens
World
Atlas

Children's World Atlas

Malcolm Watson

Consultant: Clive Carpenter

Miles Kelly

First published in 2007 by Miles Kelly Publishing Ltd
Harding's Barn, Bardfield End Green, Thaxted, Essex, CM6 3PX, UK

Copyright © Miles Kelly Publishing Ltd 2007

This edition updated 2018, printed 2019

2 4 6 8 10 9 7 5 3

Publishing Director Belinda Gallagher
Creative Director Jo Cowan
Editorial Director Rosie Neave
Editors Becky Miles, Amanda Askew
Editorial Assistant Carly Blake
Designers Simon Lee, Elaine Wilkinson
Cover Designer Simon Lee
Image Manager Liberty Newton
Production Elizabeth Collins, Jennifer Brunwin-Jones
Reprographics Stephan Davis, Callum Ratcliffe-Bingham
Assets Lorraine King

ISBN 978-1-78617-843-5 Hardback
ISBN 978-1-78617-844-2 Paperback

Printed in India

British Library Cataloguing-in-Publication Data
A catalogue record for this book is available from the British Library

All information correct at time of going to press

Made with paper from a sustainable forest

www.mileskelly.net

Contents

Using the atlas

Divided into continental areas, this atlas explores the world with amazing facts, statistics and photographs. Highly detailed maps show important cultural and geographical features, such as major towns, places of interest, mountain ranges and rivers.

1 Graticule
The coloured frame that runs around each map. It changes colour for each continental area and provides grid references that enable you to locate features on the map easily.

2 Main heading
Introduces the main countries on the page.

3 Locator globe
Highlights where in the world the countries are.

4 Introduction
Gives an insight into some of the countries that are mapped.

5 Scale
Shows the scale of the map in kilometres and miles.

6 Map
Shows towns, territories and islands, plus physical features such as mountain ranges.

7 Did You Know?
Amazing facts about people and places.

8 Image
Each photograph is accompanied by a detailed caption.

North Africa

4 The Sahara Desert dominates this region at 6000 km in width and 2000 km from north to south. Only a narrow strip of land stands next to the Mediterranean Sea, but the fertile valleys of the Atlas Mountains and the banks of the Nile river have enough water to grow crops.

Algeria, Libya and Tunisia have become wealthy by selling oil and natural gas to Europe. Egypt was the richest country in the world when the pharaohs ruled more than 3000 years ago. Egypt's well-preserved tombs and temples, especially the Great Pyramid of Giza, are a tourist attraction.

7 Did You Know?
The Sahara Desert region was wet and fertile 8000 years ago. As the climate has become drier, the desert has expanded.

8 In north Africa, many civilizations live in fortified cities, or ksars. *Aït Benhaddou* is situated near Marrakech [E2], Morocco. Few families live here now as they have moved to modern villages nearby. Scenes from films including Alexander (2004) and The Mummy (1999) have been shot here.

9 In the next minute...
...the Sun will evaporate the equivalent of 110 million bottles of water from the Nile river.

KEY TO MAPS

Country border	State border	Disputed border	Country capital	State capital	Town
		Tarfaya WESTERN	**Madrid** ⬤	Lincoln ■	• Rock Springs

Desert	Highest peak	River	Dependency/territory	Research station	Place of interest
S A H A R A	*Tahat Peak* *2918 m*	*Amazon*	*FALKLAND ISLANDS* (UK)	Casey (Australia)	◆ *Mount* *Rushmore*

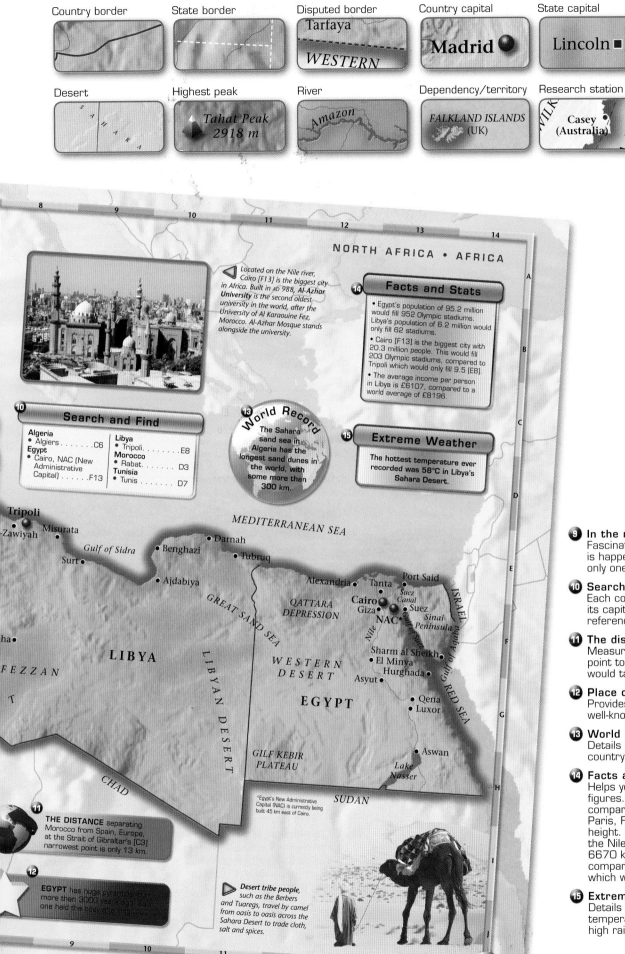

NORTH AFRICA • AFRICA

Located on the Nile river, Cairo [F13] is the biggest city in Africa. Built in AD 988, **Al-Azhar University** is the second oldest university in the world, after the University of Al Karaouine Fez, Morocco. Al-Azhar Mosque stands alongside the university.

14 Facts and Stats

• Egypt's population of 95.2 million would fill 952 Olympic stadiums. Libya's population of 6.2 million would only fill 62 stadiums.

• Cairo [F13] is the biggest city with 20.3 million people. This would fill 203 Olympic stadiums, compared to Tripoli which would only fill 9.5 [E8].

• The average income per person in Libya is £6107, compared to a world average of £8196.

10 Search and Find

Algeria	Libya
• Algiers C6	• Tripoli E8
Egypt	**Morocco**
• Cairo, NAC (New Administrative Capital) F13	• Rabat D3
	Tunisia
	• Tunis D7

13 World Record
The Sahara sand sea in Algeria has the longest sand dunes in the world, with some more than 300 km.

15 Extreme Weather
The hottest temperature ever recorded was 58°C in Libya's Sahara Desert.

MEDITERRANEAN SEA

Tripoli
-Zawiyah •Misurata
Gulf of Sidra •Darnah
Surt •Benghazi •Tubruq
•Ajdabiya

Alexandria •Tanta Port Said
QATTARA Suez Canal
DEPRESSION **Cairo**
Giza •Suez
NAC★ Sinai Peninsula

GREAT SAND SEA ISRAEL

ha•
FEZZAN LIBYA LIBYAN DESERT WESTERN DESERT
Nile Sharm al Sheikh
•El Minya
Hurghada
Asyut•

EGYPT Gulf of Suez Gulf of Aqaba RED SEA

•Qena
•Luxor

GILF KEBIR PLATEAU •Aswan

CHAD Lake Nasser

SUDAN

*Egypt's New Administrative Capital (NAC) is currently being built 45 km east of Cairo.

11 THE DISTANCE separating Morocco from Spain, Europe, at the Strait of Gibraltar's [C3] narrowest point is only 13 km.

12 EGYPT has huge pyramids built more than 3000 years ago. Each one held the body of a king.

Desert tribe people, such as the Berbers and Tuaregs, travel by camel from oasis to oasis across the Sahara Desert to trade cloth, salt and spices.

9 In the next minute...
Fascinating information about what is happening across the world in only one minute.

10 Search and Find
Each country or state is listed with its capital city and a grid reference.

11 The distance...
Measures the distance from one point to another and how long it would take to travel.

12 Place of interest
Provides extra information about a well-known sight or attraction.

13 World Record
Details a world record that a country holds.

14 Facts and Stats
Helps you to understand facts and figures. The highest peaks are compared to the Eiffel Tower in Paris, France, which is 320 m in height. Rivers are compared to the Nile river, Africa, which is 6670 km in length. Population is compared to an Olympic stadium, which would hold 100,000 people.

15 Extreme Weather
Details the highest and lowest temperatures, dramatic storms or high rainfall.

Planet Earth

Earth is a huge ball of rock with two thirds of its surface covered by seas and oceans. The third planet from the Sun in the Solar System, Earth is the only planet where life is known to exist, due to an atmosphere rich in oxygen and the water on its surface. Beneath the Earth's thin, solid crust is the liquid mantle, and at the centre is the core. The outer part of the core is liquid, but the inner core is solid metal.

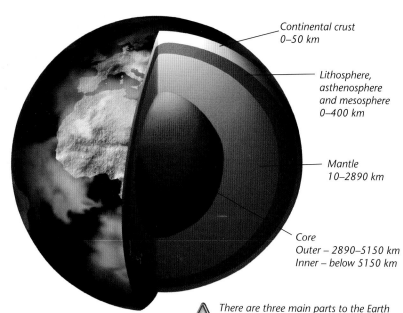

Continental crust
0–50 km

Lithosphere, asthenosphere and mesosphere
0–400 km

Mantle
10–2890 km

Core
Outer – 2890–5150 km
Inner – below 5150 km

There are three main parts to the Earth – the crust, mantle and core. Although the inner core reaches a temperature of 7000°C, it remains solid because the pressure is 6000 times greater than on the surface.

SPINNING EARTH

The Earth spins on its axis – an imaginary line through its centre – at a speed of more than 1600 km/h. It doesn't spin straight up, but leans to one side. As the Earth spins, the view of the Sun from different places on Earth constantly changes. This brings day and night, and the seasons.

In December, the South Pole leans towards the Sun. Places in the southern half of the world have summer. At the same time, places in the northern half have winter.

Seasons

There are four seasons – spring, summer, autumn and winter. Each season brings a change in temperature and weather. The changes in the seasons occur because the Earth tilts towards the Sun. When the Northern Hemisphere tilts towards the Sun, the northern part of the world has summer and the south has winter. Six months later, the opposite occurs – the Southern Hemisphere tilts towards the Sun. Then the north has winter and the south has summer. The tropics around the centre of the Earth are slightly different. They only have two seasons – wet and dry.

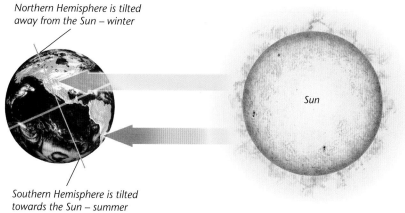

Northern Hemisphere is tilted away from the Sun – winter

Sun

Southern Hemisphere is tilted towards the Sun – summer

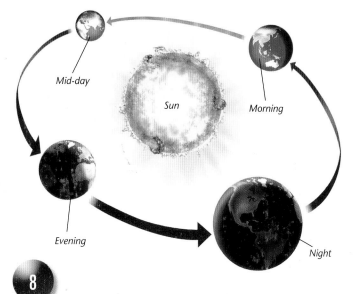

Mid-day

Sun

Morning

Evening

Night

When it is daylight on the half of the Earth facing towards the Sun, it is night on the half of the Earth facing away from it. As the Earth rotates, so the day and night halves shift gradually around the world.

Night and day

The Earth spins a complete turn on its axis every 24 hours. This gives us night and day. The Sun is the source of light for daytime. When it is night, it is dark because the Sun is shining on the opposite side of the Earth. When it is evening or early morning, the Sun is moving away or towards our part of the Earth.

Shaping the land

The Earth's crust is made up of pieces called tectonic plates, which are constantly moving, changing the shape of the land. This can create mountains and volcanoes, as well as cause natural disasters, such as earthquakes. Rocks can also be broken down or worn away by the weather, such as wind and rain, or by the movement of water, such as waves.

A volcano erupts, shooting molten magma into the air.

A sea arch, formed by waves wearing away the rock.

PLATE TECTONICS

The Earth's crust is split into several parts called tectonic plates. The plates float on the molten magma underneath, causing them to constantly move.

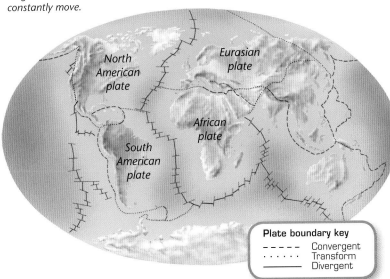

North American plate

Eurasian plate

African plate

South American plate

Plate boundary key
- - - - - Convergent
· · · · · · Transform
─────── Divergent

Divergent plate boundaries
Where two plates move away from each other, molten rock, or magma, rises to fill the gap. This usually occurs beneath the oceans, forming a spreading ocean ridge, such as the mid-Atlantic ridge.

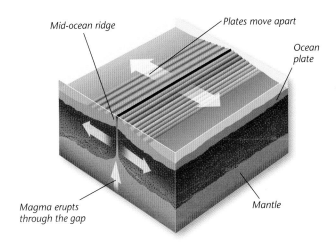

Mid-ocean ridge

Plates move apart

Ocean plate

Magma erupts through the gap

Mantle

Convergent plate boundaries
When two plates crash together, they crumple up and form major mountain chains, such as the Andes, as well as volcanoes. The Earth's crust is thin, so if cracks appear, the magma shoots up as the lava of a volcano. When an ocean plate is driven down into the Earth's magma, it is called subduction.

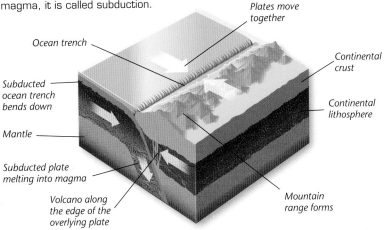

Ocean trench

Plates move together

Subducted ocean trench bends down

Continental crust

Mantle

Continental lithosphere

Subducted plate melting into magma

Volcano along the edge of the overlying plate

Mountain range forms

Transform plate boundaries
If two plates push past each other, pressure can build up, creating a break, or fault, which often causes an earthquake. Some earthquakes are so powerful that buildings collapse. Landslides can also occur, causing great damage. Undersea earthquakes can cause the massive waves of a tsunami, such as the tsunami that struck southeast Asia in 2004, killing 230,000 people.

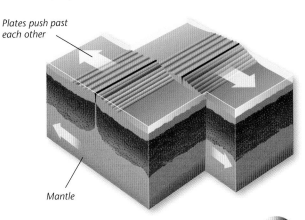

Plates push past each other

Mantle

Climate

The Earth's climate is very simple. Near the Equator, the temperature is hot, and closer to the poles, the temperature is cold. All year round, daytime temperatures at the Equator are around 33°C and there are no seasons. At the poles, the temperature is usually below freezing, and in winter there are long hours of darkness and temperatures drop to −40°C. Rain and snowfall patterns are more complex. Countries at the Equator experience heavy rain, but the poles have very little rainfall.

Global warming

The increased level of carbon dioxide in the atmosphere causes global warming because the gas traps the Sun's heat. Carbon dioxide is emitted when carbon fuels are burnt – this happens in cars and factories. The effects of global warming are becoming evident. Large areas of ice around Antarctica have already disappeared. The Sahara Desert is expanding and droughts are more common in Australia, causing rivers, such as the Murray, to dry up (see below). Sea levels are slowly rising, threatening cities such as New York City and low-lying countries such as Bangladesh with flooding. Using alternative sources of energy, such as wind and solar power, is vital to slow down these changes.

TYPES OF CLIMATE

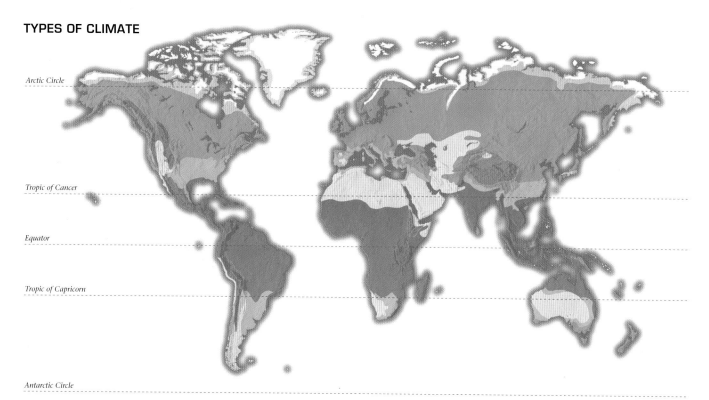

Arctic Circle

Tropic of Cancer

Equator

Tropic of Capricorn

Antarctic Circle

Polar and tundra
The lands around the Arctic Ocean and Antarctica are normally covered in snow. Northern Canada and Russia have a brief summer where the snow melts and the top layer of soil thaws to create a boggy ground called tundra.

Desert
Just north and south of the Equator lie desert areas. They have high daytime summer temperatures and are warm even in winter. Rain is very rare. Few plants grow and crops are only farmed where there are sources of water.

Cool temperate
Near the Arctic Circle, winters are cold and snowy, and summers are short. Closer to the Equator winters are milder, with little snow and warm summers. Forests are abundant and farming is common in the southern areas.

Warm temperate
In areas around the Mediterranean Sea and in some parts of North America, summers are hot and dry and winters are cool, but mild. Rainfall varies, so farming centres around growing citrus and olive trees.

Tropical
Close to the Equator, countries experience high temperatures and high rainfall for almost every month of the year. More animals and plants live in the tropical rainforests of the Amazon, central Africa and Indonesia than any other region.

Mountainous
Mountains have their own climate and snow can even be found at the Equator. At 5000 m in height, the temperature is 30°C colder than at sea level. Mountains also have more rainfall than the land surrounding them.

Population

The population of the world reached 7.6 billion in 2017. With around 250 babies being born each minute, and many people living longer due to a better quality of life, the population of the world is increasing rapidly. This rise puts pressure on the world's natural resources, and many cities are becoming overcrowded as people move in search of work. China is the most populated country with 1.39 billion people. Tokyo, the capital of Japan, is the largest city in the world with a population of 39.6 million.

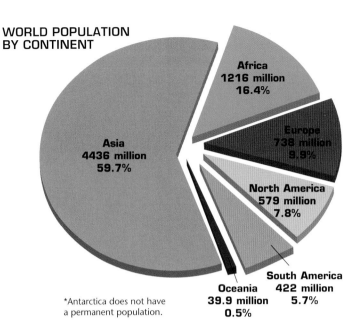

WORLD POPULATION BY CONTINENT

Asia 4436 million 59.7%
Africa 1216 million 16.4%
Europe 738 million 9.9%
North America 579 million 7.8%
South America 422 million 5.7%
Oceania 39.9 million 0.5%

*Antarctica does not have a permanent population.

TOP 10 COUNTRIES BY POPULATION DENSITY

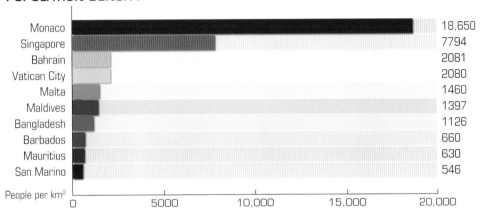

Country	People per km²
Monaco	18,650
Singapore	7794
Bahrain	2081
Vatican City	2080
Malta	1460
Maldives	1397
Bangladesh	1126
Barbados	660
Mauritius	630
San Marino	546

TOP 10 COUNTRIES BY POPULATION

1	China	1,391,700,000
2	India	1,339,200,000
3	USA	325,719,000
4	Indonesia	263,990,000
5	Pakistan	213,123,000
6	Brazil	207,661,000
7	Nigeria	193,393,000
8	Bangladesh	166,221,000
9	Russia	144,530,000
10	Mexico	129,200,000

TOP 20 CITIES BY POPULATION

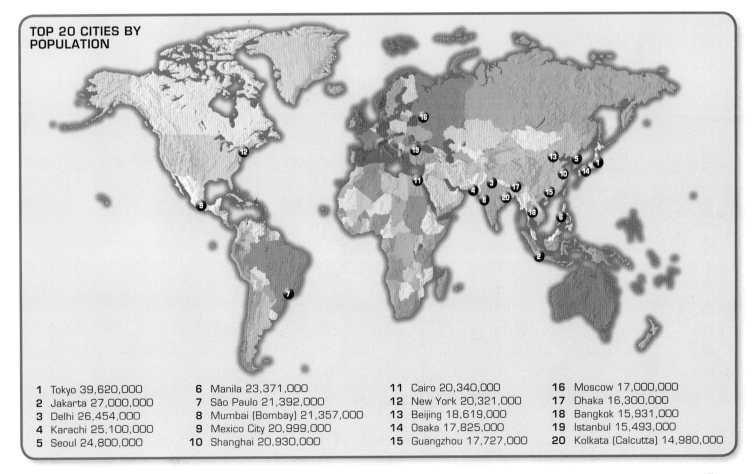

1 Tokyo 39,620,000	6 Manila 23,371,000	11 Cairo 20,340,000	16 Moscow 17,000,000
2 Jakarta 27,000,000	7 São Paulo 21,392,000	12 New York 20,321,000	17 Dhaka 16,300,000
3 Delhi 26,454,000	8 Mumbai (Bombay) 21,357,000	13 Beijing 18,619,000	18 Bangkok 15,931,000
4 Karachi 25,100,000	9 Mexico City 20,999,000	14 Osaka 17,825,000	19 Istanbul 15,493,000
5 Seoul 24,800,000	10 Shanghai 20,930,000	15 Guangzhou 17,727,000	20 Kolkata (Calcutta) 14,980,000

The Physical World

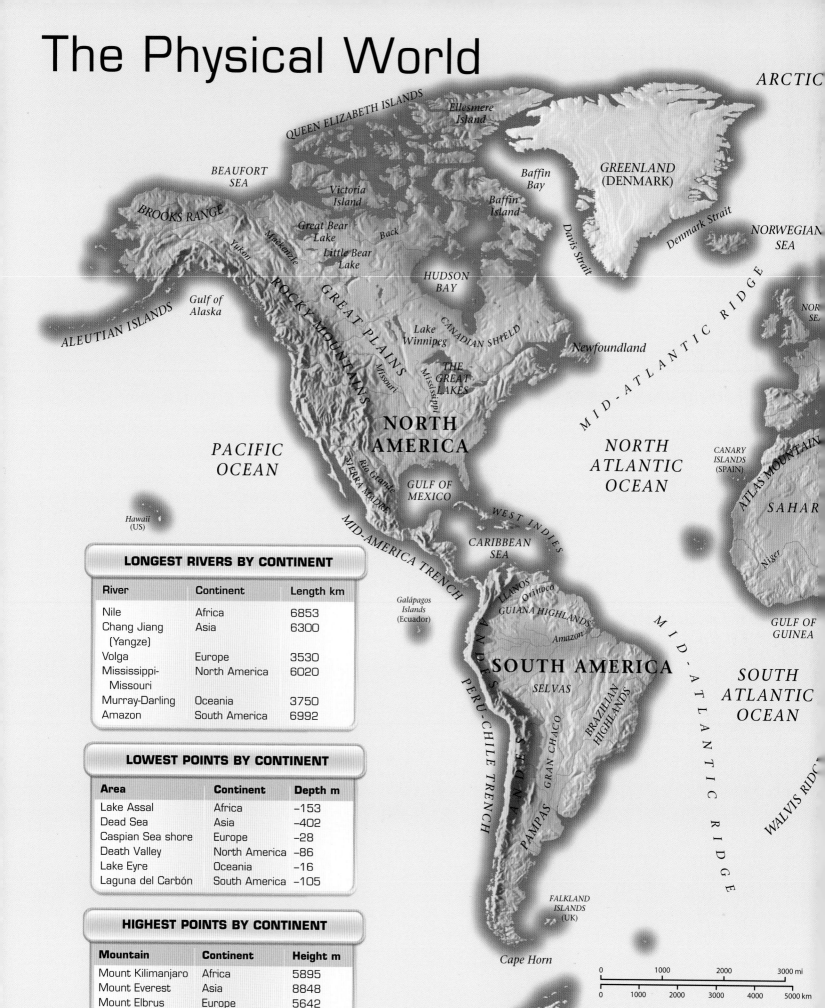

ARCTIC

QUEEN ELIZABETH ISLANDS

Ellesmere
Island

BEAUFORT
SEA

GREENLAND
(DENMARK)

Baffin
Bay

Victoria
Island

Baffin
Island

NORWEGIAN
SEA

BROOKS RANGE

Great Bear
Lake

Back

Denmark Strait

NOR
SE

Mackenzie

Little Bear
Lake

Yukon

HUDSON
BAY

Davis Strait

Gulf of
Alaska

GREAT PLAINS

CANADIAN SHIELD

Lake
Winnipeg

Newfoundland

ALEUTIAN ISLANDS

ROCKY MOUNTAINS

Missouri

THE
GREAT
LAKES

Mississippi

MID-ATLANTIC RIDGE

NORTH
AMERICA

PACIFIC
OCEAN

NORTH
ATLANTIC
OCEAN

CANARY
ISLANDS
(SPAIN)

ATLAS MOUNTAIN

Río Grande

SIERRA MADRE

GULF OF
MEXICO

SAHAR

Hawaii
(US)

WEST INDIES

Niger

MID-AMERICA TRENCH

CARIBBEAN
SEA

LONGEST RIVERS BY CONTINENT

River	Continent	Length km
Nile	Africa	6853
Chang Jiang (Yangze)	Asia	6300
Volga	Europe	3530
Mississippi-Missouri	North America	6020
Murray-Darling	Oceania	3750
Amazon	South America	6992

Galápagos
Islands
(Ecuador)

LLANOS

Orinoco

GUIANA HIGHLANDS

GULF OF
GUINEA

ANDES

Amazon

MID-ATLANTIC RIDGE

SOUTH AMERICA

SOUTH
ATLANTIC
OCEAN

SELVAS

BRAZILIAN
HIGHLANDS

LOWEST POINTS BY CONTINENT

Area	Continent	Depth m
Lake Assal	Africa	−153
Dead Sea	Asia	−402
Caspian Sea shore	Europe	−28
Death Valley	North America	−86
Lake Eyre	Oceania	−16
Laguna del Carbón	South America	−105

PERÚ-CHILE TRENCH

GRAN CHACO

WALVIS RIDG

PAMPAS

FALKLAND
ISLANDS
(UK)

HIGHEST POINTS BY CONTINENT

Mountain	Continent	Height m
Mount Kilimanjaro	Africa	5895
Mount Everest	Asia	8848
Mount Elbrus	Europe	5642
Denali	North America	6194
Puncak Jaya	Oceania	5030
Aconcagua	South America	6960

Cape Horn

0	1000	2000	3000 mi
0	1000 2000 3000	4000	5000 km

Antarctic

OCEAN

VALBARD (NORWAY)

Franz Josef Land

Novaya Zemlya

Severnaya Zemlya

LAPTEV SEA

NEW SIBERIAN ISLANDS

EAST SIBERIAN SEA

KARA SEA

BARENTS SEA

LAPLAND

Dvina

URAL MOUNTAINS

SIBERIAN LOWLAND

Ob

Yenisey

Nizhnyaya Tunguska

CENTRAL SIBERIAN PLATEAU

Lena

BALTIC SEA

TH EUROPEAN PLAIN

EUROPE

Volga

Ob

Yenisey

Angara

Lena

Aldan

BERING SEA

SEA OF OKHOTSK

Ural

ASIA

Lake Baikal

Dnieper

Irtysh

SAYAN MOUNTAINS

CARPATHIAN MOUNTAINS

Aral Sea

Lake Balkhash

GOBI DESERT

KURIL TRENCH

PS

Danube

BLACK SEA

CASPIAN SEA

TIEN MOUNTAINS

SEA OF JAPAN

MEDITERRANEAN SEA

ZAGROS MOUNTAINS

Euphrates

Tigris

HINDU KUSH

KUNLAN MOUNTAINS

Huang

TIBETAN PLATEAU

Chang Jiang

EAST CHINA SEA

PACIFIC OCEAN

DESERT

Nile

RED SEA

Arabian Peninsula

ARABIAN SEA

Indus

HIMALAYAS

Ganges

Brahmaputra

MICRONESIA

NUBIAN DESERT

GULF OF ADEN

DECCAN

BAY OF BENGAL

Mekong

SOUTH CHINA SEA

PHILIPPINE SEA

FRICA

ETHIOPIAN HIGHLANDS

Uele

MID-INDIAN RIDGE

CELEBES SEA

MELANESIA

Congo

CONGO BASIN

GREAT RIFT VALLEY

Lake Victoria

EAST INDIES

Kasai

JAVA TRENCH

INDIAN OCEAN

CORAL SEA

KALAHARI DESERT

GREAT SANDY DESERT

Orange

SOUTHWEST INDIAN RIDGE

SOUTHEAST INDIAN RIDGE

GREAT VICTORIAN DESERT

GREAT DIVIDING RANGE

OCEANIA

Cape of Good Hope

SOUTHERN OCEAN

Great Australian Bight

TASMAN SEA

WORLD'S OCEANS	
Ocean	**Area km²**
Pacific	165,240,000
Atlantic	82,440,000
Indian	73,440,000
Southern	23,325,000
Arctic	14,090,000

LARGEST DESERTS		
Desert	**Continent**	**Area km²**
Sahara	Africa	8,600,000
Arabian	Asia	2,300,000
Australian	Australia	1,550,000
Gobi	Asia	1,300,000
Kalahari	Africa	930,000

LARGEST INLAND WATER BODIES		
Lake	**Continent**	**Area km²**
Caspian Sea	Asia–Europe	371,800
Superior	North America	82,350
Victoria	Africa	69,500
Huron	North America	59,600
Michigan	North America	57,800

The Political World

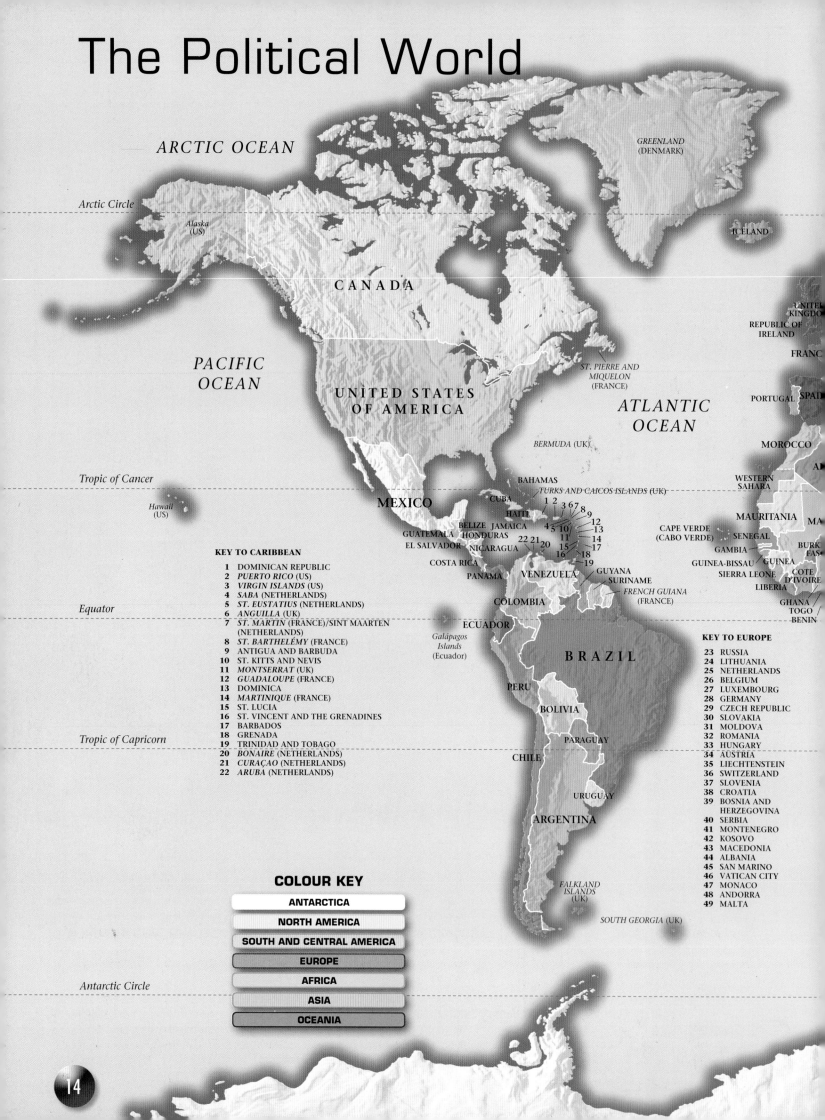

ARCTIC OCEAN

Arctic Circle

GREENLAND (DENMARK)

Alaska (US)

ICELAND

C A N A D A

PACIFIC OCEAN

ST. PIERRE AND MIQUELON (FRANCE)

UNITED STATES OF AMERICA

ATLANTIC OCEAN

UNITED KINGDOM

REPUBLIC OF IRELAND

FRANCE

PORTUGAL SPAIN

BERMUDA (UK)

MOROCCO

Tropic of Cancer

BAHAMAS

WESTERN SAHARA

TURKS AND CAICOS ISLANDS (UK)

MEXICO

CUBA

1 2

3 6 7

8

9

MAURITANIA

MALI

Hawaii (US)

HAITI

4

5 10

12

13

CAPE VERDE (CABO VERDE)

SENEGAL

GUATEMALA

BELIZE JAMAICA

HONDURAS

11

14

GAMBIA

BURKINA FASO

EL SALVADOR

NICARAGUA

22 21

20

15

17

GUINEA-BISSAU

GUINEA

16

18

SIERRA LEONE

COTE D'IVOIRE

COSTA RICA

19

LIBERIA

PANAMA

VENEZUELA

GUYANA

SURINAME

GHANA

TOGO

BENIN

COLOMBIA

FRENCH GUIANA (FRANCE)

Equator

ECUADOR

Galápagos Islands (Ecuador)

B R A Z I L

KEY TO EUROPE

23 RUSSIA

24 LITHUANIA

25 NETHERLANDS

26 BELGIUM

27 LUXEMBOURG

28 GERMANY

29 CZECH REPUBLIC

30 SLOVAKIA

31 MOLDOVA

32 ROMANIA

33 HUNGARY

34 AUSTRIA

35 LIECHTENSTEIN

36 SWITZERLAND

37 SLOVENIA

38 CROATIA

39 BOSNIA AND HERZEGOVINA

40 SERBIA

41 MONTENEGRO

42 KOSOVO

43 MACEDONIA

44 ALBANIA

45 SAN MARINO

46 VATICAN CITY

47 MONACO

48 ANDORRA

49 MALTA

PERU

BOLIVIA

Tropic of Capricorn

PARAGUAY

CHILE

URUGUAY

ARGENTINA

FALKLAND ISLANDS (UK)

SOUTH GEORGIA (UK)

KEY TO CARIBBEAN

1 **DOMINICAN REPUBLIC**
2 *PUERTO RICO* (US)
3 *VIRGIN ISLANDS* (US)
4 *SABA* (NETHERLANDS)
5 *ST. EUSTATIUS* (NETHERLANDS)
6 *ANGUILLA* (UK)
7 *ST. MARTIN* (FRANCE)/SINT MAARTEN (NETHERLANDS)
8 *ST. BARTHELÉMY* (FRANCE)
9 **ANTIGUA AND BARBUDA**
10 **ST. KITTS AND NEVIS**
11 *MONTSERRAT* (UK)
12 *GUADALOUPE* (FRANCE)
13 **DOMINICA**
14 *MARTINIQUE* (FRANCE)
15 **ST. LUCIA**
16 **ST. VINCENT AND THE GRENADINES**
17 **BARBADOS**
18 **GRENADA**
19 **TRINIDAD AND TOBAGO**
20 *BONAIRE* (NETHERLANDS)
21 *CURAÇAO* (NETHERLANDS)
22 *ARUBA* (NETHERLANDS)

COLOUR KEY

ANTARCTICA

NORTH AMERICA

SOUTH AND CENTRAL AMERICA

EUROPE

AFRICA

ASIA

OCEANIA

Antarctic Circle

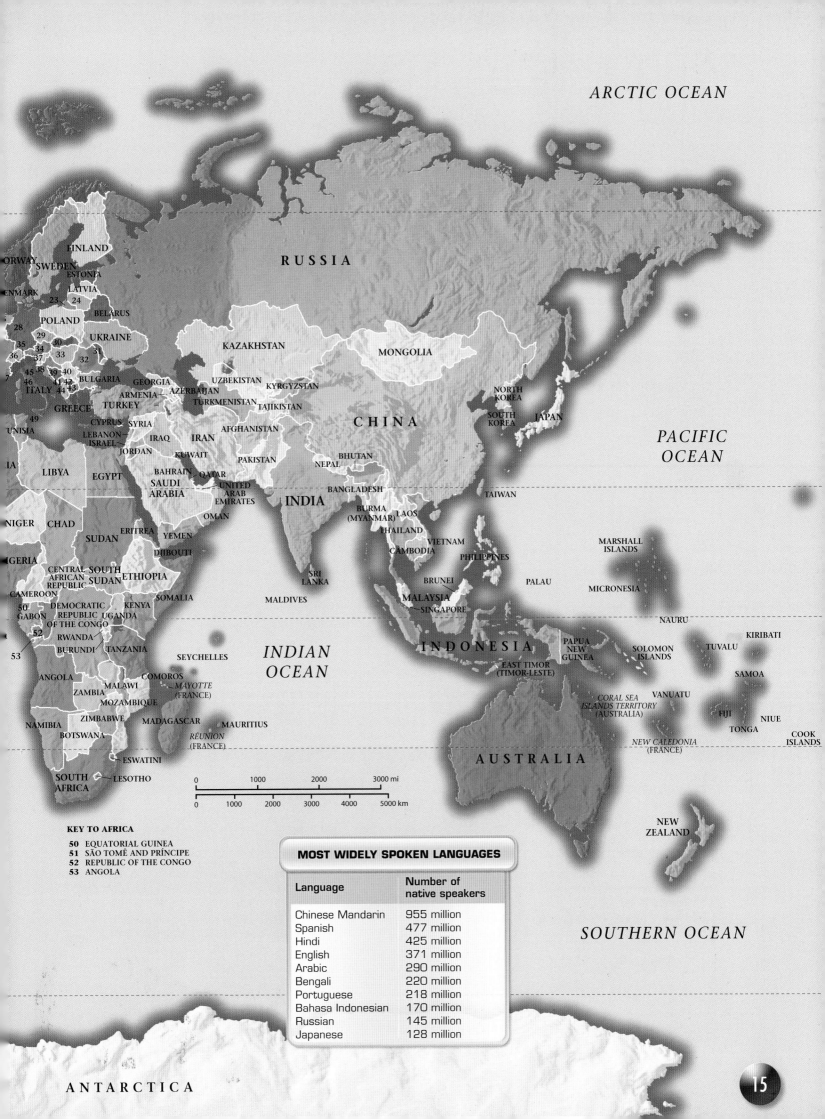

ARCTIC OCEAN

FINLAND
ORWAY
SWEDEN
ESTONIA
ENMARK
LATVIA
23   24
POLAND
BELARUS
28
29   30
UKRAINE
35   34
36   37   33   31   32
45 38 39 40
46 41 42 43
ITALY 44
GREECE
TURKEY
CYPRUS   SYRIA
49
LEBANON
UNISIA
ISRAEL
IRAQ
IRAN
JORDAN
KUWAIT
IA
LIBYA
EGYPT
BAHRAIN QATAR
SAUDI
UNITED
ARABIA
ARAB
EMIRATES
OMAN

RUSSIA

KAZAKHSTAN

MONGOLIA

NORTH
KOREA

UZBEKISTAN
KYRGYZSTAN
AZERBAIJAN
TURKMENISTAN
TAJIKISTAN
ARMENIA
GEORGIA
AFGHANISTAN

CHINA

SOUTH
KOREA
JAPAN

PACIFIC
OCEAN

PAKISTAN
NEPAL
BHUTAN
BANGLADESH
INDIA
TAIWAN

NIGER CHAD
SUDAN
ERITREA
YEMEN
DJIBOUTI
CENTRAL SOUTH
AFRICAN SUDAN ETHIOPIA
REPUBLIC
CAMEROON
50
DEMOCRATIC KENYA
GABON REPUBLIC UGANDA
OF THE CONGO
52
RWANDA
53
BURUNDI TANZANIA
ANGOLA
MALAWI
ZAMBIA
MOZAMBIQUE
NAMIBIA ZIMBABWE
BOTSWANA

BURMA
(MYANMAR) LAOS
THAILAND
VIETNAM
CAMBODIA
PHILIPPINES

SRI
LANKA

MARSHALL
ISLANDS

BRUNEI
PALAU
MICRONESIA
MALAYSIA
SINGAPORE

NAURU

MALDIVES

SEYCHELLES

INDIAN
OCEAN

INDONESIA

PAPUA
NEW
GUINEA

SOLOMON
ISLANDS

TUVALU

KIRIBATI

SAMOA

EAST TIMOR
(TIMOR-LESTE)

VANUATU

CORAL SEA
ISLANDS TERRITORY
(AUSTRALIA)

FIJI

NIUE

TONGA

COOK
ISLANDS

COMOROS
MAYOTTE
(FRANCE)

MADAGASCAR MAURITIUS
RÉUNION
(FRANCE)

NEW CALEDONIA
(FRANCE)

AUSTRALIA

ESWATINI
SOUTH LESOTHO
AFRICA

NIGERIA

IGERIA

NEW
ZEALAND

SOUTHERN OCEAN

0	1000	2000	3000 mi
0	1000	2000	3000	4000	5000 km

KEY TO AFRICA

50 EQUATORIAL GUINEA
51 SÃO TOMÉ AND PRÍNCIPE
52 REPUBLIC OF THE CONGO
53 ANGOLA

MOST WIDELY SPOKEN LANGUAGES

Language	Number of native speakers
Chinese Mandarin	955 million
Spanish	477 million
Hindi	425 million
English	371 million
Arabic	290 million
Bengali	220 million
Portuguese	218 million
Bahasa Indonesian	170 million
Russian	145 million
Japanese	128 million

ANTARCTICA

Antarctica

Just under 98 percent of Antarctica is covered by ice that is about 1.6 km thick. Although it is the coldest place on Earth, the region is heavily affected by global warming. The climate is becoming warmer due to an increased level of carbon dioxide, which traps the Sun's heat. Large areas of ice that cover the sea around Antarctica have already broken away and melted. Deep under the ice lie vast amounts of oil, coal and gold, but mining is prohibited.

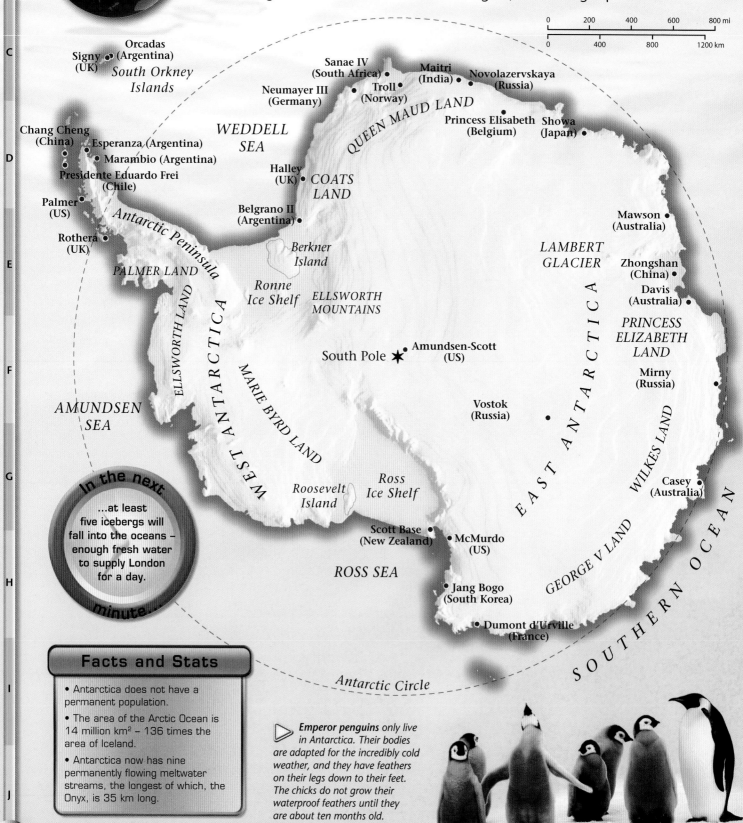

Orcadas (Argentina)
Signy (UK)
South Orkney Islands

Sanae IV (South Africa)
Maitri (India)
Novolazervskaya (Russia)
Neumayer III (Germany)
Troll (Norway)
QUEEN MAUD LAND
Princess Elisabeth (Belgium)
Showa (Japan)

Chang Cheng (China)
Esperanza (Argentina)
Marambio (Argentina)
Presidente Eduardo Frei (Chile)

WEDDELL SEA

Halley (UK)
COATS LAND

Belgrano II (Argentina)

Palmer (US)

Rothera (UK)

Antarctic Peninsula

PALMER LAND

Berkner Island

Ronne Ice Shelf

ELLSWORTH LAND

ELLSWORTH MOUNTAINS

Mawson (Australia)

LAMBERT GLACIER

Zhongshan (China)

Davis (Australia)

PRINCESS ELIZABETH LAND

South Pole ✱ Amundsen-Scott (US)

WEST ANTARCTICA

MARIE BYRD LAND

AMUNDSEN SEA

Vostok (Russia)

Mirny (Russia)

EAST ANTARCTICA

WILKES LAND

Ross Ice Shelf

Roosevelt Island

Casey (Australia)

Scott Base (New Zealand)
McMurdo (US)

ROSS SEA

GEORGE V LAND

Jang Bogo (South Korea)

Dumont d'Urville (France)

SOUTHERN OCEAN

Antarctic Circle

In the next minute... ...at least five icebergs will fall into the oceans – enough fresh water to supply London for a day.

Facts and Stats

- Antarctica does not have a permanent population.
- The area of the Arctic Ocean is 14 million km² – 136 times the area of Iceland.
- Antarctica now has nine permanently flowing meltwater streams, the longest of which, the Onyx, is 35 km long.

▷ **Emperor penguins** only live in Antarctica. Their bodies are adapted for the incredibly cold weather, and they have feathers on their legs down to their feet. The chicks do not grow their waterproof feathers until they are about ten months old.

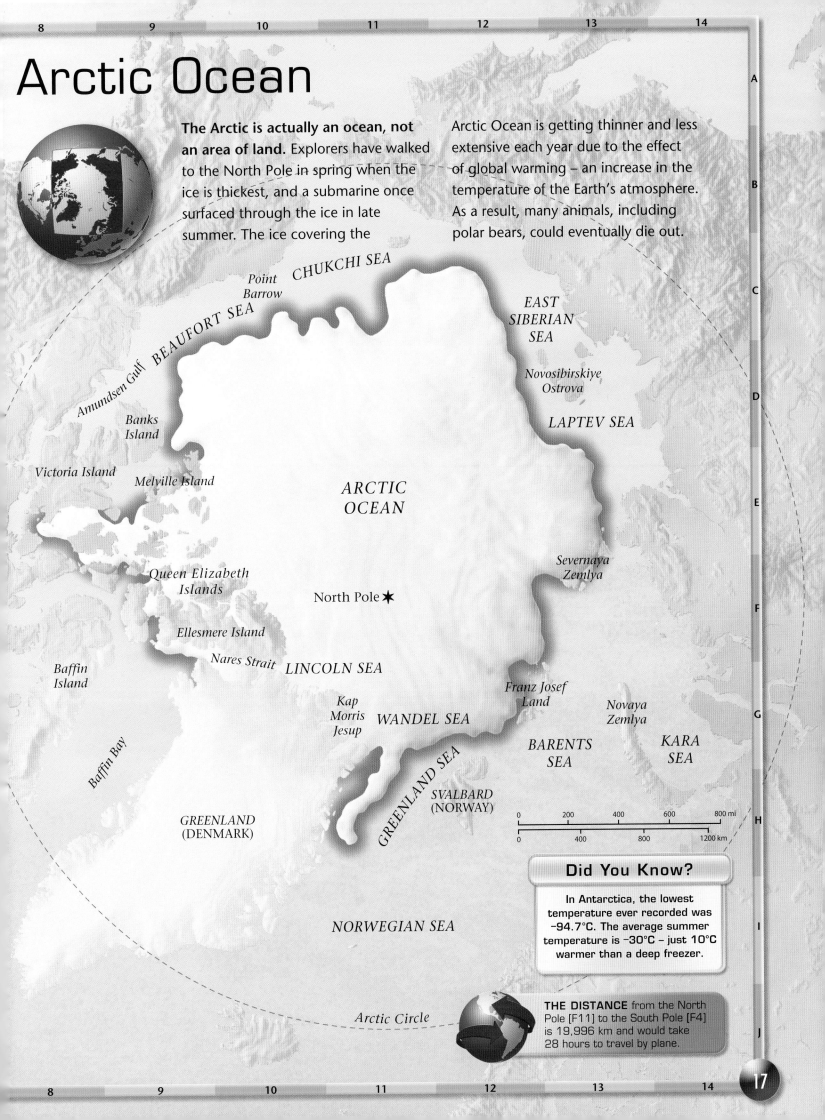

Arctic Ocean

The Arctic is actually an ocean, not an area of land. Explorers have walked to the North Pole in spring when the ice is thickest, and a submarine once surfaced through the ice in late summer. The ice covering the Arctic Ocean is getting thinner and less extensive each year due to the effect of global warming – an increase in the temperature of the Earth's atmosphere. As a result, many animals, including polar bears, could eventually die out.

Point Barrow

CHUKCHI SEA

BEAUFORT SEA

EAST SIBERIAN SEA

Amundsen Gulf

Novosibirskiye Ostrova

Banks Island

LAPTEV SEA

Victoria Island

Melville Island

ARCTIC OCEAN

Severnaya Zemlya

Queen Elizabeth Islands

North Pole ✴

Ellesmere Island

Nares Strait

LINCOLN SEA

Baffin Island

Franz Josef Land

Novaya Zemlya

Kap Morris Jesup

WANDEL SEA

BARENTS SEA

KARA SEA

Baffin Bay

GREENLAND SEA

SVALBARD (NORWAY)

GREENLAND (DENMARK)

| 0 | | 200 | | 400 | | 600 | | 800 mi |
| 0 | | 400 | | 800 | | | 1200 km | |

NORWEGIAN SEA

Did You Know?

In Antarctica, the lowest temperature ever recorded was −94.7°C. The average summer temperature is −30°C – just 10°C warmer than a deep freezer.

Arctic Circle

THE DISTANCE from the North Pole [F11] to the South Pole [F4] is 19,996 km and would take 28 hours to travel by plane.

North America

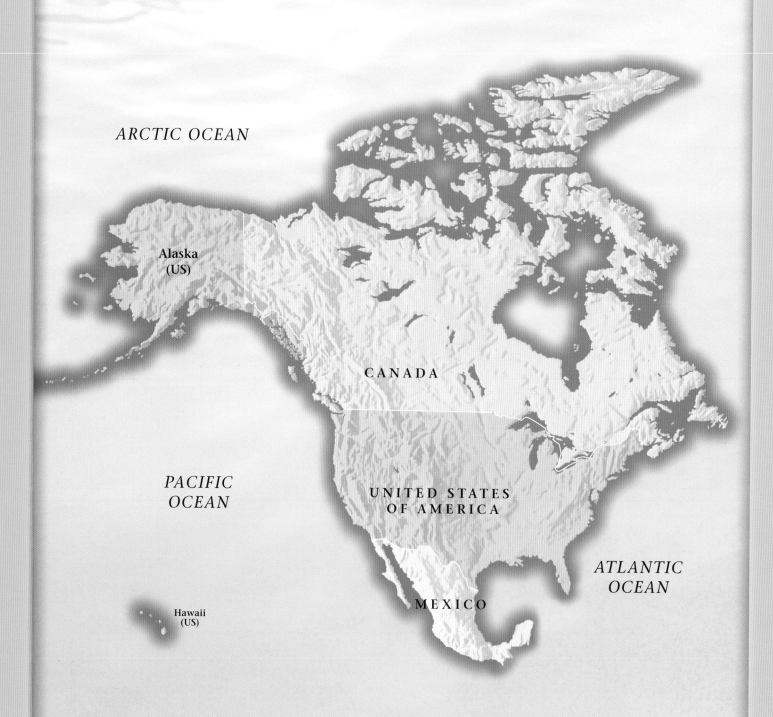

ARCTIC OCEAN

Alaska
(US)

CANADA

*PACIFIC
OCEAN*

UNITED STATES
OF AMERICA

*ATLANTIC
OCEAN*

MEXICO

Hawaii
(US)

COUNTRY FACTFILE

Country	Life expectancy	Population to nearest thousand	Population growth %	Population as urban %	Area km²	Population density per km²	Capital city	Currency	Languages
Canada	82	36,286,000	0.7	82	9,970,610	3.6	Ottawa	Canadian Dollar	English, French
Mexico	76	129,200,000	1.1	80	1,958,201	66	Mexico City	Mexican Peso	Spanish
United States of America	80	325,719,000	0.8	82	9,629,091	33.8	Washington D.C.	US Dollar	English, Spanish

NB: Central America can be found as part of the South and Central America section.

Northeast USA

The northeast is the centre of the United States' industry and commerce with many large manufacturing companies. Ford and General Motor vehicles, as well as coal mines, steel works, the New York Stock Exchange, Washington White House and the Senate buildings are all situated here. Modern black music started in Cleveland and Detroit, whilst away from the cities there are many beaches, rivers, forests and lakes.

Lake of the Woods

Isle Royale

Lake Superior

CANADA

Red Lake

NORTH DAKOTA

Marquette

Upper Peninsula

Moorhead

Duluth

MINNESOTA

WISCONSIN

MICHIGAN

Green Bay

SOUTH DAKOTA

Minnesota

Minneapolis · ■ St. Paul
Bloomington
Burnsville

Eau Claire

Green Bay
Appleton
Oshkosh · Lake Winnebago

Lake Michigan

Lower Peninsula

Saginaw

Mississippi

Mankato

Rochester

La Crosse

Grand Rapids

Flint
Lansing

Wisconsin

Waukesha

Ann Arbor
Kalamazoo

Mason City

Cedar

Madison ■
Janesville

Milwaukee

Waterloo

Rockford

IOWA

Elgin

South Bend

Sioux City

Cedar Rapids
Davenport

Aurora · Chicago
Joliet · Gary

Fort Wayne

Des Moines ■

ILLINOIS

Wabash

INDIANA

NEBRASKA

Des Moines

Peoria

Muncie

Council Bluffs

Illinois

Champaign

Anderson

MISSOURI

Mississippi

Decatur
Springfield ■

Terre Haute · ■ Indianapoli

Bloomington

Jeffersonville

East St. Louis

Evansville

There are 30 major league baseball teams in two leagues, the American League (founded 1901) and the National League (founded 1876). 1903 was the first time that the World Series, between the winners of the two leagues, was played.

Search and Find

- Washington D.C.
  . . . . H11

Connecticut
- Hartford F12

Delaware
- Dover G11

Illinois
- Springfield I5

Indiana
- Indianapolis . . . H7

Iowa
- Des Moines . . . G3

Maine
- Augusta D13

Maryland
- Annapolis . . . H11

Massachusetts
- Boston E13

Michigan
- Lansing F7

Minnesota
- St. Paul E3

New Hampshire
- Concord E13

New Jersey
- Trenton G12

New York
- Albany E12

Ohio
- Columbus H8

Pennsylvania
- Harrisburg . . . G11

Rhode Island
- Providence . . . E13

Vermont
- Montpelier . . D12

West Virginia
- Charleston I9

Wisconsin
- Madison F5

Facts and Stats

- The biggest city is New York City [F12] with 20.3 million people. This would fill 203 Olympic stadiums.
- The biggest lake is Lake Superior [C5] at 82,350 km². This is only 20 percent smaller than Iceland.
- Mount Washington [D12] is the highest mountain at 1917 m – six times higher than the Eiffel Tower.

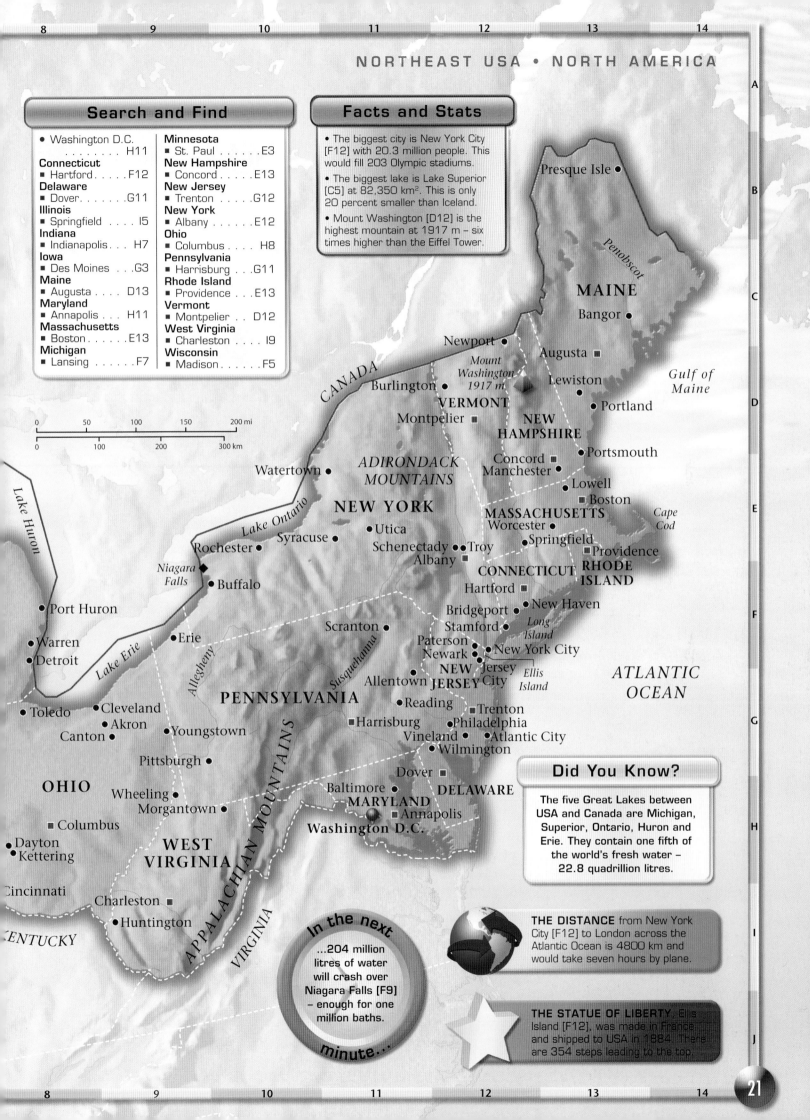

Did You Know?

The five Great Lakes between USA and Canada are Michigan, Superior, Ontario, Huron and Erie. They contain one fifth of the world's fresh water – 22.8 quadrillion litres.

In the next ...204 million litres of water will crash over Niagara Falls [F9] – enough for one million baths. **minute...**

THE DISTANCE from New York City [F12] to London across the Atlantic Ocean is 4800 km and would take seven hours by plane.

THE STATUE OF LIBERTY, Ellis Island [F12], was made in France and shipped to USA in 1884. There are 354 steps leading to the top.

Southeast USA

The warm climate of Florida and the Gulf of Mexico coastal areas makes southeast USA popular with tourists. There is Disney World in Florida for fun, Cape Canaveral for space rocket launches, Miami for beaches, New Orleans for jazz, Nashville for country music and the Mississippi river for boat trips. Farming is the main occupation – mainly of tobacco, oranges, rice, peanuts, vegetables and cotton. There are many oil and gas rigs in the Gulf of Mexico to generate energy resources.

GRACELAND, Nashville [C8], is the home of Elvis Presley (1935–1977) and is visited by around 600,000 fans a year.

THE DISTANCE from the source to the mouth of the Mississippi–Missouri river is 6020 km and would take 20 days floating on a raft.

Extreme Weather

Hurricane Katrina, the largest hurricane ever recorded in the USA, caused 80 percent of New Orleans [H6] to flood. More than one million people were evacuated and 1833 died.

The **Kentucky Derby** takes place in Louisville [B8] on the first Saturday of May. The race is 2 km in length and more than 150,000 spectators attend the two-week-long festival every year.

World Record — The largest space rocket launch site in the world is at Cape Canaveral [H11].

IOWA

ILLINOIS

St. Joseph

Independence · Columbia · St. Louis
Kansas City · Jefferson City

Owensboro

KANSAS

MISSOURI · Cape Girardeau

· Paducah

· Springfield

Clarksville ·

OZARK PLATEAU

OKLAHOMA

ARKANSAS

· Fort Smith

· Memphis

■ Little Rock

Hot Springs ·

Pine Bluff ·

Mississippi

Yazoo

Texarkana

Ouachita

· El Dorado

· Greenville

Tuscaloosa ·

MISSISSIPPI

TEXAS

· Monroe

Meridian ·

· Shreveport

Jackson ■

Pearl

LOUISIANA

Natchez ·

Hattiesburg ·

Red

· Alexandria

Prichard ·

Mobile

Biloxi ·

Baton Rouge ■

Lafayette ·

· New Orleans

· Lake Charles

Marsh Island

Mississippi Delta

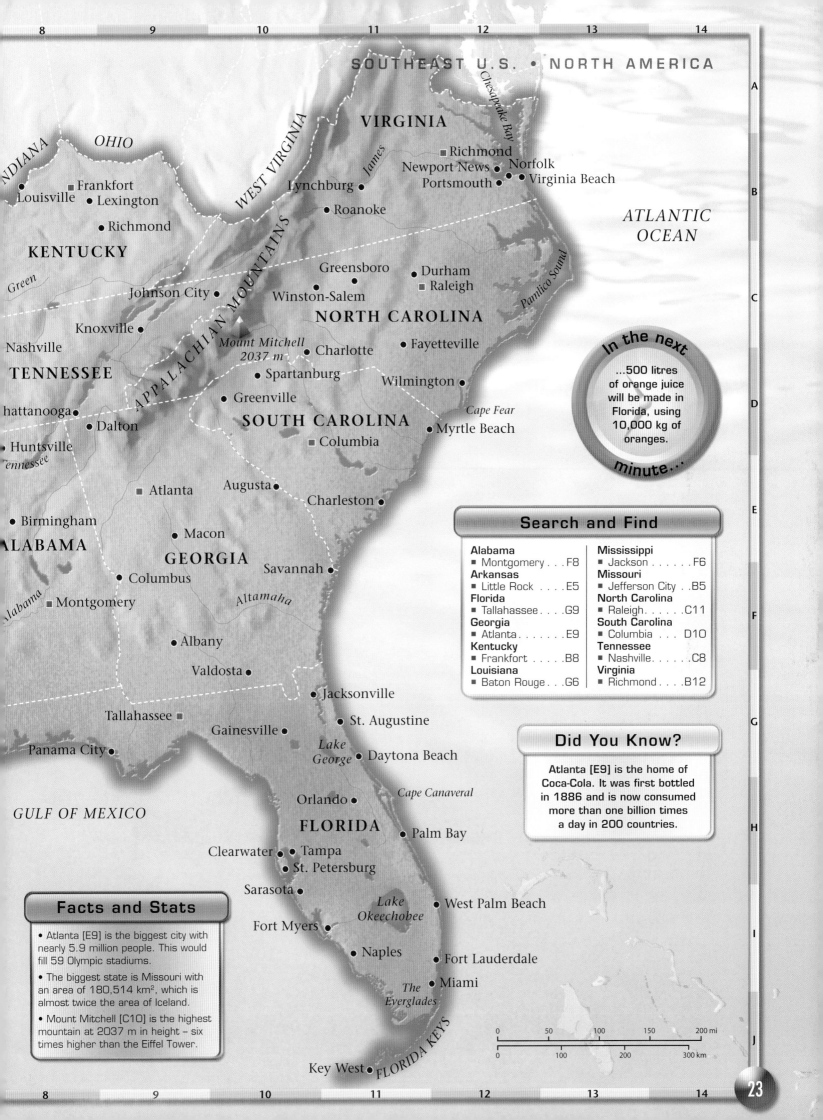

INDIANA

OHIO

KENTUCKY

Louisville
• Frankfort
• Lexington
• Richmond

TENNESSEE
Nashville
• Knoxville
• Johnson City
Chattanooga
• Dalton
• Huntsville
Tennessee

WEST VIRGINIA

VIRGINIA

• Lynchburg
• Roanoke

■ Richmond
Newport News • • Norfolk
Portsmouth • • Virginia Beach

ATLANTIC OCEAN

Chesapeake Bay
James

APPALACHIAN MOUNTAINS

Greensboro • • Durham
Winston-Salem • Raleigh

NORTH CAROLINA

Mount Mitchell 2037 m
• Charlotte
• Fayetteville

• Spartanburg
Wilmington •

• Greenville

SOUTH CAROLINA
■ Columbia

Pamlico Sound

Cape Fear
• Myrtle Beach

Green

ALABAMA
• Birmingham

• Atlanta
Augusta •

GEORGIA
• Macon

• Columbus
■ Montgomery

Savannah •

Charleston •

Altamaha

Alabama

• Albany

Valdosta •

• Jacksonville
• St. Augustine

GULF OF MEXICO

Tallahassee ■
Gainesville •
Lake George • Daytona Beach

Panama City •

FLORIDA

Orlando •

Cape Canaveral

• Palm Bay

Clearwater • • Tampa
• St. Petersburg
Sarasota •

Lake Okeechobee
• West Palm Beach

Fort Myers •

• Naples
• Fort Lauderdale

The Everglades
• Miami

Key West • FLORIDA KEYS

In the next
...500 litres of orange juice will be made in Florida, using 10,000 kg of oranges.
minute...

Search and Find

Alabama	**Mississippi**
■ Montgomery . . . F8	■ Jackson F6
Arkansas	**Missouri**
■ Little Rock E5	■ Jefferson City . . B5
Florida	**North Carolina**
■ Tallahassee G9	■ Raleigh. C11
Georgia	**South Carolina**
■ Atlanta E9	■ Columbia . . . D10
Kentucky	**Tennessee**
■ Frankfort B8	■ Nashville. C8
Louisiana	**Virginia**
■ Baton Rouge . . .G6	■ Richmond B12

Did You Know?

Atlanta [E9] is the home of Coca-Cola. It was first bottled in 1886 and is now consumed more than one billion times a day in 200 countries.

Facts and Stats

• Atlanta [E9] is the biggest city with nearly 5.9 million people. This would fill 59 Olympic stadiums.

• The biggest state is Missouri with an area of 180,514 km², which is almost twice the area of Iceland.

• Mount Mitchell [C10] is the highest mountain at 2037 m in height – six times higher than the Eiffel Tower.

0   50   100   150   200 mi
0   100   200   300 km

Northwest USA and Alaska

Inland areas in northwest USA are either stunning mountain scenery or vast ranches. Washington's Seattle is the only large urban area, with the Boeing aircraft factory, and the headquarters of Microsoft, UPS, Starbucks and Amazon. The USA's biggest apple-growing region stretches from the Pacific Ocean to the Great Plains of the Dakotas. Alaska is the USA's largest state. However, vast areas are uninhabited due to long, severe winters. Alaska is one of the leading oil-producing regions in the world.

In the next

...Wyoming will produce 300 tonnes of coal – enough to produce electricity to power ten million TVs.

minute...

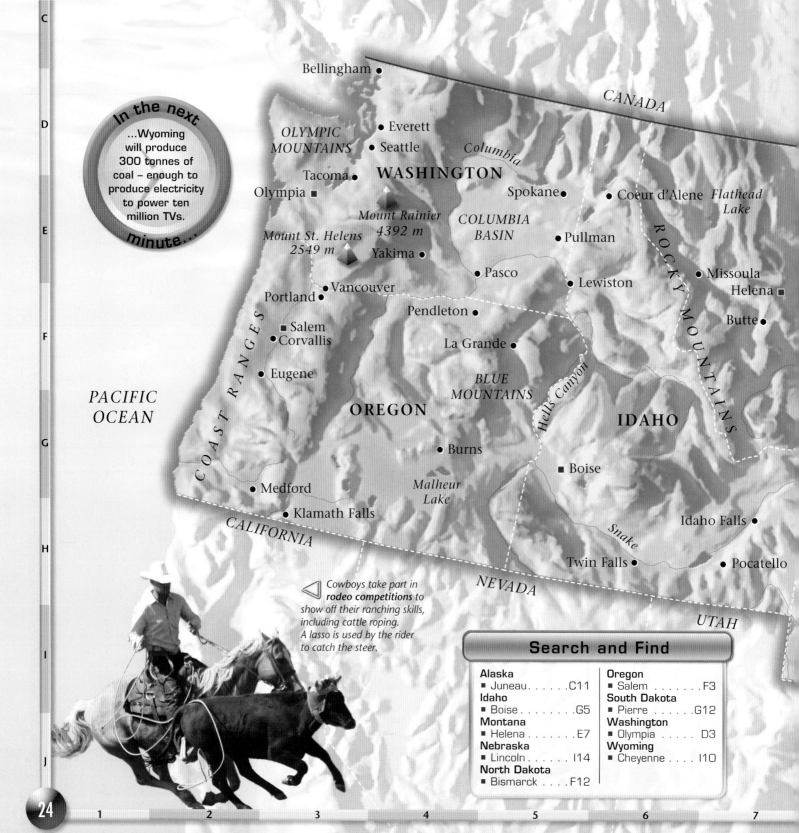

CANADA

Bellingham

OLYMPIC MOUNTAINS

Everett

Seattle

Columbia

Tacoma

WASHINGTON

Olympia

Spokane

Coeur d'Alene   Flathead Lake

Mount Rainier 4392 m

COLUMBIA BASIN

Pullman

Mount St. Helens 2549 m

Yakima

Pasco

Lewiston

ROCKY MOUNTAINS

Missoula

Helena

Vancouver

Portland

Pendleton

La Grande

Butte

Salem

Corvallis

COAST RANGES

Eugene

BLUE MOUNTAINS

OREGON

Hells Canyon

IDAHO

PACIFIC OCEAN

Burns

Boise

Medford

Malheur Lake

Klamath Falls

Snake

Idaho Falls

CALIFORNIA

NEVADA

Twin Falls

Pocatello

UTAH

Cowboys take part in **rodeo competitions** to show off their ranching skills, including cattle roping. A lasso is used by the rider to catch the steer.

Search and Find

ALASKA

CHUKCHI SEA

Wainwright
Point Hope
Barrow
Noatak
Colville
St. Lawrence Island
Kobuk
Nome
Koyukuk
St. Matthew Island
BERING SEA
Hooper Bay
Alakanuk
Yukon
Tanana
Fort Yukon
St. Paul Island
Nunivak Island
Bethel
Kwethluk
Fairbanks
Near Islands
St. George Island
Denali 6194 m
Anchorage
Rat Islands
Aleutian Islands
Dillingham
Kenai
Seward
Cordova
Andreanof Islands
Fox Islands
Unimak Island
Kodiak
CANADA
Kodiak Island
Gulf of Alaska
Yakutat
PACIFIC OCEAN
Juneau
Sitka
Ketchikan

0 100 200 300 400 500 mi
0 200 400 600 800 km

Facts and Stats

- Montana is 380,847 km² in area – 3.5 times the area of Iceland.
- Seattle [D4] is the biggest city with almost 3.9 million people. This would fill 39 Olympic stadiums.
- Alaska's Denali [B11] is the highest mountain at 6194 m – 19 times higher than the Eiffel Tower.

Did You Know?

In 1867, the USA bought Alaska from Russia for $7.2 million (£3.7 million) – cheaper than a modern New York apartment.

0 50 100 150 200 mi
0 100 200 300 km

Great Falls
Fort Peck Lake
Missouri
Williston
Minot
Grand Forks
MONTANA
Lake Sakakawea
NORTH DAKOTA
GREAT PLAINS
Miles City
Bismarck
Jamestown
Fargo
MINNESOTA
Bozeman
Billings
Lake Oahe
Aberdeen
Watertown
Yellowstone National Park
Cody
BIGHORN MOUNTAINS
Gillette
Cheyenne
Pierre
SOUTH DAKOTA
Jackson
Rapid City
White
Sioux Falls
WYOMING
Mount Rushmore
Lake Francis Case
Casper
Yanktown
Niobrara
SAND HILLS
Norfolk
IOWA
Loup
Rock Springs
NEBRASKA
Laramie
Cheyenne
COLORADO
North Platte
Grand Island
Omaha
Platte
Lincoln
Hastings

KANSAS

THE DISTANCE of the USA's Pacific coastline is 12,268 km and would take a migrating whale about 50 days to swim.

Southwest USA and Hawaii

The nation's most dramatic landscape belongs to southwest USA, which is covered by the Rocky Mountains. Southern California, Nevada and Arizona are desert – the driest place being Death Valley. Texas is the home of the oil industry, and Nevada's Las Vegas attracts tourists visiting casinos and nearby scenery, such as the Grand Canyon. California has boomed due to the Hollywood film studios, Silicon Valley's large number of computer firms, and some of the most productive farmland in the country. Tropical Hawaii is a popular surfing and beach island 4800 km southwest of California.

Search and Find

Arizona
- Phoenix F7

California
- Sacramento . . . C4

Colorado
- Denver C10

Hawaii
- Honolulu H3

Kansas
- Topeka D13

Nevada
- Carson City . . . C5

New Mexico
- Santa Fe F10

Oklahoma
- Oklahoma City . F13

Texas
- Austin H13

Utah
- Salt Lake City . . C8

PACIFIC OCEAN

OREGON

IDAHO

Mount Shasta 4322 m

Eureka

Redding

Winnemucca

Humboldt

Elko

Great Salt Lake

COAST RANGES

Reno

Carson City

Sacramento

Santa Rosa

Oakland

Stockton

San Francisco

Palo Alto

Modesto

Yosemite National Park

Sunnyvale

San Jose

SIERRA NEVADA

NEVADA

Tonopah

GREAT BASIN

Cedar City

Salinas

Monterey

Fresno

Mount Whitney 4418 m

San Luis Obispo

Bakersfield

CALIFORNIA

Las Vegas

DEATH VALLEY

Hoover Dam

Grand Canyon

Santa Barbara

ARIZONA

Oxnard

Pasadena

San Bernardino

Los Angeles

Riverside

Long Beach

Anaheim

Prescott

Oceanside

Phoenix

San Diego

Gila

Mesa

Yuma

Did You Know?

If California were its own country, it would have the fifth largest economy in the world.

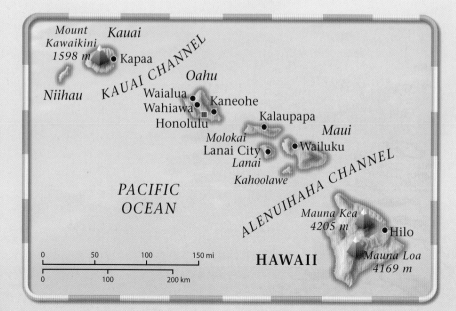

Mount Kawaikini 1598 m

Kauai

Kapaa

KAUAI CHANNEL

Oahu

Niihau

Waialua

Wahiawa

Kaneohe

Honolulu

Kalaupapa

Maui

Molokai

Lanai City

Wailuku

Lanai

ALENUIHAHA CHANNEL

Kahoolawe

PACIFIC OCEAN

Mauna Kea 4205 m

Hilo

HAWAII

Mauna Loa 4169 m

0   50   100   150 mi
0   100   200 km

Facts and Stats

- Texas is 691,027 km² in area – 6.5 times the area of Iceland.

- Los Angeles [F5] is the biggest city with 13.35 million people. This would fill 134 Olympic stadiums.

- Mount Whitney [D5] is the highest mountain at 4418 m in height – 14 times higher than the Eiffel Tower.

▷ The Colorado river has carved a gorge over millions of years to form the **Grand Canyon** [E7]. It is up to 446 km in length and 1.6 km in depth.

0 50 100 150 200 mi

0   100   200   300 km

Brigham City

Ogden

WYOMING

Salt Lake City

Provo

UTAH

Fort Collins • Sterling •

Greeley •

Boulder •

South Platte

Lakewood ■ Denver •

COLORADO

St. Joseph •

NEBRASKA

Kansas City •

Grand Junction •

Aspen •

R O C K Y

Hays •

Salina •

Kansas

Topeka ■

Colorado Springs •

Mount Elbert 4399 m

KANSAS

MISSOURI

Colorado

Pueblo •

Arkansas

Durango •

Lamar •

Hutchinson •

Wichita •

Farmington •

Dodge City •

M O U N T A I N S

umphreys Peak 3851 m

Cimarron

Ponca City •

Enid •

Flagstaff

Gallup •

Los Alamos •

Santa Fe ■

North Canadian

Tulsa •

Muskogee •

Winslow •

Albuquerque •

OKLAHOMA

Oklahoma City ■

NEW MEXICO

Amarillo •

Elk City •

Norman •

Clovis •

Lawton •

Rio Grande

Lubbock •

Wichita Falls •

Durant •

Silver City •

Roswell •

Plano •

Fort Worth •

Dallas •

Sabine

Tucson

Deming •

Las Cruces •

Hobbs •

Carlsbad •

Abilene •

Arlington •

Longview •

Tyler •

Douglas •

El Paso •

Odessa •

Midland •

TEXAS

Brazos

Waco •

Trinity

MEXICO

Pecos •

Pecos

San Angelo •

Leon

LOUISIANA

ARKANSAS

In the next ...the Hoover Dam's [E6] power station will generate enough electricity to power 34.6 million light bulbs. **minute...**

S T O C K T O N P L A T E A U

E D W A R D S P L A T E A U

Colorado

Austin ■

Beaumont

Houston •

Port Arthur •

Del Rio •

San Antonio •

Galveston •

Eagle Pass •

San Antonio

THE DISTANCE across the Rocky Mountains [E9] is 1700 km and once took horse-drawn wagon trains more than six months to travel.

MEXICO

Laredo •

Corpus Christi •

GULF OF MEXICO

McAllen •

Brownsville •

Canada

Canada is the second largest country in the world. The Rocky Mountains of western Canada reach more than 3600 m above sea level and create stunning scenery. Tourists sail along the coast to see icebergs and to view migrating whales. The largest Canadian cities are Toronto and Montreal in the east, and Vancouver in the west. Quebec differs from the rest of Canada because of the large French-speaking population that lives there. Canada has a wealth of natural resources, including wood and petroleum, and is one of the top ten richest nations.

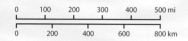

Did You Know?

Canada has 10 percent of the world's forests. These are inhabited by a wide range of wildlife, including bears and moose.

Facts and Stats

• Canada is the second largest country in the world with an area of 9,970,610 km² – 97 times the area of Iceland.

• Toronto [J11] is the biggest city with a population of 5.9 million – this would fill 60 Olympic stadiums.

Deep in the Canadian Rockies is **Banff National Park** in Alberta, which was founded in 1885, and is Canada's oldest national park. Peyto Lake is a popular attraction as the water turns turquoise in colour as the surrounding glaciers melt.

ARCTIC OCEAN

BEAUFORT SEA

Banks Island

• Inuvik

Mackenzie

Kugluktuk •

ALASKA (US)

Dawson •

Norman Wells •

YUKON TERRITORY

MACKENZIE MOUNTAINS

NORTHWEST TERRITORIES

Mount Logan 5959 m

■ Whitehorse

Yellowknife ■

Gulf of Alaska

ROCKY

Fort Resolution •

Fort Smith •

PACIFIC OCEAN

BRITISH COLUMBIA

Peace

C A N

COAST

• Hazelton

• Prince Rupert

• Peace River

Haida Gwaii

MOUNTAINS

• Grande Prairie

Prince George •

ALBERTA

■ Edmonto

Vancouver Island

Fraser

MOUNTAINS

• Red Deer

• Kamloops

• Calgary

Vancouver •

Medicine Hat •

Victoria ■

Lethbridge •

UNITED STATE

Aurora Borealis can be seen in the Northern Hemisphere. Also known as the Northern Lights, the bands of shimmering light are caused by atmospheric particles crashing into the Earth's atmosphere.

Search and Find

Alberta
- Edmonton H7

British Columbia
- Victoria I5

Canada
- Ottawa I12

Manitoba
- Winnipeg I9

New Brunswick
- Fredericton . . . I13

Newfoundland and Labrador
- St. John's . . . H14

Northwest Territories
- Yellowknife F7

Nova Scotia
- Halifax I13

Nunavut
- Iqaluit. F11

Ontario
- Toronto J11

Prince Edward Island
- Charlottetown . I13

Quebec
- Quebec I12

Saskatchewan
- Regina I8

Yukon Territory
- Whitehorse F5

In the next ...Canadians will consume 25 litres of maple syrup – a natural sugar from the sugar maple tree. minute...

GREENLAND (DENMARK)

Ellesmere Island
Axel Heiberg Island
Bathurst Island
Devon Island
Baffin Bay
Prince of Wales Island
Baffin Island
Victoria Island
Iqalukyuuttiaq
NUNAVUT
Southampton Island
Salliit
Iqaluit
LABRADOR SEA
Kangiqtiniq (Rankin Inlet)
Coats Island
Mansel Island
Ungava Peninsula
Hudson Strait
Feuilles
HUDSON BAY
LABRADOR
Nain
NEWFOUNDLAND AND LABRADOR
Churchill
Churchill
Nelson
Goose Bay
Gander
St. John's
Newfoundland
La Grande Rivière
Flin Flon
Prince Albert
MANITOBA
Severn
James Bay
QUEBEC
Anticosti Island
ST. PIERRE AND MIQUELON (FRANCE)
ONTARIO
Fort Albany
Gaspé
PRINCE EDWARD ISLAND
Saskatoon
Albany
Chicoutimi
NEW BRUNSWICK
Charlottetown
Regina
Winnipeg
Fredericton
St. John
Halifax
Moose Jaw
Brandon
Thunder Bay
Trois-Rivières
Sherbrooke
Bay of Fundy
NOVA SCOTIA
F AMERICA
Montreal
Sudbury
Quebec
ATLANTIC OCEAN
Ottawa
Georgian Bay
Toronto
Oshawa
Kitchener
Hamilton
London
Windsor

CHEWAN
ADA

THE DISTANCE from St. John's [H14] to Vancouver [I6] is further than St. John's to Prague, Europe.

Mexico

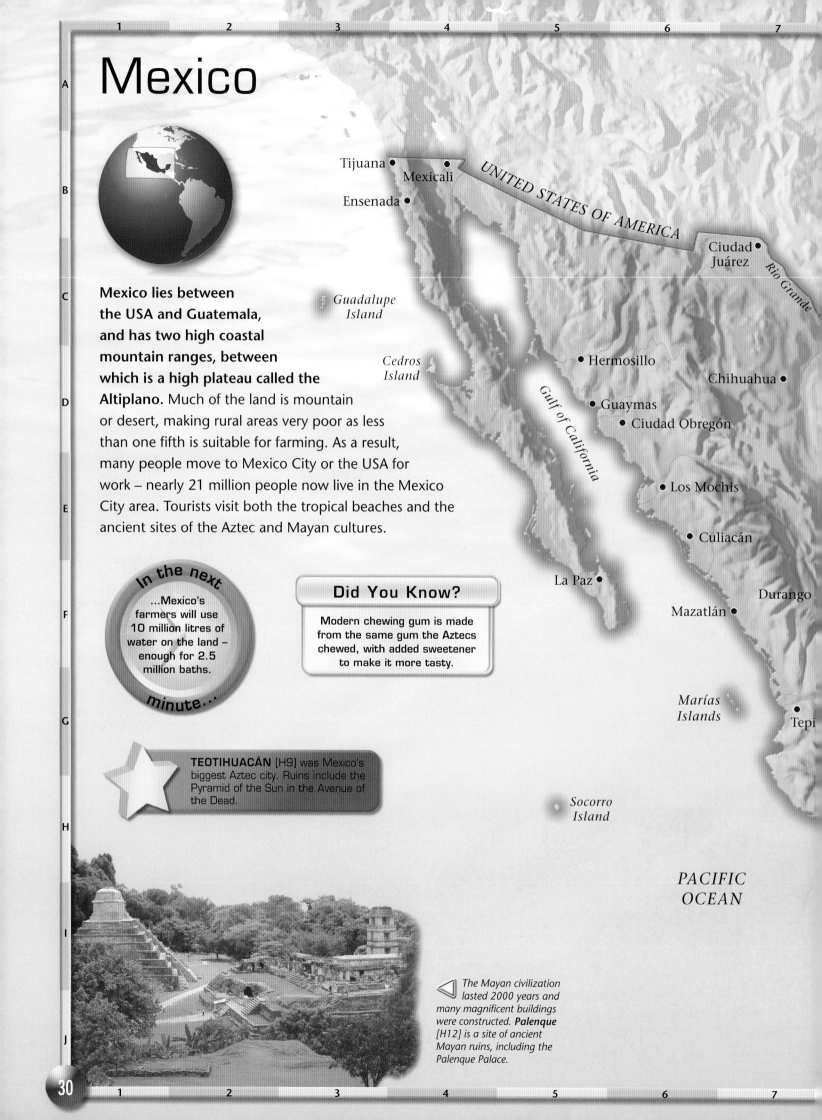

Mexico lies between the USA and Guatemala, and has two high coastal mountain ranges, between which is a high plateau called the **Altiplano**. Much of the land is mountain or desert, making rural areas very poor as less than one fifth is suitable for farming. As a result, many people move to Mexico City or the USA for work – nearly 21 million people now live in the Mexico City area. Tourists visit both the tropical beaches and the ancient sites of the Aztec and Mayan cultures.

In the next
...Mexico's farmers will use 10 million litres of water on the land – enough for 2.5 million baths.
minute...

Did You Know?

Modern chewing gum is made from the same gum the Aztecs chewed, with added sweetener to make it more tasty.

TEOTIHUACÁN [H9] was Mexico's biggest Aztec city. Ruins include the Pyramid of the Sun in the Avenue of the Dead.

Tijuana
Mexicali
Ensenada

UNITED STATES OF AMERICA

Ciudad Juárez

Rio Grande

Guadalupe Island

Cedros Island

Hermosillo

Chihuahua

Gulf of California

Guaymas
Ciudad Obregón

Los Mochis

Culiacán

La Paz

Durango

Mazatlán

Marías Islands

Tepi

Socorro Island

PACIFIC OCEAN

The Mayan civilization lasted 2000 years and many magnificent buildings were constructed. **Palenque** [H12] is a site of ancient Mayan ruins, including the Palenque Palace.

The stories of the ancient Mexican cultures are retold through ornately dressed **folk dancers**. The costumes and performances represent ancient Mayan dances for the gods.

Facts and Stats

• Mexico City [H9] has a population of nearly 21 million people – this would fill 210 Olympic stadiums.

• The Rio Grande [C7] is 3060 km in length – less than half the length of the Nile river.

• The highest mountain is Volcan Pico de Orizaba [H10] at 5700 m in height. It is 18 times higher than the Eiffel Tower.

THE DISTANCE from east to west across Mexico City [H9] is only 30 km, but it takes more than three hours by car at peak times.

The Xochimilco area of Mexico City [H9] has many **ancient canals**. During festivals, boats are covered with flowers to attract tourists.

UNITED STATES OF AMERICA

Nuevo Laredo

Gómez Palacio   Monclova

Terreón   Monterrey   Reynosa
                         Matamoros
Saltillo

MEXICO

Ciudad Victoria

GULF OF MEXICO

Ciudad Madero
San Luis Potosí   Tampico
Aguascalientes

Cancún

Mérida   Cozumel
                          Island
León
Querétaro   Chichén
                          Itzá
Guadalajara
            Pachuca   Yucatán
Teotihuacán   Volcan Pico Peninsula
               de Orizaba
Morelia   Ecatepec 5700 m   Chetumal
Toluca   Bay of Campeche
Colima
        Mexico City   Veracruz
Cuernavaca   Puebla Orizaba
                    Coatzacoalcos   Villahermosa

Chilpancingo
                              Palenque
        Oaxaca
                                          BELIZE
Acapulco   Tuxtla Gutiérrez
                                    GUATEMALA

Gulf of Tehuantepec

0   100   200   300 mi
0   200   400 km

South and Central America

BAHAMAS

CUBA

DOMINICAN
REPUBLIC

BELIZE

GUATEMALA

HONDURAS

2

1

3

4

EL SALVADOR

NICARAGUA

5

6

7

9

COSTA RICA

8

10

GUYANA

PANAMA

VENEZUELA

SURINAME

COLOMBIA

ECUADOR

PERU

B R A Z I L

BOLIVIA

PACIFIC
OCEAN

CHILE

PARAGUAY

URUGUAY

ATLANTIC
OCEAN

ARGENTINA

KEY
1 HAITI
2 JAMAICA
3 ST. KITTS AND NEVIS
4 ANTIGUA AND BARBUDA
5 DOMINICA
6 ST. LUCIA
7 ST. VINCENT AND THE GRENADINES
8 GRENADA
9 BARBADOS
10 TRINIDAD AND TOBAGO

COUNTRY FACTFILE

Country	Life expectancy	Population to nearest thousand	Population growth %	Population as urban %	Area km²	Population density per km²	Capital city	Currency	Languages
Antigua and Barbuda	77	95,000	1.2	59	442	214.9	St. John's	East Caribbean Dollar	English, Creole
Argentina	77	44,045,000	0.9	92	2,766,890	15.9	Buenos Aires	Argentine Peso	Spanish
Bahamas	73	391,000	0.8	87	13,939	28.1	Nassau	Bahamian Dollar	English, Creole
Barbados	76	284,000	0.3	52	430	660.5	Bridgetown	Barbadian Dollar	English, Bajan (Creole)
Belize	69	398,000	1.8	52	22,965	17.3	Belmopan	Belizean Dollar	English, Creole, Spanish
Bolivia	70	11,146,000	1.5	69	1,098,581	10.1	La Paz, Sucre	Boliviano	Spanish, Quechua, Aymara
Brazil	74	207,661,000	0.7	87	8,502,728	24.4	Brasília	Real	Portuguese
Chile	80	17,574,000	0.8	88	756,626	23.2	Santiago, Valparaiso	Chilean Peso	Spanish
Colombia	74	48,292,000	1.0	81	1,141,748	43.1	Bogotá	Colombian Peso	Spanish
Costa Rica	79	4,948,000	1.2	79	51,100	96.8	San José	Costa Rican Colon	Spanish
Cuba	79	11,239,000	-0.3	77	110,861	101.4	Havana	Cuban Peso	Spanish
Dominica	77	74,000	0.2	71	739	100.1	Roseau	East Caribbean Dollar	English, French Creole
Dominican Republic	75	10,169,000	1.2	81	48,311	210.5	Santo Domingo	Domincan Peso	Spanish
Ecuador	77	16,777,000	1.3	79	269,178	62.3	Quito	US Dollar	Spanish, Quechua
El Salvador	75	6,582,000	0.3	72	21,041	312.8	San Salvador	US Dollar	Spanish
Grenada	75	108	0.4	40	344	314	St. George's	East Caribbean Dollar	English, French Creole
Guatemala	73	16,584	1.8	52	108,889	152	Guatemala City	Quetzal	Spanish
Guyana	69	778,000	0.3	36	215,083	3.6	Georgetown	Guyanese Dollar	English, Creole
Haiti	64	10,981,000	1.3	59	27,750	405.7	Port-au-Prince	Gourde	French, Creole
Honduras	71	8,866,000	1.8	57	112,088	78.8	Tegucigalpa	Lempira	Spanish
Jamaica	74	2,729,000	0.7	56	10,991	248.5	Kingston	Jamaican Dollar	English, Creole
Nicaragua	74	6,328,000	1.0	59	130,670	48.4	Managua	Gold Cordoba	Spanish
Panama	79	4,098,000	1.3	75	74,177	55.2	Panama City	Balboa, US Dollar	Spanish, English
Paraguay	77	6,954,000	1.2	62	406,752	17.1	Asunción	Guarani	Spanish, Guarani
Peru	74	29,328,000	1.0	79	1,285,216	22.9	Lima	New Sol	Spanish, Quechua
St. Kitts and Nevis	76	55,000	0.7	44	269	204.5	Basseterre	East Caribbean Dollar	English, Creole
St. Lucia	78	179,000	0.3	59	617	290.1	Castries	East Caribbean Dollar	English, French Creole
St. Vincent and the Grenadines	76	110,000	0	55	398	282.8	Kingstown	East Caribbean Dollar	English, Creole
Suriname	73	563,000	1.0	75	163,820	3.4	Paramaribo	Suriname Dollar	Dutch, Sranantonga, Hindi
Trinidad and Tobago	73	1,328,000	0	72	5128	259	Port-of-Spain	Trinidad and Tobago Dollar	English, Creole
Uruguay	77	3,493,000	0.3	95	175,016	20	Montevideo	Uruguayan Peso	Spanish
Venezuela*	76	28,930,000	1.5	88	916,445	34.3	Caracas	Sovereign Bolivar	Spanish

*Likely to change due to uncertain economic and political situation.

Central America and the Caribbean

Central America is a narrow area of land where the mountain chain continues from Antarctica up to Alaska. The only gap, which joins the Atlantic and Pacific Oceans, is the Panama Canal.

The manmade canal shortens the journey between the oceans by 13,000 km. The Caribbean islands are mainly agricultural, but their sandy beaches, warm seas and links to the USA and Europe make them popular tourist destinations.

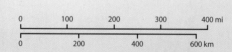 In many places in Central America, **weaving** is still done by hand rather than by machine. Colourful rugs and tapestries from the region are sold around the world.

Havana
Pinar del Río
Cárdenas
Nueva Gerona
Santa Clara
Cienfuegos
Sancti Spíritus
CUB
Camagüey
Isla de la Juventud

CAYMAN ISLANDS (UK)

Montego Bay
JAMAICA
Spani
Tow

MEXICO
BELIZE
Belize City
Belmopan
MAYA MOUNTAINS
Quezaltenango
San Antonio
GUATEMALA
Guatemala City
San Pedro Sula
La Ceiba
El Progreso
Escuintla
HONDURAS
San Salvador
Tegucigalpa
EL SALVADOR
Chinandega
Estelí
León
NICARAGUA
Managua

COSTA RICA
Puntarenas
Heredia
San José
Cerro Chirripó Grande 3819 m
Gulf of Darien
Barranqu
Cartagena
Panama Canal
Colón
San Miguelito
Sincelejo
David
CORDILLERA CENTRAL
Panama City
Montería
PANAMA
Gulf of Panama

Medellín
Quibdó
Manizales
Pereira
Armenia
Ibagué
Buenaventura
Cali
Popayán
Pasto
ECUADOR
CORDILLERA C

Scale:
| 0 | 100 | 200 | 300 | 400 mi |
| 0 | 200 | 400 | 600 km |

Search and Find

Facts and Stats

• Colombia has a population of nearly 48.3 million people – this would fill 483 Olympic stadiums.

• The life expectancy of people in Haiti is only 64 years, compared to 79 years in Cuba and a world average of 69 years.

• The average income per person in Haiti is £586 and £23,682 in the Bahamas, compared to a world average of £8196.

A

Nassau

BAHAMAS

▷ There are two lakes in the craters of the **Poas volcano**, Costa Rica. Due to geothermal activity, it is believed that the lakes are turning into geysers. Since 1828, the volcano has erupted 46 times.

B

TURKS AND
CAICOS ISLANDS
(UK)

• Holguín
Bayamo
• Guantánamo
ntiago Cap-Haïtien
Cuba Gonaïves

DOMINICAN
REPUBLIC

Santiago San Francisco
de Macorís
La Vega
La Romana

Port-au-Prince
ngston Santo
Les Cayes Jacmel **Domingo**

HAITI

C

VIRGIN
ISLANDS
(UK)

VIRGIN
ISLANDS
(US)

ANGUILLA (UK)

ST. MARTIN (FRANCE)/SINT MAARTEN (NETH.)
ST. BARTHELÉMY (FRANCE)
ST. EUSTATIUS (NETH.)

PUERTO
RICO (US)

SABA
(NETH.)

**ANTIGUA AND
BARBUDA**

Basseterre
ST. KITTS AND NEVIS St. John's
MONTSERRAT (UK)

D

GUADELOUPE
(FRANCE)

DOMINICA
Roseau

MARTINIQUE (FRANCE)

Castries
ST. LUCIA

In the next
...Colombia, will pack 1313 kg of coffee into bags for export – that's nearly 200,000 cups.
minute...

CARIBBEAN SEA

ARUBA
(NETHERLANDS)

CURAÇAO
(NETHERLANDS)

ST. VINCENT AND
THE GRENADINES Kingstown

BARBADOS
Bridgetown

E

GRENADA St. George's

BONAIRE
(NETHERLANDS)

Port-of-Spain

World Record
At more than 979 m in height, Angel Falls [G11] is the highest waterfall in the world.

nta
arta
Pico Cristobal Colon
5800 m

oledad
• Maracaibo

Caracas Cumaná

**TRINIDAD
AND TOBAGO**

F

Barquisimeto
Valencia Maracay Barcelona
Valera
• Guanare
• Barinas

Cúcuta
• San Cristóbal

• Ciudad Guayana
Ciudad Bolívar

• Bucaramanga
Barrancabermeja

VENEZUELA

Georgetown

G

• Tunja
Río Meta

Angel Falls ◆

GUIANA
HIGHLANDS

Paramaribo

FRENCH
GUIANA
(FRANCE)

Bogotá
• Villavicencio

Puerto Ayacucho

GUYANA

SURINAME

H

COLOMBIA

Río Vaupés

BRAZIL

Río Apaporis

BRAZIL

BRAZIL

I

Río Caquetá

Did You Know?

PERU

THE DISTANCE from one end of the Panama Canal [F6] to the other is only 77 km, but it saves 18 days sailing time.

The Bermuda Triangle is an area in the Atlantic Ocean, northeast of the Caribbean. Many ships and aircraft have disappeared here without a trace.

J

South America

Stretching from the tropical forests of the Amazon to just a short distance from icy Antarctica, South America is a continent of contrasts. The Andes stretch the length of the continent, but the main feature is the Amazon rainforest. The rainforest is home to more plant and animal species than any other habitat in the world. However, around 25,000 km² of the rainforest is destroyed each year to make room for farmland. The forest not only provides a home to many animals, but it is also the source of many plant-derived medicines. By absorbing carbon dioxide, the forest helps to reduce global warming.

At 6992 km in length, the **Amazon river** crosses the full width of Brazil. A wide range of wildlife live in the river, including the endangered boto, or Amazon river dolphin.

Search and Find

Argentina	Ecuador
● Buenos Aires . . G8	● Quito B5
Bolivia	**Paraguay**
● La Paz D7	● Asunción E8
● Sucre. E7	**Peru**
Brazil	● Lima D5
● Brasília. D10	**Uruguay**
Chile	● Montevideo G8
● Santiago. G7	
● Valparaíso. G6	

In the next ...9000 tonnes of the Amazon rainforest will be destroyed – about 100 trees and other plants. minute...

The statue of Jesus, **Christ the Redeemer**, stands at the top of Mount Corcovado, Rio de Janeiro [E10]. At 38 m in height, it is one of the most famous landmarks in the world.

VENEZUEL

Esmeraldas
Ibarra
Manta   **Quito**
Portoviejo   Ambato
Guayaquil   Riobamba
ECUADOR
COLOMBIA
Negro
Amazon
Iquitos
AMAZON BASIN
Piura
Chiclayo
Trujillo   Pucallpa   Porto Velho
Chimbote   **PERU**   Rio Branco
Huacho   **Lima**
Callao   Huancayo
Ayacucho   Cusco   **BOLIVIA**
Ica   Lake
Juliaca   Titicaca
Arequipa   Puno   Cochabamb
La Paz   Oruro   Sant
Arica   **Sucre**
Nevado Sajama   6520 m   Potosi
Iquique
Tarija
Calama   San Salvad
ATACAMA de Jujuy
Antofagasta   DESERT
PACIFIC OCEAN
CHILE   GRA
San Miguel de Tucumán
ARGI
La Serena   Córdob
Coquimbo
San Juan
Godoy Cruz   Río Cuart
Vina del Mar
Valparaíso   Mendoza
Santiago   Cerro
Rancagua   Aconcagua   6959 m
Talcahuano
Concepción   Chillan
Los Angeles
Temuco   Neuquén
Valdivia
Osorno   Comodor
Puerto Montt   Rivadavia
PATAGONIA
Puerto Madry
Río Gallego
Punta Arenas
Ushuai

GUYANA
SURINAME
FRENCH GUIANA (FRANCE)

Boa Vista
Amapá
Macapá
Manaus
Amazon
Marajó Island
Belém
São Luis
Parnaíba
Madeira
Santarém
Altamira
Fortaleza
Marabá
Imperatriz
Teresina
Mossoró
Natal
Campina Grande
João Pessoa
Recife
Araguaína
Juazeiro do Norte
BRAZIL
Tocantins
Juazeiro
Maceio
Aracaju
Feira de Santana
Salvador
Chiabá
Brasília
Itabuna
MATO GROSSO PLATEAU
Anápolis
Goiânia
Campo Grande
Uberlândia
Uberaba
Governador Valadares
Rio Préto
Belo Horizonte
Vitoria
Nova Iguaçu
Niteroi
Campinas
São Paulo
Rio de Janeiro
Pedro Juan Caballero
Santos
PARAGUAY
Curitiba
Asunción
Ciudad del Este
HACO
Resistencia
Florianópolio
Corrientes
NTINA
Porto Alegre
Salto
Rivera
Pelotas
anta Fe
Rio Grande
Rosario
URUGUAY
Buenos Aires
Montevideo
Lomas e Zamora
La Plata
Bahía Blanca
Mar del Plata
Punta Alta

ATLANTIC OCEAN

Cruz

0   200   400   600   800 mi
0   400   800   1200 km

FALKLAND ISLANDS
(UK)

SOUTH GEORGIA
(UK)

ape Horn

Facts and Stats

- Brazil's population is 207.6 million and would fill 2077 Olympic stadiums. In comparison, Uruguay's population is only 3.3 million.
- There are only 5 doctors per 10,000 people in Bolivia, compared to 39 doctors in Uruguay and a world average of 15 doctors.
- The average income per person in Uruguay is £12,405 and £2592 in Bolivia, compared to a world average of £8196.

Did You Know?

The Amazon river holds two thirds of all the flowing water in the world and is 270 km in width where it meets the sea.

Extreme Weather

Chile's Atacama Desert [E7] has an average rainfall of less than 0.5 mm a year. The city of Calama [E7] has never recorded a single drop. It's too dry for animals to survive.

USHUAIA [J7] is the most southern city in the world. It has a ski resort and a base for supply ships to Antarctica.

THE DISTANCE from Chile to the next land mass of Australia is 10,400 km and would take 12 hours by plane.

One of the largest **street carnivals** in the world is held every February in Rio de Janeiro [E10]. People dress in elaborate costumes and parades take place in the city centre. More than 200,000 people take part.

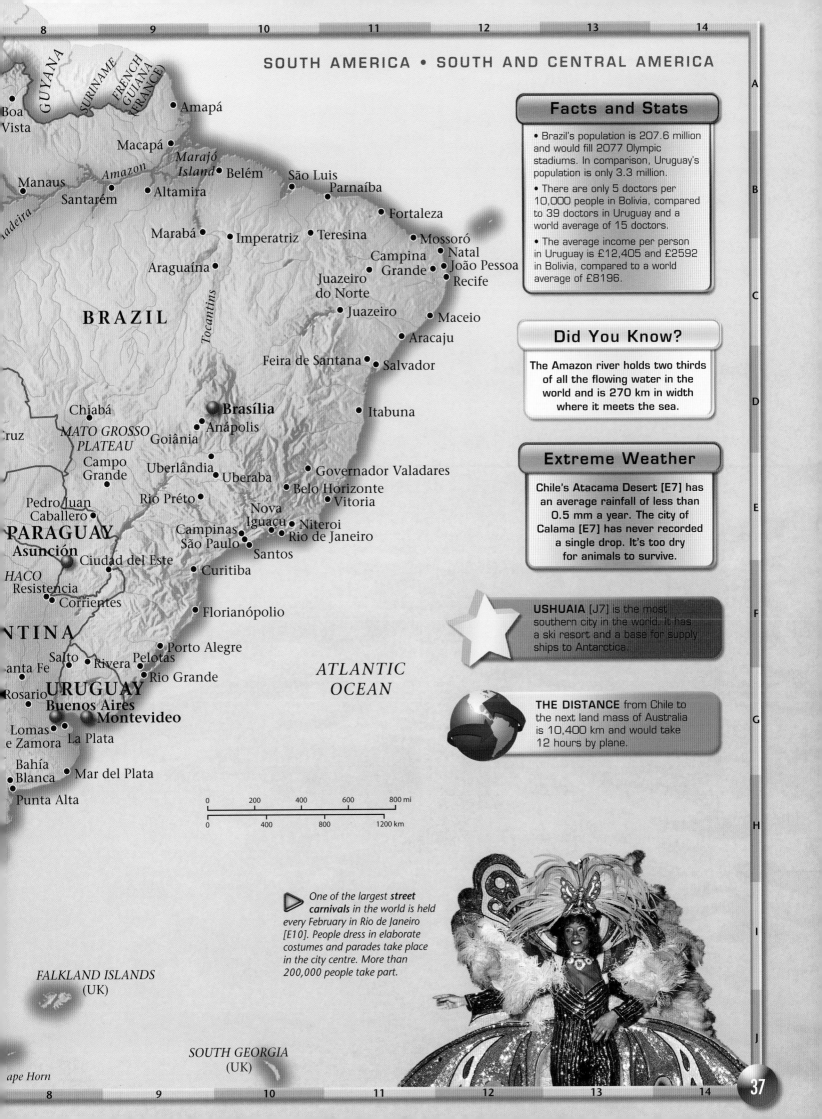

Europe

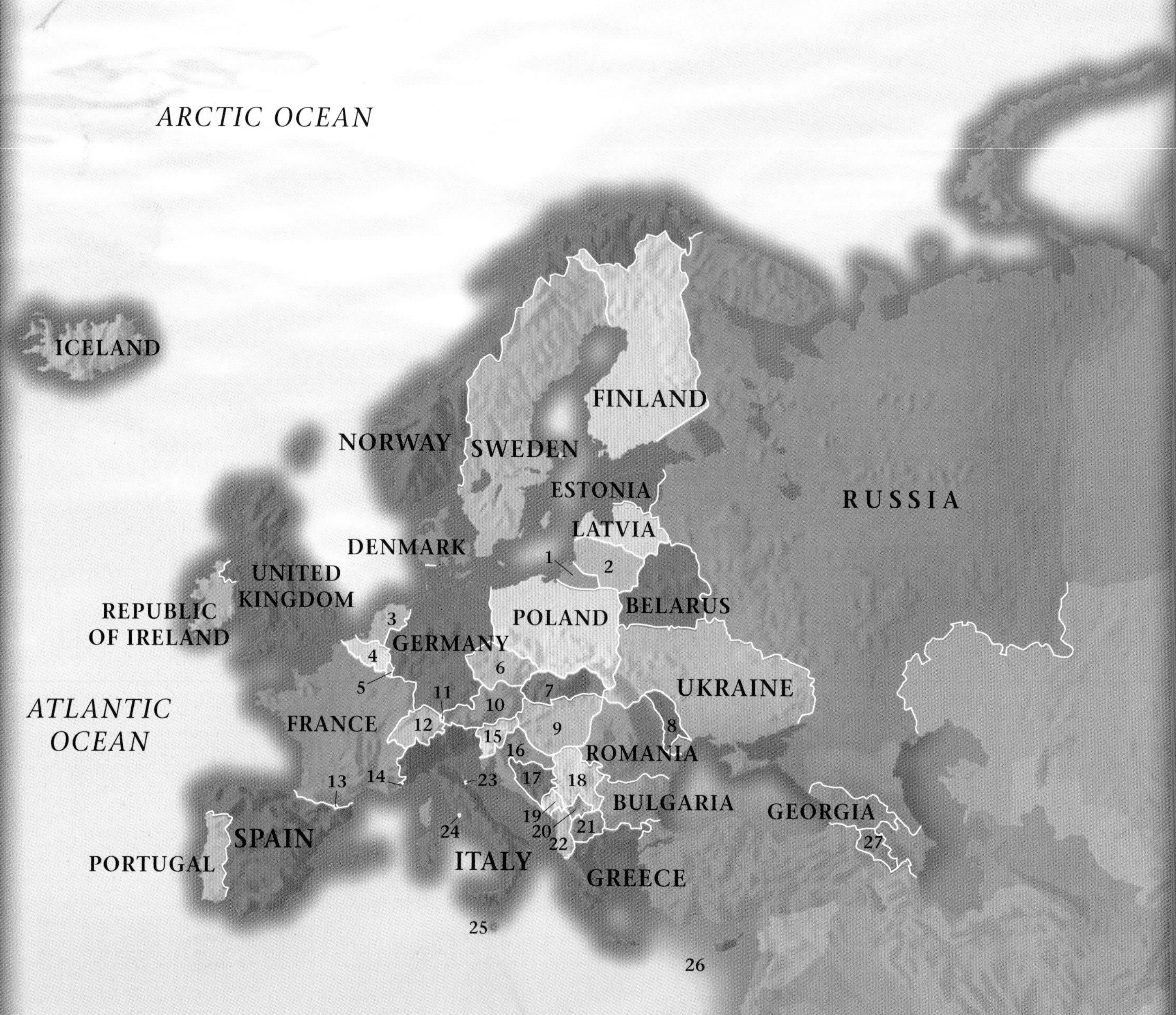

ARCTIC OCEAN
ICELAND
FINLAND
NORWAY
SWEDEN
ESTONIA
RUSSIA
LATVIA
DENMARK
1
2
UNITED KINGDOM
BELARUS
REPUBLIC OF IRELAND
3
POLAND
GERMANY
4
6
5
11
7
UKRAINE
ATLANTIC OCEAN
10
FRANCE
12
15
9
8
ROMANIA
16
13
14
23
17
18
BULGARIA
GEORGIA
19
24
20
21
SPAIN
22
27
PORTUGAL
ITALY
GREECE
25
26

KEY
1 RUSSIA
2 LITHUANIA
3 NETHERLANDS
4 BELGIUM
5 LUXEMBOURG
6 CZECH REPUBLIC
7 SLOVAKIA
8 MOLDOVA
9 HUNGARY
10 AUSTRIA
11 LIECHTENSTEIN
12 SWITZERLAND
13 ANDORRA
14 MONACO
15 SLOVENIA
16 CROATIA
17 BOSNIA AND HERZEGOVINA
18 SERBIA
19 MONTENEGRO
20 KOSOVO
21 MACEDONIA
22 ALBANIA
23 SAN MARINO
24 VATICAN CITY
25 MALTA
26 CYPRUS
27 ARMENIA

* Crimea is legally part of Ukraine but has been annexed by Russia. See page 58 for detailed map.

COUNTRY FACTFILE

Country	Life expectancy	Population to nearest thousand	Population growth %	Population as urban %	Area km²	Population density per km²	Capital city	Currency	Languages
Albania	79	2,870,000	0	60	28,748	99.9	Tiranë	Lek	Albanian
Andorra	83	75,000	0	95	468	161.1	Andorra la Vella	Euro	Catalan, Spanish
Armenia	75	2,973,000	–0.2	70	29,743	100	Yerevan	Dram	Armenian
Austria	82	8,823,000	0.5	68	83,879	105.2	Vienna	Euro	German
Belarus	73	9,492,000	–0.2	79	207,546	45.7	Minsk	Belarusian Rouble	Belarusian, Russian
Belgium	81	11,376,000	0.7	98	30,528	367.2	Brussels	Euro	Dutch, Flemish, French
Bosnia and Herzegovina	77	3,438,000	–0.2	49	51,129	67.1	Sarajevo	Marka	Croat, Serb
Bulgaria	75	7,050,000	–0.6	75	111,036	63.5	Sofia	Lev	Bulgarian, Turkish
Croatia	76	4,154,000	–0.5	77	56,542	73.4	Zagreb	Kuna	Croat
Cyprus*	79	1,141,000	1.3	70	9251	123.3	Nicosia	Euro	Greek, Turkish, English
Czech Republic	79	10,610,000	0.1	75	78,864	134.5	Prague	Czech Koruna	Czech
Denmark	80	5,781,000	0.2	88	43,094	134.1	Copenhagen	Danish Krone	Danish
Estonia	77	1,319,000	0	69	45,227	30.3	Tallinn	Euro	Estonian, Russian
Finland	81	5,513,000	0.4	85	338,145	16.4	Helsinki	Euro	Finnish, Swedish
France	82	66,448,000	0.4	85	639,176	102.4	Paris	Euro	French
Georgia	76	4,015,000	–0.02	68	69,492	57.8	Tbilisi	Lari	Georgian
Germany	81	82,522,000	0	88	357,021	230.9	Berlin	Euro	German
Greece	81	10,768,000	–0.1	79	131,957	81.6	Athens	Euro	Greek
Hungary	76	9,798,000	–0.3	71	93,022	105.3	Budapest	Forint	Hungarian
Iceland	83	348,000	1.1	94	102,819	3.4	Reykjavik	Icelandic Krona	Icelandic
Ireland, Republic of	81	4,758,000	1.2	63	70,285	67.7	Dublin	Euro	English, Irish (Gaelic)
Italy	82	60,484,000	0	71	301,277	201	Rome	Euro	Italian
Kosovo	77	1,799,000	0.3	51	10,828	166.1	Pristina	Euro	Albanian
Latvia	75	1,934,000	–1.1	69	64,610	30	Riga	Euro	Latvian, Russian
Liechtenstein	82	38,000	0.7	45	160	238.1	Vaduz	Swiss Franc	German
Lithuania	75	2,810,000	–1.1	68	65,301	43	Vilnius	Euro	Lithuanian, Russian
Luxembourg	82	602,000	2	91	2586	232.8	Luxembourg	Euro	Letzeburgish, German, French
Macedonia	70	2,074,000	0.2	67	25,713	80.7	Skopje	Macedonian Denar	Macedonian, Albanian
Malta	81	476,000	0.3	95	316	1511.1	Valletta	Euro	Maltese, English
Moldova	71	3,503,000	–1.1	48	33,873	103.5	Chisinau	Moldovan Leu	Romanian (Moldovan), Russian, Ukrainian
Monaco	89	37,000	0.3	100	2	18,650	Monaco	Euro	French, Monegasque, Italian
Montenegro	75	622,000	–0.3	67	13,894	44.8	Podgorica	Euro	Serb, Albanian, Montenegrin
Netherlands	81	17,184,000	0.4	92	41,546	413.6	Amsterdam, The Hague	Euro	Dutch, Frisian
Norway	82	5,214,000	1	82	323,878	16.1	Oslo	Norwegian Krone	Norwegian
Poland	78	38,434,000	–0.1	66	312,685	122.9	Warsaw	Zloty	Polish
Portugal	79	10,291,000	0	65	92,391	111.4	Lisbon	Euro	Portuguese
Romania	75	19,524,000	0	57	237,500	82.4	Bucharest	Leu	Romanian, Hungarian
Russia	71	144,530,000	0	78	17,075,400	8.5	Moscow	Rouble	Russian, Tatar, Ukrainian
San Marino	83	33,000	0.7	97	61	545.9	San Marino	Euro	Italian
Serbia	76	7,021,000	–0.5	56	77,468	90.5	Belgrade	Serbian Dinar	Serb, Hungarian
Slovakia	77	5,435,000	0	57	49,036	110.8	Bratislava	Euro	Slovak, Hungarian
Slovenia	78	2,067,000	0	55	20,273	101.9	Ljubljana	Euro	Slovenian
Spain	82	46,572,000	0.8	80	504,782	92.2	Madrid	Euro	Spanish (Castilian), Catalan, Basque, Gallego
Sweden	82	10,120,000	0.8	87	449,964	22.5	Stockholm	Swedish Krona	Swedish
Switzerland	83	8,484,000	0.7	74	41,285	205.5	Bern	Swiss Franc	German, French, Italian
Ukraine	72	44,737,000	–0.4	70	603,700	74.4	Kiev	Hryvnia	Ukrainian, Russian
United Kingdom	81	66,040,000	0.5	83	244,088	270.6	London	British Pound	English
Vatican City	N/A	1000	0	100	0.44	2080	Vatican City	Euro	Italian, Latin

*Cyprus is part of Europe, but the mapping can be found in the Asia section.

Britain and Ireland

The United Kingdom (England, Scotland, Wales and Northern Ireland) and the Republic of Ireland make up the British Isles. The UK has become one of the most influential and prosperous countries in the world. By 1900, the British Empire ruled many countries, including Canada, South Africa, India and Australia, which is why so many nations speak English. Ireland declared independence in 1919, but it only came into effect in 1922. Scotland, Wales and Northern Ireland now have their own parliaments. Manufacturing was once the major industry, but most wealth is now generated by banking, insurance and high-tech equipment.

The **Giant's Causeway** [E7] in Northern Ireland is made up of 40,000 columns created by a volcanic eruption. The columns measure up to 12 m in height. According to legend, the giant Finn McCool began to build the causeway towards Scotland, but he fell asleep before he finished it.

Search and Find

England
- London H10

Northern Ireland
- Belfast F7

Republic of Ireland
- Dublin G7

Scotland
- Edinburgh E8

Wales
- Cardiff H8

THE DISTANCE from Land's End [I7] to John o'Groats [C9] once took a cyclist 41 hours and a runner 12 days to complete.

ATLANTIC OCEAN

Lewis

Outer Hebrides

Skye

Giant's Causeway

Londonderry

NORTHERN IRELAND

Sligo

Belfa

Armagl

REPUBLIC OF IRELAND

IRISH SEA

Drogheda

Galway

Shannon

Liffey

Dubli

Limerick

WICKLOW MOUNTAINS

ST. GEORGE'S CHANNEL

Carrantuohill 1041 m

Waterford

Cork

Isles of Scilly

Land's End

Edinburgh [E8], Scotland, is the second most visited city after London. More than 4 million people are attracted to the city each year to see historical sights, such as Edinburgh Castle, or to attend the Edinburgh Festival in August.

8 9 10 11 12 13 14

A

Shetland
Islands

Lerwick

Orkney
Islands

John o'Groats

Snowdonia National Park [G8], Wales, was created in 1951 and covers 2142 km² of land. More than 26,000 people actually live within the area and it receives more than six million visitors a year. The area is a mixture of forest, open land, coast and mountains – making it popular with hikers.

B

C

0   50   100   150 mi
0   100   200 km

Inverness

SCOTLAND

Ben Nevis
1343 m

RAMPIAN MOUNTAINS

Aberdeen

Perth   Dundee

Falkirk

gow   Edinburgh

Motherwell

Ayr

NORTH
SEA

D

THE TOWER OF LONDON [H10] has been a castle, a royal palace, a prison, a zoo and the home of the crown jewels.

Newcastle
upon Tyne

Carlisle   Sunderland

Scafell Pike
977 m

PENNINES

Middlesbrough

ISLE
OF MAN
(UK)

York

Blackpool   Leeds   Hull

Snowdon   Liverpool   Manchester
1085 m

Chester   ENGLAND   Sheffield

Wrexham   Stoke-on-Trent

WALES

Aberystwyth

Derby   Nottingham

Leicester   Peterborough

Birmingham

Coventry

Northampton   Cambridge

CAMBRIAN
MOUNTAINS

Wye   Severn

Trent

Ouse

Norwich

Ipswich

Colchester

Swansea   Gloucester

Newport   Swindon   Oxford

Cardiff

Bristol

Thames

London

Avebury Stone Circle

Reading

Stonehenge

Dover

Southampton   Portsmouth

Bournemouth

Brighton

Exeter

Plymouth

Isle of
Wight

ENGLISH CHANNEL

Guernsey
CHANNEL   Jersey
ISLANDS (UK)

In the next ...148 passengers will arrive or depart from London's Heathrow Airport, one of the busiest airports in the world. *minute...*

E

Facts and Stats

• London [H10] is the biggest city with nearly 10.5 million people. This would fill 1048 Olympic stadiums.

• The Shannon [G6] is the longest river at 386 km in length. However, it is more than 17 times shorter than the Nile river.

• Ben Nevis [D8] is the highest mountain at 1343 m in height – four times higher than the Eiffel Tower.

F

G

Did You Know?

Avebury Stone Circle [I9] is 6000 years old, and is the largest ancient stone monument in the world.

H

I

The **Millennium Bridge**, London [H10], was opened in 2000, and is used as a pedestrian footbridge. It has been designed to hold 5000 people at any one time. St. Paul's Cathedral is situated at its north end and the Tate Modern art gallery is at the south end.

J

Scandinavia

Norway, Sweden, Denmark, Finland and Iceland are Europe's most northerly and least populated countries. Mainland Scandinavia stretches from Norway's mountainous Atlantic coast in the west to Finland's low-lying forested countryside in the east. More than one third lies within the Arctic Circle where, during a 73-day winter period, the Sun never rises. Norway and Iceland are not members of the European Union. Living standards are high due to vast natural resources, such as oil, gas, timber and iron. Scandinavia has a reputation for stylish designs with brands such as Bang and Olufsen, Ikea and Volvo.

In the next minute...

...Sweden will make more than two million matches – enough to fill 40,000 boxes.

World Record

Finland has more of its territory covered by lakes than any other country – 187,888 lakes cover 10 percent of the country.

Facts and Stats

- Sweden's population of 10.1 million would fill 101 Olympic stadiums.
- The life expectancy of people in Sweden is 82 years, compared to 80 years in Denmark and a world average of 69 years.
- The average income per person in Norway is £57,452, compared to a world average of £8196.

Did You Know?

The first Legoland was opened in Billund [I6], Denmark, in 1968. On average, every person in the world owns 52 Lego bricks.

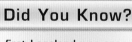
Sognefjord [F5], Norway, is the second largest fjord in the world. Towns are situated on the fjord and the stunning scenery attracts many tourists, which helps to support the economy.

Lofoten Islands   Bodø

ATLANTIC OCEAN

Kristiansund   Trondheim   Östersund

Ålesund

NORWAY

Sognefjord   Galdhøpiggen 2469 m

Bergen   Voss

Lillehammer

Hamar

Haugesund

Oslo

Drammen

Stavanger

Skien   Fredrikstad   Karlstad

Örebro

Kristiansand

Linköping

Skagerrak

Göteborg   Borås

NORTH SEA

Jönköping

Ålborg   Kattegat   Halmstad   Växjö

DENMARK

Randers

Århus   Helsingborg   Karlshamn

Billund

Copenhagen   Karlskron

Esbjerg

Lund

Kolding   Odense

Roskilde   Malmö

BORNHOLM (DENMARK)

GERMANY

ARCTIC OCEAN

North Cape

Vadsø

Tromsø

Narvik

Kiruna

L A P L A N D

Gällivare

Rovaniemi

SWEDEN

Kemi

Luleå
Piteå

Oulu

Skellefteå

G U L F   O F   B O T H N I A

Umeå

Kokkola

Örnsköldsvik

Kuopio

Vaasa

Sundsvall

Jyväskylä

RUSSIA

FINLAND

Söderhamn

Pori   Tampere

Gävle   Hämeenlinna   Lahti

Åland   Vantaa
Islands   Turku   Kotka

Mariehamn   Espoo   Helsinki

Uppsala

Västerås

Stockholm

Södertälje

Norrköping

Västervik

Visby
Gotland

Borgholm
Öland

BALTIC SEA

Sweden's **Ice Hotel** near Kiruna [C8] is only open from December to April and is rebuilt each year. The hotel has more than 80 rooms and even has a church. Everything in the hotel, down to the glasses, is made of ice.

Search and Find

Denmark
- Copenhagen . . . I7

Finland
- Helsinki G10

Iceland
- Reykjavik. I11

Norway
- Oslo G6

Sweden
- Stockholm. G8

THE DISTANCE from Norway's North Cape [A9] to the North Pole is shorter than the distance from Oslo [G6] to southern Italy.

LAPLAND [C9] is said to be where Santa Claus lives. In December, many tourists visit the region to see Santa with his elves and reindeer.

0   50   100   150 mi
0   100   200 km

Isafjördhur

Olafsfjördhur

Húsavik   Akureyri   Myvatn

Seydisfjördhur

Eskifjördhur

ICELAND

Ólafsvik

VATNAJÖKULL

Hvitá   Thórsá

Akranes   Hvannadalshnúkur
                2119 m   Höfn

Keflavik   Reykjavik

Kopavogur

NORWEGIAN SEA

ATLANTIC OCEAN

Vestmannaeyar

0   50   100   150   200 mi
0   100   200   300 km

Spain and Portugal

The Iberian Peninsula is occupied by Spain and Portugal. Africa is less than 16 km from the Strait of Gibraltar, and to the north Spain is bordered by France and the mountain state of Andorra. Spain also includes the Balearic Islands in the Mediterranean Sea and the Canary Islands, including Tenerife and Gran Canaria, which lie 100 km west of Africa in the Atlantic Ocean. Well-known for olive, orange and lemon groves, as well as hot weather and sandy beaches, these countries attract millions of tourists each year.

▷ The costas of Spain are popular coastal regions. **Costa Brava** [C13] in northeast Spain is in the vicinity of Barcelona. S'Agaró is an exclusive resort, and its hotels have even been used in films.

THE DISTANCE from the east to the west side of the border between Spain and Gibraltar [I7] is only 800 m.

BILBAO [B9] is home to many museums including the Fine Arts Museum and the world-famous Guggenheim Museum.

Facts and Stats

- Spain's population of nearly 46.6 million would fill 466 Olympic stadiums. However, the population of Andorra is only 67,000 and would only fill half a stadium.
- The life expectancy of people in Spain is 82 years, compared to a world average of 69 years.
- The average income per person in Andorra is £29,787, compared to a world average of £8196.

Did You Know?

Sardines are the most popular Portuguese seafood. The average consumption for a person is 6 kg a year.

El Ferrol
La Coruña
Gijón
Oviedo
Lugo
Santiago de Compostela
CANTABRIAN M
Sil
León
Vigo
Orense
Esla
Braga
Duero
Zamora
Guimaraes
Tormes
Porto
Salamanca
Aveiro
SIERR
Coimbra
Tajo (Tagu
Santarém
Tajo (Tagus)
Cáceres
PORTUGAL
Mérida
Estoril
Lisbon
Badajoz
Almada
Évora
Setúbal
Beja
Guadiana
Guadalquivir
Lagos
Huelva
Seville
ATLANTIC OCEAN
Faro
Moron de la Frontera
Arcos
Jerez de la Frontera
Ronda
Cádiz
GIBRALTA (UK)
Algeciras
Strait of Gibraltar
CEUTA (SPAIN)
MOROCCO

BAY OF BISCAY

Santander
Bilbao
San Sebastián
...NTAINS
Vitória-Gasteiz Pamplona
FRANCE
Pico de Aneto
3405 m
PYRENEES
ANDORRA
Logroño
Burgos
Andorra
la Vella
Palencia
Soria
Zaragoza
Lleida
Girona
Manresa
Terrasa Mataró
Barcelona
Valladolid
Duero
Ebro
Gállego
Cinca
Costa Brava
Reus Tarragona
Costa Dorada
Segovia
Ávila
Tortosa
E GREDOS
Guadalajara
Alcalá de Henares
Morella
Costa del Azahar
Menorca
Mahón
Madrid
Teruel
Mallorca
Aranjuez Cuenca
Castellón de la Plana
Toledo
Turia
Sagunto
Palma
Valencia
SPAIN
Júcar
Gulf of
Valencia
BALEARIC ISLANDS
Ibiza
Ciudad Real
Albacete
Ibiza
Alcoy
Benidorm
Formentera
Segura
Alicante
Elche
Linares
Costa Blanca
Córdoba
Murcia
Jaén
Lorca Cartagena
Genil
Granada
SIERRA NEVADA
Motril Almería
Málaga
Marbella Costa del Sol
MEDITERRANEAN SEA
MELILLA
(SPAIN)

Search and Find

Andorra
● Andorra la Vella C12
Portugal
● Lisbon G4

Spain
● Madrid E8

0   50   100 mi
0   80   160 km

In the next
...the bark of Portugal's and Spain's cork trees will produce enough cork for 136,000 wine bottles.
minute...

▷ Bullfighting is popular in Spain. **Toreros** are performers who fight and kill bulls. There are various types, including matadors, depending on the skills used during the fight. Performances and costumes are elaborate, attracting tourists from all over the world.

France and Monaco

The third largest country in Europe, France has the third highest population. Despite having a rural landscape, more than 85 percent of the population lives in towns, with more than one sixth in Paris. France has an excellent health, education and social care system, and is the fifth wealthiest country in the world. Northern France is an industrialized, low-lying region, and the south has the snow-capped peaks of the Alps and Pyrenees as well as the sunny beaches of the Mediterranean Sea. Monaco is a tiny, independent, French-speaking country. One of the richest countries in the world, Monaco boasts more than 2000 millionaires and no taxes. Only three hours from the mainland by boat is the mountainous island of Corsica.

Search and Find

France	Monaco
● Paris C9	● Monaco H11

PARIS [C9] is one of the most visited places in the world, with attractions such as the Eiffel Tower and the Louvre.

THE DISTANCE from Calais [A9] to Dover, England, is 41 km and has been swum in less than eight hours.

*The Gothic cathedral **Notre Dame de Paris** [C9] was mainly constructed in the 13th and 14th centuries, but is constantly being restored. The famous Emmanuel bell weighs 13 tonnes.*

In the next ...France will provide the UK with enough electricity to power one light bulb in every home. minute...

Île d'Ouessant
Brest ●
St. Malo ●
Quimper ●
Laval ●
Lorient ●
Rennes ●
Belle-Île
Angers ●
St. Nazaire ●
● Nantes
Loir
Île d'Yeu
Poitiers ●
Île de Ré
● La Rochelle
BAY OF BISCAY
Cognac ●
Angoulême ●
Périgueux ●
Bordeaux ●
Dordogne
Bergerac
Garonne
Mont-de-Marsan ●
Agen ●
Bayonne ●
Adour
Montauban
● Pau
Toulou
● Tarbes
● Lourdes
Ariège
PYRENEES
SPAIN
ANDORRA
Cherbour
Bo

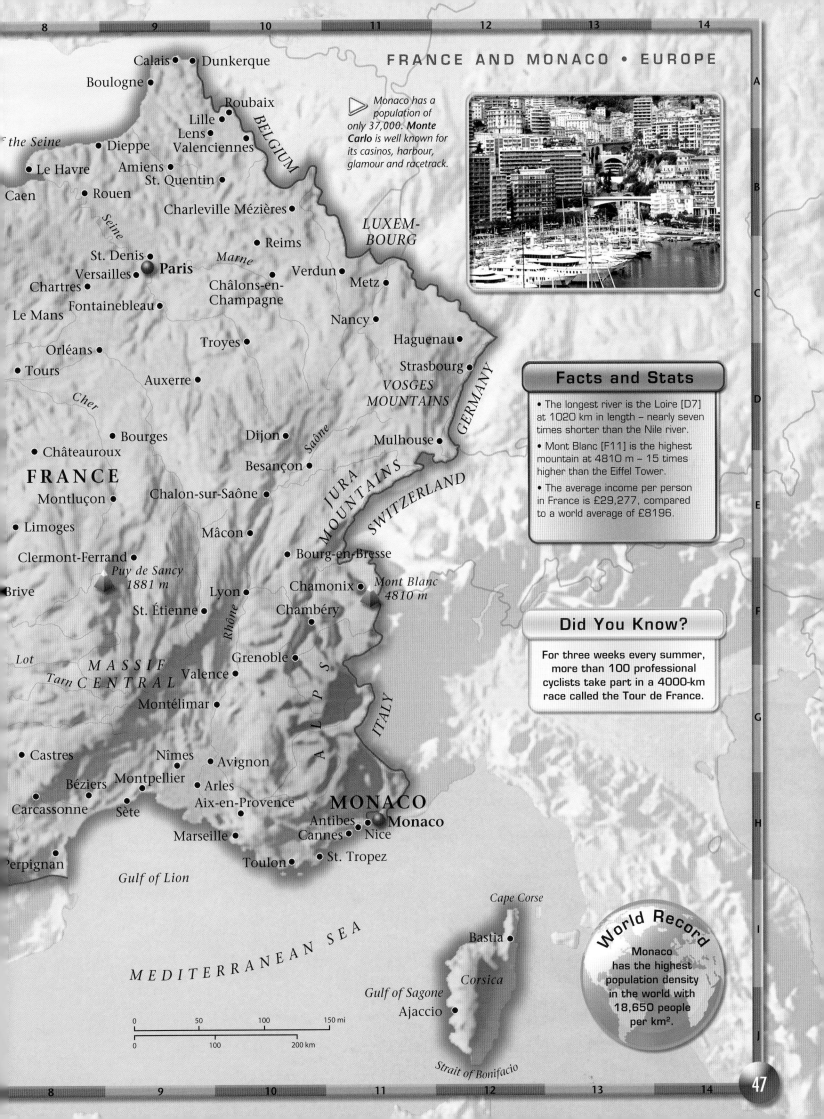

Monaco has a population of only 37,000. **Monte Carlo** is well known for its casinos, harbour, glamour and racetrack.

Calais • **Dunkerque**
Boulogne •
Roubaix •
Lille •
Lens •
Dieppe • **Valenciennes** •
Amiens •
St. Quentin •
Le Havre •
Caen • **Rouen** •
the Seine
BELGIUM
Charleville Mézières •
LUXEM-
BOURG
Reims •
St. Denis • Marne
Verdun •
Versailles • **Paris**
Metz •
Chartres • **Châlons-en-Champagne**
Fontainebleau •
Nancy •
Le Mans
Haguenau •
Orléans • **Troyes** •
Strasbourg •
VOSGES
MOUNTAINS
• **Tours**
GERMANY
Auxerre •
Cher
Bourges • **Dijon** •
Mulhouse •
• **Châteauroux**
Saône
Besançon •
FRANCE
JURA
MOUNTAINS
Montluçon • **Chalon-sur-Saône** •
SWITZERLAND
Limoges •
Mâcon •
Clermont-Ferrand •
• **Bourg-en-Bresse**
Puy de Sancy
1881 m
Chamonix • Mont Blanc
4810 m
Brive
Lyon •
St. Étienne • **Chambéry** •
Rhône
Lot
Grenoble •
MASSIF
Tarn CENTRAL **Valence** •
A
L
P
S
Montélimar •
ITALY
• **Castres**
Nîmes •
• **Avignon**
Béziers • **Montpellier** •
Arles
Carcassonne
Aix-en-Provence •
MONACO
Sète •
Antibes • • **Monaco**
Marseille • **Cannes** • **Nice**
Perpignan
Toulon • • **St. Tropez**
Gulf of Lion
Cape Corse
MEDITERRANEAN SEA
Bastia •
Corsica
Gulf of Sagone
Ajaccio •
Strait of Bonifacio

Facts and Stats

- The longest river is the Loire [D7] at 1020 km in length – nearly seven times shorter than the Nile river.

- Mont Blanc [F11] is the highest mountain at 4810 m – 15 times higher than the Eiffel Tower.

- The average income per person in France is £29,277, compared to a world average of £8196.

Did You Know?

For three weeks every summer, more than 100 professional cyclists take part in a 4000-km race called the Tour de France.

World Record
Monaco has the highest population density in the world with 18,650 people per km².

0   50   100   150 mi
0   100   200 km

Italy and the Balkans

Northern Italy is highly industrialized and produces many famous brands, such as Ferrari and Armani, while the south is mainly agricultural. Croatia, Bosnia and Herzegovina, Serbia, Montenegro, Kosovo and Macedonia were once part of Yugoslavia, but they have each become independent since 1991. Greece is one of Europe's oldest nations. The dry climate, steep slopes and thin soil limit farming to grapes, olives and citrus fruit. This area was home to the ancient Greek and Roman empires, which produced monuments such as Rome's Colosseum and the Parthenon in Athens, as well as Olympia – home to the first Olympic Games in 776 BC.

Facts and Stats

• Italy's population of 60.5 million would fill 605 Olympic stadiums. Montenegro's population of 622,000 would fill six stadiums.

• The life expectancy of people in San Marino is 83 years, compared to 76 years in Serbia and a world average of 69 years.

• The average income per person in Italy is £24,313, compared to £2963 in Kosovo and a world average of £8196.

In the next ...Italy will produce 5603 kg of pasta – that's about 70,000 adult portions! minute...

One of the most prominent sights in *Zagreb* [B8], the capital of Croatia, is the cathedral. The spires are 105 m in height and were built after an earthquake in 1880, which damaged much of the original structure.

Did You Know?

It costs the Italian government more money to keep the Tower of Pisa [D5] leaning than it would to straighten it.

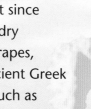

SWITZERLAND

AUSTRIA

SLOVENIA

FRANCE

Bolzano

Aosta • Como • Lecco • Trento
Monza • Bergamo
Novara • Milan • Brescia Verona • Vicenza
Turin • Lodi • Cremona • Padua • Venice
Alessandria • Piacenza • Mantua • Chioggia
Parma • Adria
Genoa • Reggio nell' • Ferrara
Savona • Emilia • Bologna
San Remo • La Spezia • Carrara • Forli • Ravenna
Massa • Pistoia • Rimini
Viareggio • Prato
Pisa • Florence • SAN MARINO
Livorno • Empoli • San Marino
Siena • Arezzo • Ancona
Piombino • Perugia
Elba • Grosseto • ITALY
Terni • Teramo
Civitavecchia • Pesca
Rome • VATICAN CITY (in Rome)
Latina • Campobasso
Gaeta • Benevento
Gulf of Gaeta • Naples
Salerno
Gulf of Salerno

Kranj
Udine • Ljubljana
Treviso • Trieste
Koper
Rijeka
Gulf of Venice • Pula

Sassari

Nuoro

Sardinia

Cagliari

TYRRHENIAN SEA

Palermo • Messin
Trapani
Mount Etna 3326 m
Caltanissetta • Catania
Agrigento • Sicily
Ragusa • Siracu

Pantelleria

MALTA
Vallett

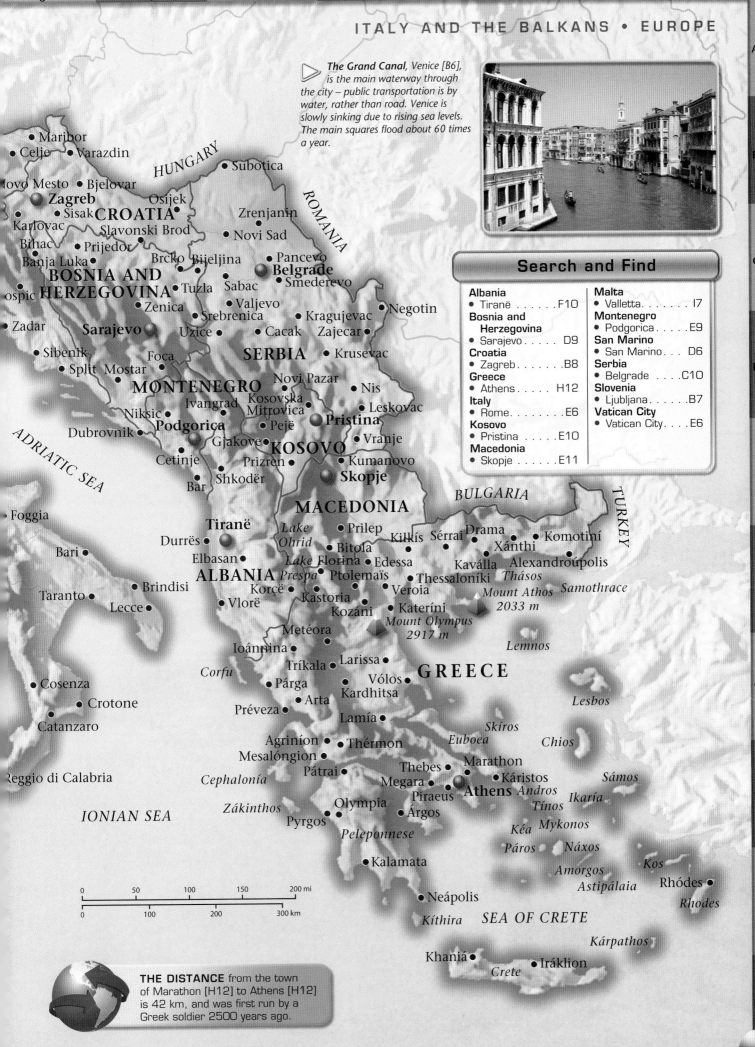

The Grand Canal, Venice [B6], is the main waterway through the city – public transportation is by water, rather than road. Venice is slowly sinking due to rising sea levels. The main squares flood about 60 times a year.

Search and Find

Albania
- Tiranë F10

Bosnia and Herzegovina
- Sarajevo D9

Croatia
- Zagreb B8

Greece
- Athens H12

Italy
- Rome E6

Kosovo
- Pristina E10

Macedonia
- Skopje E11

Malta
- Valletta I7

Montenegro
- Podgorica E9

San Marino
- San Marino . . . D6

Serbia
- Belgrade C10

Slovenia
- Ljubljana B7

Vatican City
- Vatican City E6

Maribor
Celje · Varazdin
Novo Mesto · Bjelovar
Zagreb   Osijek
Sisak   CROATIA
Karlovac
Bihac · Prijedor
Banja Luka   Brcko Bijeljina
BOSNIA AND   Pancevo
HERZEGOVINA   Belgrade
ospic   Tuzla   Sabac   Smederevo
Zenica   Valjevo
Zadar   Srebrenica   Kragujevac   Negotin
Sarajevo   Uzice   Cacak   Zajecar
Sibenik   Foca   SERBIA   Krusevac
Split Mostar   Novi Pazar
MONTENEGRO   Nis
Niksic   Ivangrad Mitrovica   Leskovac
Dubrovnik   Podgorica   Pejë   Pristina
Gjakove   Vranje
Cetinje   KOSOVO
Bar   Prizren   Kumanovo
Shkodër   Skopje

Subotica
Zrenjanin
Novi Sad
HUNGARY
ROMANIA
Slavonski Brod

ADRIATIC SEA

Foggia
Bari
Taranto
Brindisi
Lecce

Cosenza
Crotone
Catanzaro
Reggio di Calabria

IONIAN SEA

BULGARIA   TURKEY
MACEDONIA
Tiranë   Prilep   Kilkís   Sérrai   Drama   Komotiní
Durrës   Bitola   Xánthi
Elbasan   Lake Florina   Edessa   Kaválla   Alexandroúpolis
ALBANIA   Prespa   Ptolemaïs   Thessaloníki   Thásos
Korçë   Kastoria   Veroia   Mount Athos   Samothrace
Vlorë   Kozáni   Kateríni   2033 m
Metéora   Mount Olympus
Ioánnina   2917 m   Lemnos
Tríkala   Larissa
Corfu   Vólos   GREECE
Párga   Kardhitsa   Lesbos
Préveza   Arta
Lamía   Skíros   Chios
Agrínion   Thérmon   Euboea
Mesalóngion
Thebes   Marathon   Sámos
Pátrai   Megara   Káristos
Olympia   Piraeus   Andros   Ikaría
Zákinthos   Árgos   Athens   Tínos
Pyrgos   Kéa   Mykonos
Peleponnese   Páros   Náxos
Kalamata   Amorgos   Kos
Astipálaia   Rhódes
Neápolis   Rhodes
Kíthira   SEA OF CRETE
Khaniá   Kárpathos
Crete   Iráklion

Lake Ohrid

0   50   100   150   200 mi
0   100   200   300 km

THE DISTANCE from the town of Marathon [H12] to Athens [H12] is 42 km, and was first run by a Greek soldier 2500 years ago.

Germany and the Low Countries

Luxembourg, Belgium and the Netherlands are the three nations that make up the low countries. Much of the Netherlands is below sea level, and it relies on massive sea walls called dykes and thousands of pumps to drain the land. Brussels, the capital of Belgium, is home to the European Union's main centre of government, and Antwerp is the centre of the world's diamond-cutting industry. Luxembourg has the second-highest income per person in the world due to its banking industry. Germany has the fourth largest economy in the world after the United States, China and Japan, and produces machinery and cars such as BMW, Mercedes and Porsche. Parts of the former East Germany, which reunited with the West in 1990, are still not as prosperous.

Search and Find

Belgium
- Brussels E5

Germany
- Berlin D11

Luxembourg
- Luxembourg . . . G6

Netherlands
- Amsterdam . . . D6
- The Hague . . . D5

◁ *Amsterdam [D6] is well-known for its network of canals. The tall, leaning buildings were once used for storage. Hooks at the top of each house enabled goods to be pulled up to the top rooms.*

Facts and Stats

- Germany's population of 82.5 million would fill 825 Olympic stadiums. Luxembourg's population of 602,000 would only fill 60 stadiums.
- Mount Zugspitze [I9] is the highest mountain at 2964 m – nine times higher than the Eiffel Tower.
- The average income per person in Luxembourg is £79,314, compared to a world average of £8196.

COLOGNE [E7] holds one of the biggest carnivals in the world. Every November, more than one million people take part in the festival.

THE DISTANCE from the source of the Rhine river [F7] in the Swiss Alps to its mouth at the North Sea is 1320 km.

NORTH SEA

Terschelling · Ameland · Ea
Vlieland · Waddenzee
Texel · Groninge
Den Helder · Leeuwarden
Alkmaar · **NETHERLANDS** · Assen
Northeast Polder · Emmen
Haarlem · **Amsterdam** · *Flevoland Polder* · Zwolle
Leiden · Hilversum · Apeldoorn
The Hague · Utrecht · Enschede
Delft · Gouda · Arnhem
Rotterdam · Waal Nijmegen · Münste
Dordrecht
Vlissingen · Breda · Tilburg · 's-Hertogenbosch
Zeebrugge
Ostend · Bruges · Eindhoven · *Maas (Meuse)*
Ghent · Antwerp · Duisburg · Dortmun
Roeselare · Aalst · Mechelen · Krefeld · Essen
Kortrijk · Leuven · Genk · Düsseldorf · Wuppert.
Scheldt · Solingen
Brussels · Hasselt · Maastricht · Cologne
Tournai · Namur · Aachen
Charleroi · Liège · Bonn
Mons · Verviers · Rhine
Meuse (Maas) · Dinant
FRANCE · **BELGIUM** · HUNSRÜCK · Koblenz
Bastogne
LUXEMBOURG
Luxembourg · Trier
Esch-sur-Alzette
Kaiserslauten
Saarbrücken · FRANCE
Karlsruhe
Baden-Bade
B L F O
SWIT.
Freiburg im Breisga

| 0 | 50 | 100 | 150 | 200 mi |
| 0 | 100 | 200 | 300 km |

Sylt
DENMARK
Flensburg•
Schleswig•
Kiel Bay
Fehmarn
Kiel•
Mecklenburg Bay
Rügen
risian Islands
Cuxhaven•
Lübeck•
Rostock•
Greifswald•
Vilhelmshaven•
Bremerhaven•
Hamburg•
Schwerin•
Oldenburg•
Bremen•
Lüneburg•
Neubrandenburg•
Ems
Elbe
Osnabrück•
Hannover•
Wolfsburg•
Brandenburg•
Berlin•
Bielefeld•
Braunschweig•
Potsdam•
Hamm•
Hameln•
Paderborn•
Magdeburg•
Frankfurt an der Oder•
Elbe
POLAND
Dessau•
Göttingen•
Cottbus•
Kassel•
Halle•
GERMANY
Leipzig•
Siegen•
Eisenach•
Weimar•
Meissen•
Görlitz•
Erfurt•
Dresden•
Giessen•
Jena•
Chemnitz•
Freital•
Fulda•
Gera•
Zwickau•
Wies aden•
Frankfurt am Main•
Main
Plauen•
CZECH REPUBLIC
Offenbach•
Mainz•
Darmstadt•
Bamberg•
Worms•
Würzburg•
Bayreuth•
Mannheim•
udwigshafen•
Heidelberg•
Fürth••
Nuremberg•
BOHEMIAN FOREST
Heilbronn•
Pforzheim•
Regensburg•
Stuttgart•
Tübingen•
Ingolstadt•
K
Reutlingen•
Passau•
S T
SWABIAN JURA
Ulm•
Augsburg•
Danube
Munich•
Lake Constance
BAVARIAN ALPS
Mount Zugspitze 2964 m
Berchtesgaden•
RLAND
AUSTRIA

In the next
…the Netherlands will make 1648 kg of cheese – enough for 83,700 cheese slices.
minute…

World Record
The Netherlands has a greater percentage of its land below sea level – 26% – than any other country.

▷ **Cologne Cathedral** [E7] is one of the tallest and most magnificent Gothic buildings in the world. Its construction began in the 13th century, but wasn't completed until the late 19th century. The cathedral has 12 bells, and 509 steps lead to the top of the south tower, nearly 100 m above the ground.

Switzerland and Austria

Landlocked Switzerland, Austria and Liechtenstein are dominated by the Alps, creating stunning mountain scenery. Millions of tourists are attracted to the natural beauty, spectacular mountain vistas and popular Alpine skiing. Switzerland guards its independence and was not involved in either of the two World Wars. As a neutral, independent state, Switzerland is part of the United Nations and many charitable and banking organizations. As a result, it is a very wealthy country. Many composers come from Austria, including Mozart, Haydn, Schubert and Strauss.

The Belvedere Palace, Vienna *[E13], was built in the 17th and 18th centuries. Archduke Franz Ferdinand was the last person to live at the palace. It is now a museum and gallery, exhibiting many important collections, including the works of Renoir, Monet and Van Gogh.*

In the next ...14,509 kg of chocolate will be eaten worldwide. The Swiss are the world's biggest consumers. **minute...**

FRANCE

GERMANY

Basel • — Rhine — • Schaffhausen
Aarau • • Baden • Winterthur
Olten • • Lake Constance
• Solothurn Zürich •
Biel • St. Gallen • • Bregenz
Neuchâtel • Zug • • Feldkirch
Lake Neuchâtel Lucerne • Vaduz
Yverdon • Thun • **SWITZERLAND** **LIECHTENSTEIN** Innsbruck •
Fribourg • • St. Anton
Lausanne • Interlaken Chur • • Galtür
Lake Geneva Saanen • Andermatt • BERNESE ALPS LEPONTINE ALPS Davos •
Montreux • **Bern** •
Geneva •
Sion • Brig • St. Moritz •
Mount Dufourspitze 4634 m
Zermatt • Bellinzona •
Mount Matterhorn 4478 m Locarno •
ITALY ITALY
• Lugano

Did You Know?

The Swiss invented the quartz watch, wristwatch and waterproof watch. Switzerland produces expensive watches, such as Rolex, and watch-making is its third largest industry.

Leukerbad, in the heart of the Bernese Alps [G3], is the largest thermal spa in Europe. Dating back to Roman times, the complex contains 3.9 million litres of water and is surrounded by picturesque mountain scenery.*

BERN [F3] is the city where Albert Einstein worked, the Toblerone chocolate bar is made, and Emmental cheese is manufactured.

THE DISTANCE of the St. Moritz [G5] bobsleigh run is 1585 m and it takes just 70 seconds to travel from one end to the other.

Search and Find

Extreme Weather

In 1999, the biggest avalanche in Austria for 400 years smashed into the town of Galtür [G6], killing 31 people.

0   50   100 mi

0   80   160 km

CZECH REPUBLIC

SLOVAKIA

Zwettl Stadt

Inn

Braunau

Linz

Krems

Danube

Wels

Amstetten

Klosterneuburg

Steyr

Sankt Pölten

Vienna

Gmunden

Enns

Salzburg

Baden

Hallein

Bad Ischl

Wiener Neustadt

Neusiedler See

AUSTRIA

Kufstein

Kitzbühel

Schwaz

Mount Grossglockner 3797 m

Leoben

Kapfenberg

HOHE TAUERN

NIEDERE TAUERN

Knittelfeld

Judenburg

Mur

HUNGARY

Graz

Gleisdorf

Spittal

Wolfsberg

Drau

ITALY

Villach

Klagenfurt

SLOVENIA

Facts and Stats

• The population of Liechtenstein is only 38,000 and wouldn't even fill half an Olympic stadium.

• Switzerland's Mount Dufourspitze [H3] is the highest mountain at 4634 m in height – 14 times higher than the Eiffel Tower.

• The average income per person in Switzerland is £61,156 compared to a world average of £8196.

▷ Switzerland is split into federal states, or cantons. Bern is the second largest Swiss canton, and is dominated by mountains, glaciers and waterfalls. The small village of **Gstaad** near Saanen [G2] is a popular ski resort with fantastic Alpine scenery.

Hungary, Romania and Bulgaria

Bulgaria and Romania became members of the European Union in 2007, with Hungary joining in 2004. These countries are now experiencing rapid economic growth after decades of communist rule. Romania is the largest of the three and Europe's longest river, the Danube, flows along its southern border to the Black Sea. Hungary's capital, Budapest, has a lively arts and music scene, and is host to a range of cultural and sporting festivals. The countryside is scenic with many lakes, historic towns and villages. Bulgaria also borders the Black Sea, but it is mainly mountainous and rural, and relatively undeveloped.

SLOVAKIA

Miskolc

AUSTRIA

Gyor • • Esztergom

• **Budapest**

Szombathely

Székesfehérvár • **HUNGARY**

SLOVENIA

Lake Balaton • Dunaujvaros • Kecskemét

Kaposvár • *Tisza*

Danube Szeged • Arad

CROATIA Pécs • Timisoara

SERBIA

Facts and Stats

• The Danube [D6/G10] is the longest river at 2860 km in length. The Nile river is twice as long.

• Mount Musala [I10] is the highest mountain at 2925 m, which is nine times higher than the Eiffel Tower.

• The average income per person in Hungary is £10,844, compared to a world average of £8,196.

▷ On the bank of the Danube river in Budapest [C6] is **Hungary's Parliament building.** *Hungarian architect, Imre Steindl, designed the building, although he went blind before the project was completed. More than 40 kg of gold was used in its construction.*

◁ **Bran Castle** *in Romania is more commonly known as Dracula's Castle because Bram Stoker based his novel around the building. In 2007, the castle was put up for sale for £40 million.*

Did You Know?

One of the few Bulgarian commercial crops is the rose. The petals are used in the perfume industry.

THE DISTANCE from the source to the mouth of the Danube river [D6/G10] is 2888 km – almost all of it is accessible to boats.

ESZTERGOM [C5] is a former capital of Hungary and home to the nation's largest church, the Esztergom Basilica.

Search and Find

Bulgaria	Romania
● Sofia I9	● Bucharest F11
Hungary	
● Budapest C6	

In the next ...61,000 litres of water will enter the Black Sea from the Danube river. minute...

UKRAINE

Nyíregyháza

● Satu Mare

Debrecen
● Baia Mare

● Oradea

Suceava ●

CARPATHIAN MOUNTAINS

MOLDOVA

Iasi ●

● Cluj-Napoca

● Bacău

● Târgu Mures

ROMANIA

UKRAINE

Mures ● Alba Iulia

● Sibiu   *Olt*
● Brasov   Focsani ●

TRANSYLVANIAN ALPS

Galati ●
Braila ●

● Tulcea

● Resita

● Ploiesti

Pitesti ●

Bucharest ●

Calarasi ●   Constanta ●

● Drobeta-Turnu Severin
● Craiova

Jiu

Giurgiu ●
● Ruse

Dobrich ●

Vidin ●   *Danube*

● Montana   ● Pleven   Shumen ●   Varna ●

SERBIA

BULGARIA

Iskur

● Vratsa   Gabrovo ●

BALKAN MOUNTAINS   Sliven ●   Burgas ●

● Sofia   Stara Zagora ●   ● Yambol

Pernik ●

Mount Musala 2925 m

BLACK SEA

● Kyustendil   Plovdiv ●   Dimitrovgrad ●

● Blagoevgrad

RHODOPE MOUNTAINS   Khaskovo ●   *Maritsa*   TURKEY

Struma

MACEDONIA

GREECE

0	50	100 mi
0	80	160 km

Poland, Czech Republic and Slovakia

Poland, Slovakia and the Czech Republic are among the newest members of the European Union. Standards of living are much lower than western Europe and many workers have moved to the United Kingdom and Ireland for better-paid jobs. However, since joining the EU, Slovakia has become a major car producer, and has seen minimal emigration. The Baltic coast of Poland is industrial with steelworks and shipyards, but low-wage rates and money from the EU have attracted new industries. Prague, the capital of the Czech Republic, is situated on the Vltava river and receives more than 9 million tourists a year.

The **Prague Astronomical Clock** *[G5] is mounted on the wall of the Old Town City Hall. The astronomical dial represents the Sun and Moon. The 12 figures of the Apostles appear every hour, and all 12 are seen at 12 p.m. Finally, the calendar dial represents the months.*

In the next
...Poland will mine 249 tonnes of coal, generating enough electricity for 9.9 million light bulbs.
minute...

Zygmunt's Column sits in the centre of **Castle Square, Warsaw** *[E10]. Built in 1644, the monument represents King Zygmunt III Waza. Markets, street entertainment and concerts take place here, making it a popular tourist site.*

BALTIC SEA

Koszalin

Szczecin

Notéc

Gorzow Wielkopolski

Warta

Poznan

Zielona Gora

Kalisz

Oder

Legnica

Wroclaw

Opole

Liberec

Walbrzych

Ústí nad Labem

Hradec Kralove

GERMANY

Karlovy Vary

Cheb

Elbe

Prague

Pardubice

Plzen

CZECH REPUBLIC

Vltava

Olomouc

Jihlava

BOHEMIAN FOREST

Zlin

Ceské Budejovice

Brno

Morava

AUSTRIA

Trencir

Trnava

Bratislava

Komárno

8 9 10 11 12 13 14

0 — 50 — 100 mi
0 — 80 — 160 km

A
B
C
D
E
F
G
H
I
J

Search and Find

Czech Republic
● Prague G5

Poland
● Warsaw E10

Slovakia
● Bratislava J7

AUSCHWITZ [G8] was the centre of the Holocaust mass killings. Now a World Heritage site, it has more than 2 million visitors a year.

THE DISTANCE across the Charles Bridge, Prague [G5] is 516 m. The bridge is lined with 30 statues dating from around 1700.

Facts and Stats

• The longest river is the Vistula river [G10] at 1047 km in length – six times shorter than the Nile river.

• The highest mountain is Gerlachovsky Stit [H9] at 2655 m – eight times higher than the Eiffel Tower.

• The average income per person in Poland is £10,530, compared to a world average of £8196.

Did You Know?

Under the town of Wieliczka [G9] is one of the oldest salt mines in the world. The mine is so large that it has passages, lakes, buildings and a church. It is now a popular tourist attraction.

Gulf of Danzig

KALININGRAD (RUSSIA)

LITHUANIA

BELARUS

● Gdynia

Gdansk ●

● Elblag

Suwalki ●

Vistula

● Olsztyn

Narew

Bialystok ●

● Bydgoszcz

● Torun

Bug

Wloclawek ●

● Plock

● **Warsaw**

POLAND

Lodz ●

Pilica

● Radom

● Lublin

Chelm ●

● Czestochowa

Vistula

San

Bytom ●

● Sosnowiece

liwice ● ● Katowice

Auschwitz ◆

Ostrava ● ● Bielsko-Biala

● Kraków ● Tarnow
● Wieliczka

● Rzeszow

UKRAINE

Gerlachovsky Stit 2655 m

Vàh

● Zilina

Martin ●

● Poprad

● Presov

TATRA MOUNTAINS

Bojnice ●

● Banská Bystrica

Kosice ●

SLOVAKIA

Nitra ●

● Levice

HUNGARY

anube

▷ *Bojnice Castle [I8] is the most visited Slovakian castle, attracting more than 200,000 visitors a year. Many films have been shot here and the International Festival of Ghosts and Monsters takes place every spring.*

Eastern Europe

The former Soviet states of Estonia, Latvia and Lithuania are now democratic, independent countries. The area is mainly flat, low-lying land that is covered in snow during winter, but a fertile grain- and dairy-farming region in summer. Without industries to compete with western Europe, these countries remain poor. Russia controls much of Europe's natural gas supplies, but has struggled to improve its standard of living. In 2014, Russia annexed the Crimean peninsula from Ukraine. Armenia and Georgia are part of the Caucasus range with the Caucasus Mountains providing a border between Europe and Asia.

*The town of Trakai, Lithuania, can be found west of Vilnius [G5]. Out of the area's 200 lakes, Lake Galve is the largest at 47 m in depth. Built in the 14th and 15th centuries on the lake, **Trakai Island Castle** can only be reached by a drawbridge.*

Search and Find

Armenia
- Yerevan J8

Belarus
- Minsk G6

Estonia
- Tallinn E5

Georgia
- Tbilisi I8

Latvia
- Riga F5

Lithuania
- Vilnius G5

Moldova
- Chisinau H6

Russia
- Moscow F7

Ukraine
- Kiev G6

*A kremlin is a Russian castle, the most famous is the **Moscow Kremlin** [F7] on the bank of the Moskva river. Surrounded by a wall, the Kremlin includes four palaces, four golden-domed cathedrals and 20 towers.*

In the next

...Russia will export enough natural gas to supply 96.4 homes for a minute.

minute...

BARENTS

- Murmansk

FINLAND

Whi

Onega •

Lake Onega
• Petrozavods

Vyborg • Lake Ladoga
Gulf of Finland • St. Petersburg

BALTIC SEA

Tallinn
ESTONIA • Novgorod
Tartu • Lake
Gulf of Peipus Rybinsk •
Riga Yaroslavl •
Liepaja • **Riga** Tver •

LATVIA Vitsyebsk • **Moscow**
LITHUANIA • Smolensk Ryazan •
RUSSIA **Vilnius** • Kirov Tul
Kaliningrad Kaunas **BELARUS**
Minsk
POLAND Hrodna • Bryansk
Pripyat Marshes • Homyel Lipetsk •
Rivne • **Kiev** Dnieper Voronezh •
Lviv • **UKRAINE** Kharkiv
SLOVAKIA Prut Dnipropetrovsk
Kryvyy Rih
MOLDOVA Dniester Zaporizhzhya Donetsk •
Chisinau Rostov-
ROMANIA Tiraspol Odessa na-Donu
Crimea Sea of
Sevastopol Krasnodar Azov

BLACK SEA

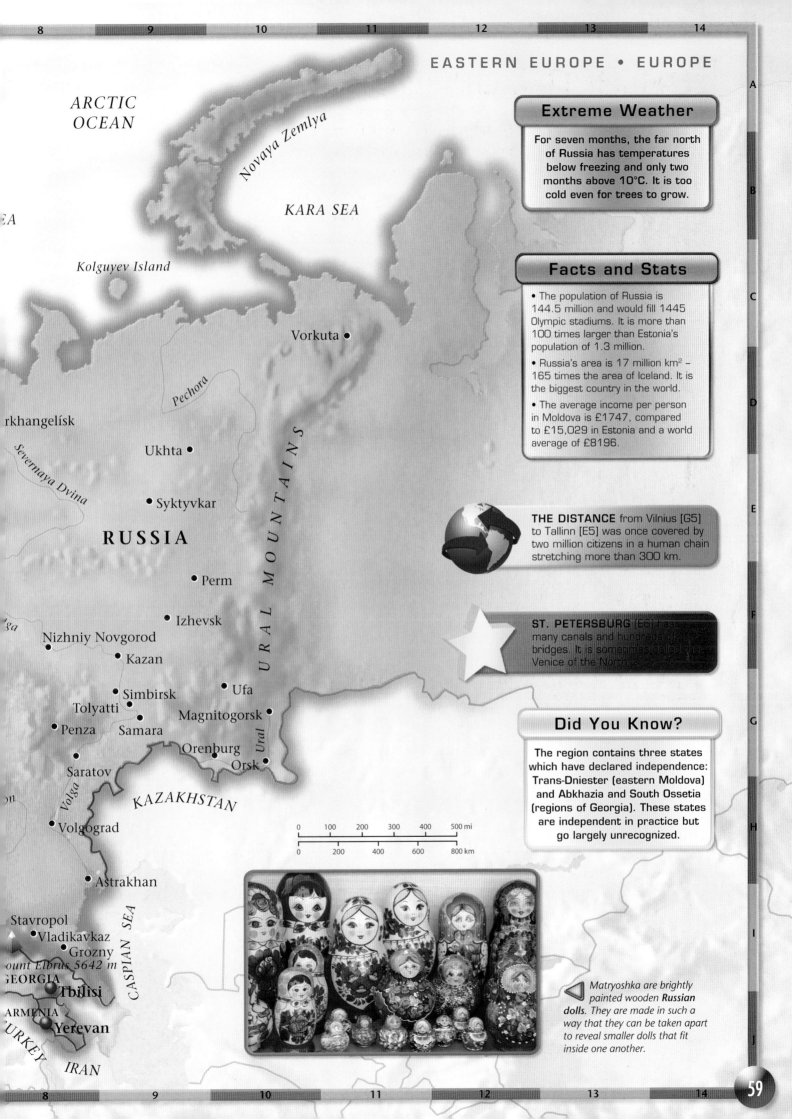

8 9 10 11 12 13 14

A
B
C
D
E
F
G
H
I
J

Extreme Weather

For seven months, the far north of Russia has temperatures below freezing and only two months above 10°C. It is too cold even for trees to grow.

Facts and Stats

- The population of Russia is 144.5 million and would fill 1445 Olympic stadiums. It is more than 100 times larger than Estonia's population of 1.3 million.
- Russia's area is 17 million km² – 165 times the area of Iceland. It is the biggest country in the world.
- The average income per person in Moldova is £1747, compared to £15,029 in Estonia and a world average of £8196.

THE DISTANCE from Vilnius [G5] to Tallinn [E5] was once covered by two million citizens in a human chain stretching more than 300 km.

ST. PETERSBURG [E6] has many canals and hundreds of bridges. It is sometimes called the Venice of the North.

Did You Know?

The region contains three states which have declared independence: Trans-Dniester (eastern Moldova) and Abkhazia and South Ossetia (regions of Georgia). These states are independent in practice but go largely unrecognized.

Matryoshka are brightly painted wooden Russian dolls. They are made in such a way that they can be taken apart to reveal smaller dolls that fit inside one another.

ARCTIC OCEAN

Novaya Zemlya

KARA SEA

Kolguyev Island

Vorkuta

Pechora

Ukhta

rkhangelísk

Severnaya Dvina

Syktyvkar

RUSSIA

URAL MOUNTAINS

Perm

Izhevsk

'ga

Nizhniy Novgorod

Kazan

Simbirsk

Ufa

Tolyatti

Magnitogorsk

Penza

Samara

Orenburg

Ural

Saratov

Orsk

KAZAKHSTAN

Volga

Volgograd

0   100   200   300   400   500 mi
0   200   400   600   800 km

Astrakhan

CASPIAN SEA

Stavropol

Vladikavkaz

Grozny

ount Elbrus 5642 m

GEORGIA

Tbilisi

ARMENIA

Yerevan

TURKEY

IRAN

Africa

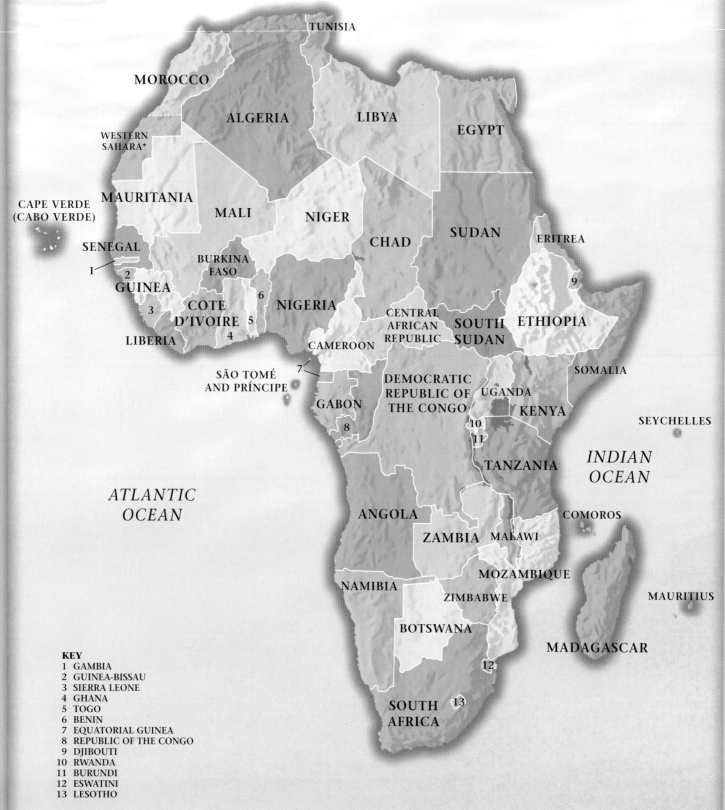

TUNISIA

MOROCCO

ALGERIA

LIBYA

EGYPT

WESTERN SAHARA*

CAPE VERDE (CABO VERDE)

MAURITANIA

MALI

NIGER

SUDAN

ERITREA

SENEGAL

1

2

GUINEA

BURKINA FASO

6

NIGERIA

CHAD

9

3

COTE D'IVOIRE

5

CENTRAL AFRICAN REPUBLIC

SOUTH SUDAN

ETHIOPIA

4

LIBERIA

CAMEROON

SOMALIA

SÃO TOMÉ AND PRÍNCIPE

7

DEMOCRATIC REPUBLIC OF THE CONGO

UGANDA

GABON

8

KENYA

SEYCHELLES

10

11

INDIAN OCEAN

TANZANIA

ATLANTIC OCEAN

COMOROS

ANGOLA

ZAMBIA

MALAWI

MOZAMBIQUE

NAMIBIA

ZIMBABWE

MAURITIUS

BOTSWANA

12

MADAGASCAR

SOUTH AFRICA

13

KEY
1 GAMBIA
2 GUINEA-BISSAU
3 SIERRA LEONE
4 GHANA
5 TOGO
6 BENIN
7 EQUATORIAL GUINEA
8 REPUBLIC OF THE CONGO
9 DJIBOUTI
10 RWANDA
11 BURUNDI
12 ESWATINI
13 LESOTHO

*Western Sahara is a disputed territory in the Maghreb region of North Africa.

COUNTRY FACTFILE

Country	Life expectancy	Population to nearest thousand	Population growth %	Population as urban %	Area km²	Population density per km²	Capital city	Currency	Languages
Algeria	77	41,320,000	1.7	80	2,381,741	17.3	Algiers	Algerian Dinar	Arabic, Berber, French
Angola	60	29,250,000	3.5	66	1,252,145	23.4	Luanda	Kwanza	Portuguese, Umbundu
Benin	62	11,179,000	2.7	47	112,622	99.3	Porto-Novo, Cotonou	CFA Franc	French, Fon, Yoruba
Botswana	63	2,303,000	1.6	69	581,730	4	Gaborone	Pula	English, Tswana
Burkina Faso	56	19,632,000	3	30	270,764	74.8	Ouagadougou	CFA Franc	French, Mossi
Burundi	61	10,864,000	3.3	13	27,816	390.1	Bujumbura	Burundi Franc	Kirundi, French
Cameroon	59	22,189,000	2.6	58	466,715	47.5	Yaoundé	CFA Franc	French, English, Fang
Cape Verde (Cabo Verde)	75	538,000	1.3	66	4033	133.4	Praia	Cape Verdean Escudo	Portuguese, Crioulo
Central African Republic	53	4,660,000	2.1	41	622,436	7.5	Bangui	CFA Franc	French, Sangho
Chad	51	14,900,000	1.9	28	1,284,000	11.6	N'Djamena	CFA Franc	French, Arabic, Sara
Comoros	65	814,000	1.6	32	1862	437.2	Moroni	Comoran Franc	Comorian, French, Arabic
Congo, Democratic Republic of the	57	86,026,000	2.4	45	2,344,856	36.7	Kinshasa	Congolese Franc	French, Lingala, Swahili
Congo, Republic of the	60	5,260,000	2.1	67	342,000	15.4	Brazzaville	CFA Franc	French, Monokutuba, Kongo
Côte d'Ivoire (Ivory Coast)	59	24,295,000	1.8	54	320,783	75.7	Yamoussoukro, Abidjan	CFA Franc	French, Akan
Djibouti	64	1,049,000	2.2	85	23,200	45.2	Djibouti	Djiboutian Franc	Somali, French, Akan
Egypt	73	95,203,000	2.5	45	996,490	95.5	Cairo, NAC*	Egyptian Pound	Arabic
Equatorial Guinea	65	1,268,000	2.4	72	28,051	45.2	Ciudad de la Paz, Malabo	CFA Franc	Spanish, French, Fang
Eritrea	65	6,536,000	0.9	40	121,115	54	Asmara	Nakfa	Tigrinya, Arabic, Afar
Eswatini	52	1,093,000	1.1	34	17,363	62.9	Mbabane, Lobamba	Lilangeni	Swazi, English
Ethiopia	63	104,960,000	2.9	21	1,063,637	98.7	Addis Ababa	Birr	Amharic, Oromo, Tigrinya
Gabon	62	2,025,000	1.9	89	267,667	7.6	Libreville	CFA Franc	French, Fang
Gambia	65	2,100,000	2.1	61	10,689	195.6	Banjul	Dalasi	English, Malinke
Ghana	67	29,614,000	2.2	56	238,533	121.2	Accra	Cedi	Hausa, English, Akan
Guinea	61	12,720,000	2.6	37	245,857	51.7	Conakry	Guinean Franc	Fulani, French, Malinke
Guinea-Bissau	51	1,860,000	1.9	49	36,125	51.5	Bissau	CFA Franc	Crioulo, Portuguese, Balante
Kenya	64	49,700,000	1.7	30	582,646	85.3	Nairobi	Kenyan Shilling	Swahili, English, Kikuyu
Lesotho	53	2,230,000	0.3	27	30,355	73.5	Maseru	South African rand	Sesotho, English
Liberia	63	4,730,000	2.5	60	111,370	48.7	Monrovia	US Dollar, Liberian Dollar	Krio, English
Libya	77	6,375,000	1.6	88	1,777,060	3.6	Tripoli	Libyan Dinar	Arabic
Madagascar	66	25,570,000	2.5	37	587,041	43.6	Antananarivo	Madagascar Ariary	Malagasy, French
Malawi	62	17,373,000	3.3	20	118,484	146.6	Lilongwe	Malawian Kwacha	Chichewa, English
Mali	60	18,540,000	3	42	1,248,574	14.8	Bamako	CFA Franc	French, Bambara
Mauritania	63	3,984,000	2.2	59	1,030,700	3.9	Nouakchott	Ouguiya	Arabic
Mauritius	76	1,264,000	0.6	48	2040	629.8	Port Louis	Mauritius Rupee	French Creole, Bhojpuri, English
Morocco	77	34,665,000	1.0	63	446,550	77.6	Rabat	Moroccan Dirham	Arabic, Berber
Mozambique	54	28,862,000	2.5	38	801,590	36.1	Maputo	Metical	Emakhuwa, Portuguese
Namibia	64	2,414,000	2	50	824,269	2.9	Windhoek	Namibian Dollar	English, Ovambo, Nama
Niger	56	21,467,000	3.2	21	1,186,408	18.1	Niamey	CFA Franc	French, Hausa
Nigeria	54	193,393,000	2.4	50	923,103	209.5	Abuja	Naira	English, Hausa, Yoruba
Rwanda	64	12,210,000	2.7	28	25,314	482.3	Kigali	Rwandan Franc	Rwanda, French, English
São Tomé and Príncipe	66	202,000	1.7	73	1001	201.8	São Tomé	Dobra	Portuguese, Crioulo
Senegal	62	15,726,000	2.4	47	196,712	79.9	Dakar	CFA Franc	French, Wolof, Fulani
Seychelles	75	97,000	0.8	59	455	215.4	Victoria	Seychelles Rupee	Creole, English
Sierra Leone	59	7,092,000	2.4	42	71,740	98.9	Freetown	Leone	English, Krio, Mende
Somalia	53	14,700,000	2	45	637,657	23.1	Mogadishu	Somali Shilling	Somali, Arabic
South Africa	64	57,726,000	1	66	1,224,691	47.3	Pretoria, Cape Town	Rand	Xhosa, English, Zulu, Afrikaans
South Sudan	52	11,868,000	3.8	20	619,745	18.4	Juba	South Sudanese Pound	English, Dinka, Arabic
Sudan	64	37,960,000	1.6	40	1,840,687	22	Khartoum	Sudanese Dinar	Arabic, Nubian
Tanzania	63	50,144,000	2.8	34	945,037	56.6	Dar es Salaam, Dodoma	Tanzanian Shilling	Swahili, English
Togo	65	7,315,000	2.6	43	56,785	129.2	Lomé	CFA Franc	French, Ewe
Tunisia	76	11,304,000	1	69	163,610	69.1	Tunis	Tunisian Dinar	Arabic, French
Uganda	56	37,674,000	3.2	24	241,551	151.8	Kampala	Ugandan Shilling	Swahili, English, Ganda
Zambia	53	16,405,000	2.9	44	752,614	21.8	Lusaka	Zambian Kwacha	English, Bemba
Zimbabwe	58	13,573,000	1.6	38	390,757	34.7	Harare	US dollar	English, Shona

*New Administrative Capital.

North Africa

The Sahara Desert dominates this region at 6000 km in width and 2000 km from north to south. Only a narrow strip of land stands next to the Mediterranean Sea, but the fertile valleys of the Atlas Mountains and the banks of the Nile river have enough water to grow crops.

Algeria, Libya and Tunisia have become wealthy by selling oil and natural gas to Europe. Egypt was the richest country in the world when the pharaohs ruled more than 3000 years ago. Egypt's well-preserved tombs and temples, especially the Great Pyramid of Giza, are a tourist attraction.

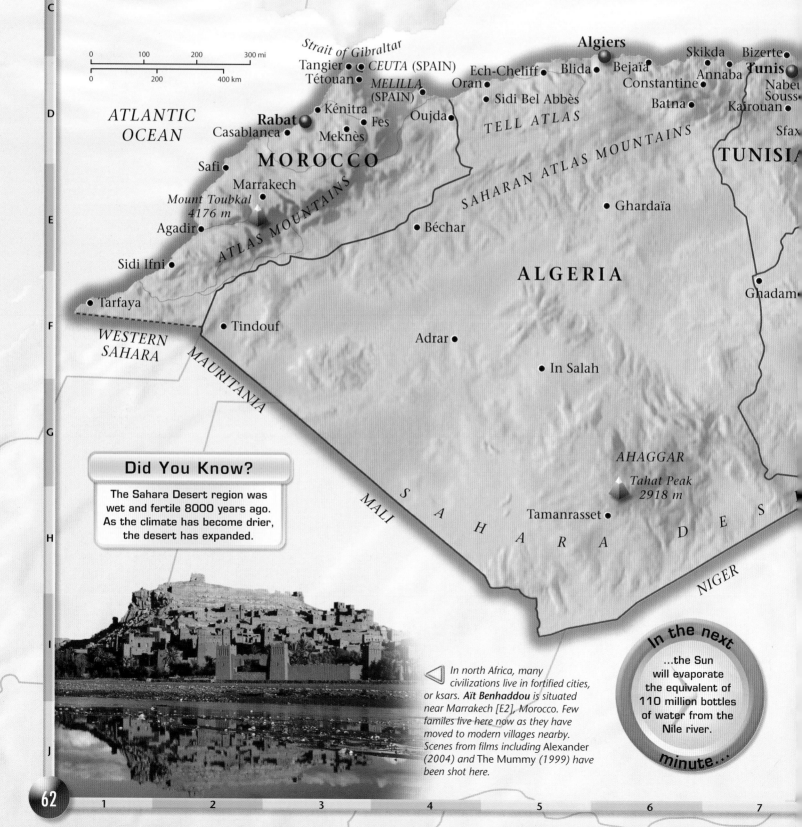

0   100   200   300 mi
0   200   400 km

ATLANTIC
OCEAN

Strait of Gibraltar
Tangier   CEUTA (SPAIN)
Tétouan
MELILLA
(SPAIN)
Kénitra
Rabat
Casablanca   Fes
Meknès
Safi   MOROCCO
Marrakech
Mount Toubkal
4176 m
Agadir
Sidi Ifni

Tarfaya

WESTERN
SAHARA

MAURITANIA

Tindouf

MALI

Oujda
Ech-Cheliff   Blida
Oran
Sidi Bel Abbès

Algiers
Bejaïa
Constantine
Batna

Skikda   Bizerte
Annaba   Tunis
Nabeu
Sousse
Kairouan
Sfax

TELL ATLAS

SAHARAN ATLAS MOUNTAINS

ATLAS MOUNTAINS

Béchar

Ghardaïa

ALGERIA

TUNISIA

Ghadam

Adrar

In Salah

AHAGGAR
Tahat Peak
2918 m

Tamanrasset

S A H A R A   D E S

NIGER

Did You Know?

The Sahara Desert region was wet and fertile 8000 years ago. As the climate has become drier, the desert has expanded.

In north Africa, many civilizations live in fortified cities, or ksars. *Aït Benhaddou* is situated near Marrakech [E2], Morocco. Few familes live here now as they have moved to modern villages nearby. Scenes from films including Alexander (2004) and The Mummy (1999) have been shot here.

In the next
...the Sun will evaporate the equivalent of 110 million bottles of water from the Nile river.
minute...

Located on the Nile river, Cairo [F13] is the biggest city in Africa. Built in AD 988, **Al-Azhar University** is the second oldest university in the world, after the University of Al Karaouine Fez, Morocco. Al-Azhar Mosque stands alongside the university.

Facts and Stats

- Egypt's population of 95.2 million would fill 952 Olympic stadiums. Libya's population of 6.2 million would only fill 62 stadiums.

- Cairo [F13] is the biggest city with 20.3 million people. This would fill 203 Olympic stadiums, compared to Tripoli which would only fill 9.5 [E8].

- The average income per person in Libya is £6107, compared to a world average of £8196.

Search and Find

Algeria
- Algiers C6

Egypt
- Cairo, NAC (New Administrative Capital) F13

Libya
- Tripoli E8

Morocco
- Rabat D3

Tunisia
- Tunis D7

World Record

The Sahara sand sea in Algeria has the longest sand dunes in the world, with some more than 300 km.

Extreme Weather

The hottest temperature ever recorded was 58°C in Libya's Sahara Desert.

MEDITERRANEAN SEA

Tripoli

Misurata

Az-Zawiyah

Gulf of Sidra

Benghazi

Darnah

Tubruq

Surt

Ajdabiya

Port Said

Alexandria

Tanta

Suez Canal

Suez

QATTARA DEPRESSION

Cairo

Giza

NAC*

Sinai Peninsula

GREAT SAND SEA

Nile

Gulf of Suez

ISRAEL

Sharm al Sheikh

Gulf of Aqaba

El Minya

Hurghada

Asyut

WESTERN DESERT

RED SEA

Sabha

LIBYA

FEZZAN

LIBYAN DESERT

EGYPT

Qena

Luxor

Aswan

GILF KEBIR PLATEAU

Lake Nasser

CHAD

SUDAN

*Egypt's New Administrative Capital (NAC) is currently being built 45 km east of Cairo.

THE DISTANCE separating Morocco from Spain, Europe, at the Strait of Gibraltar's [C3] narrowest point is only 13 km.

EGYPT has huge pyramids, built more than 3000 years ago. Each one held the body of a king.

Desert tribe people, such as the Berbers and Tuaregs, travel by camel from oasis to oasis across the Sahara Desert to trade cloth, salt and spices.

West Africa

Stretching from the heart of the Sahara Desert to the tropical forests of southern Nigeria, this region is one of the poorest in the world. In the north, Mali and Niger are plagued by drought, famine and insurgency. The southern countries of Sierra Leone, Liberia, Côte d'Ivoire and Nigeria have suffered armed unrest, government corruption and civil wars. Oil provides 65 percent of Nigeria's income, but this fails to lift the rapidly growing population out of poverty.

Extreme Weather

Southern Nigeria has eight times as much rain as London. However, parts of northern Mali have almost no rain.

CANARY ISLANDS
(SPAIN)

Las Palmas de Gran Canaria

MOROCCO

El Aaiún

WESTERN SAHARA *

ALGERIA

Dakhla

Zouérat

SAHARA

Nouadhibou

CAPE VERDE
(CABO VERDE)

MAURITANIA

MALI

Mindelo

Nouakchott

Senegal

Tombouctou

Praia

St. Louis   Kaédi

Touba

Dakar   Thiès

SENEGAL

Kayes

Mopti

Djenné

Banjul   GAMBIA

Ségou

ATLANTIC
OCEAN

Bissau   GUINEA-
BISSAU

Bamako

Ouagadougou

BURKIN

*Western Sahara is a disputed territory partially controlled by Morocco.

GUINEA

Sikasso

Conakry   Kankan

Bobo Dioulasso

Freetown   SIERRA
LEONE

COTE
D'IVOIRE

Tamale

Bo

Man   Bouaké

Gbarnga   Daloa

Kumasi   Vo

Monrovia   Harbel

Yamoussoukro   GHANA

Buchanan

LIBERIA   Abidjan   Accra

Cape Palmas   Sekondi-Takorad

GULF O

Search and Find

0   100   200   300   400 mi

0   200   400   600 km

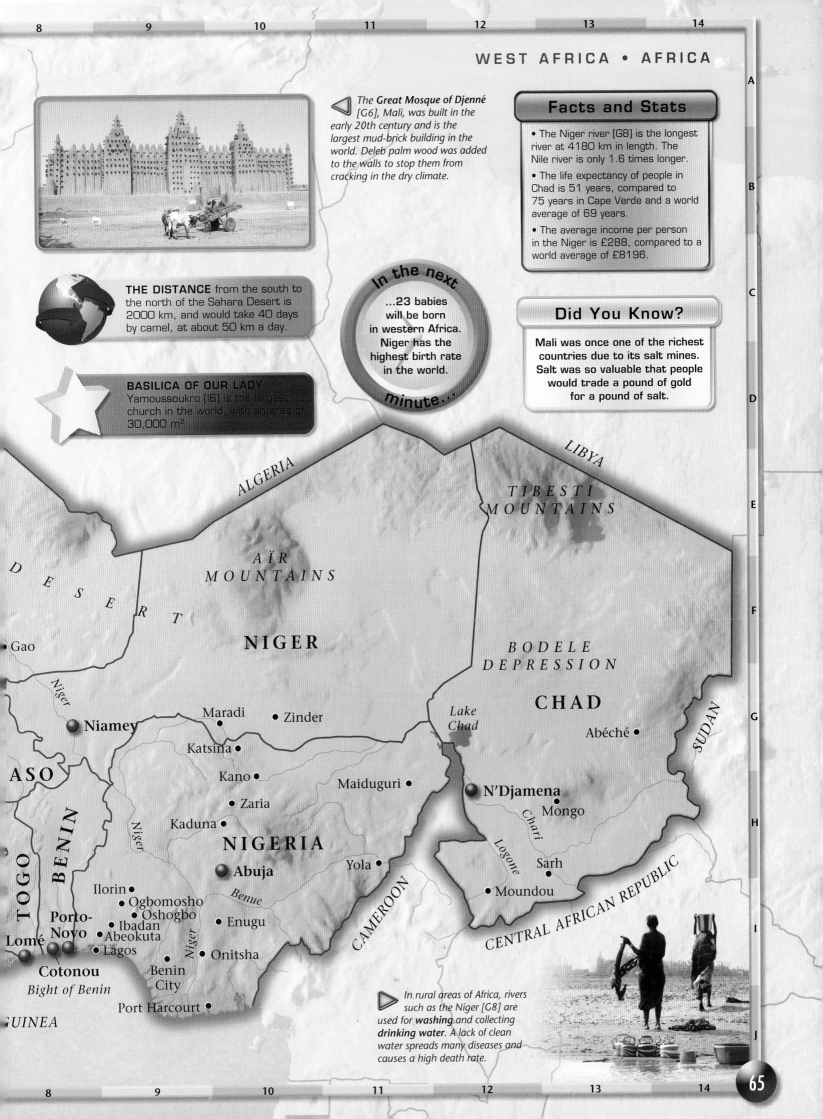

The **Great Mosque of Djenné** [G6], Mali, was built in the early 20th century and is the largest mud-brick building in the world. Deleb palm wood was added to the walls to stop them from cracking in the dry climate.

Facts and Stats

- The Niger river [G8] is the longest river at 4180 km in length. The Nile river is only 1.6 times longer.
- The life expectancy of people in Chad is 51 years, compared to 75 years in Cape Verde and a world average of 69 years.
- The average income per person in the Niger is £288, compared to a world average of £8196.

THE DISTANCE from the south to the north of the Sahara Desert is 2000 km, and would take 40 days by camel, at about 50 km a day.

In the next ...23 babies will be born in western Africa. Niger has the highest birth rate in the world. minute...

Did You Know?

Mali was once one of the richest countries due to its salt mines. Salt was so valuable that people would trade a pound of gold for a pound of salt.

BASILICA OF OUR LADY. Yamoussoukro [I6] is the largest church in the world, with an area of 30,000 m².

ALGERIA

LIBYA

TIBESTI MOUNTAINS

AÏR MOUNTAINS

DESERT

NIGER

BODELE DEPRESSION

CHAD

Gao

Niger

Maradi · Zinder

Niamey

Lake Chad

Abéché ·

Katsina ·

ASO

Kano ·

Maiduguri ·

N'Djamena

SUDAN

Zaria ·

Mongo ·

BENIN

Niger

Kaduna ·

NIGERIA

Chari

Logone

Sarh ·

TOGO

Abuja

Yola ·

Moundou ·

CAMEROON

CENTRAL AFRICAN REPUBLIC

Ilorin ·

Ogbomosho ·

Oshogbo ·

Benue

Porto-Novo

Ibadan ·

· Enugu

Lomé

Abeokuta ·

· Lagos

Niger

Onitsha

Cotonou

Benin City

Bight of Benin

Port Harcourt ·

GUINEA

In rural areas of Africa, rivers such as the Niger [G8] are used for **washing** and collecting **drinking water**. A lack of clean water spreads many diseases and causes a high death rate.

East Africa

Due to the high altitude of Kenya, Tanzania and Uganda, the climate is suited to growing crops. These countries have strong economies based on exporting crops, such as tea and coffee, which are grown on large plantations run by European companies. The countries of Ethiopia, Somalia and Sudan are poorer as they have harsher climates and a history of unrest. The droughts that have repeatedly affected this southern fringe of the Sahara Desert have caused millions of deaths as well as the destruction of crops and animals.

Lesser flamingos are the smallest of the flamingo family. They are numerous throughout Africa and are always found in large groups called 'pats'. The colour of flamingos comes from their food – unhealthy birds are pale in colour.

Facts and Stats

- Mount Kilimanjaro [H9] is the highest mountain at 5895 m. It is 18 times higher than the Eiffel Tower.
- Sudan's area is 1.8 million km². This is 18 times the area of Iceland.
- Ethiopia has a population of 104.9 million. This would fill 1050 Olympic stadiums. Djibouti's population is 1 million and would fill 10 Olympic stadiums.

Extreme Weather

The Danakil Valley [D10], Ethiopia, has the hottest average daily temperature of 55°C.

Did You Know?

Somaliland declared itself independent from Somalia in 1991 but although it has been a separate country for 25 years, no other nation has recognized its independence.

*The **Maasai people** of Kenya and Tanzania wear toga-like garments called shukkas, which can be bought at roadside shops. The official colour of the Maasai tribe is red, and is always worn as clothing or jewellery.*

EGYPT

LIBYA

LIBYAN DESERT

Wadi Halfa

Nile

CHAD

Japal Marrah 3089 m

• El Fasher

El Obeid •

• Nyala

DARFUR   **SUDAN**

BAHR AL-GHAZAL

CENTRAL AFRICAN REPUBLIC

• Wau

SOUTH SUDAN

• Yambio

DEMOCRATIC REPUBLIC OF THE CONGO

Arua

Lake Albert

Lake Edward

RWANDA

Kigali

Lake Kivu

BURUNDI

Bujumbura

Kigoma •

Lake Tanganyika

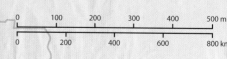

| 0 | 100 | 200 | 300 | 400 | 500 mi |
| 0 | 200 | 400 | 600 | 800 km |

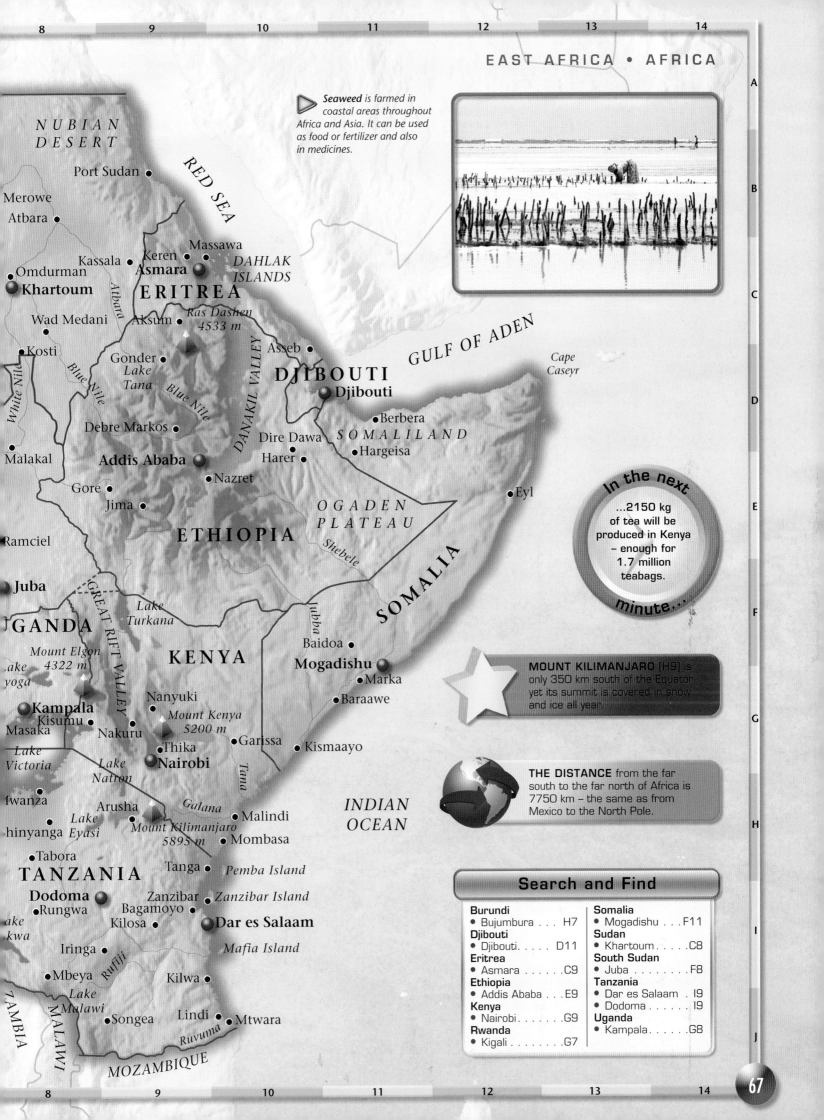

NUBIAN DESERT

Port Sudan

Merowe
Atbara

RED SEA

Omdurman
Khartoum
Kassala
Keren
Massawa
Asmara

Wad Medani

ERITREA

Kosti

Aksum
Ras Dashen 4533 m

DAHLAK ISLANDS

Asseb

DJIBOUTI

Gonder
Lake Tana

Blue Nile

Djibouti

GULF OF ADEN

Cape Caseyr

White Nile

Blue Nile

Debre Markos

Berbera

SOMALILAND

Malakal

Dire Dawa
Harer
Hargeisa

Addis Ababa

Nazret

DANAKIL VALLEY

Gore
Jima

ETHIOPIA

OGADEN PLATEAU

Shebele

Ramciel

Eyl

Juba

GREAT RIFT VALLEY

Lake Turkana

GANDA

Mount Elgon 4322 m

Jubba

SOMALIA

Lake yoga

KENYA

Baidoa

Mogadishu

Nanyuki

Marka

Kampala
Kisumu

Masaka
Nakuru

Mount Kenya 5200 m

Baraawe

Garissa

Thika
Nairobi

Kismaayo

Lake Victoria

Lake Natron

Tana

Galana

INDIAN OCEAN

wanza

Arusha

Malindi

Lake Eyasi

hinyanga

Mount Kilimanjaro 5895 m

Mombasa

Tabora

Tanga
Pemba Island

TANZANIA

Dodoma
Rungwa

Zanzibar
Zanzibar Island

Bagamoyo
Kilosa

Dar es Salaam

ake kwa

Iringa

Mafia Island

Mbeya
Rufiji

Kilwa

Lake Malawi

Songea
Lindi
Mtwara

Ruvuma

MOZAMBIQUE

> **Seaweed** is farmed in coastal areas throughout Africa and Asia. It can be used as food or fertilizer and also in medicines.

In the next ...2150 kg of tea will be produced in Kenya – enough for 1.7 million teabags. minute...

MOUNT KILIMANJARO [H9] is only 350 km south of the Equator, yet its summit is covered in snow and ice all year.

THE DISTANCE from the far south to the far north of Africa is 7750 km – the same as from Mexico to the North Pole.

Search and Find

Central and southern Africa

This region stretches from the tropical rainforests of Cameroon to the rich agricultural lands of South Africa. Only those countries with mineral wealth have prospered. Political unrest is widespread, bringing great poverty to the Central African Republic, DR Congo and Zimbabwe. Once an exporter of food and tobacco, Zimbabwe is now reliant on international aid. Farming, commerce, and gold and diamond mining have brought prosperity to many South Africans.

Victoria Falls [G8] on the Zambezi river tumbles more than 128 m into the gorge below, creating the largest sheet of falling water in the world. The local people called the waterfall 'the smoke that thunders'.

Facts and Stats

• The longest river is the Congo [C7]. At 4700 km in length, the Nile river is only 1.5 times longer.

• Mont Ngaliema (Mount Stanley) [C9] is the highest mountain at 5109 m in height – 16 times higher than the Eiffel Tower.

• The life expectancy of people in Eswatini is 52 years, compared to 76 years in Mauritius and a world average of 69 years.

Did You Know?

The Namib Desert [H6] is the oldest desert in the world. It covers 270,000 km² – more than twice the area of Iceland. Some parts have fewer than 2 cm of rain a year.

The quiver tree is a species of aloe found in southern Africa, especially throughout Namibia. Native people use the branches and bark of the tree to make containers, or quivers, for their arrows.

NIGERIA
Garoua
CHAD
Garba
CENT
AFRICAN R
Mount Cameroon 4071 m
Bamenda
Bouar   Bambari
CAMEROON
Berbérati
Malabo
Douala
Bangui
Bioko Island
Yaoundé
EQUATORIAL GUINEA
SÃO TOMÉ AND PRÍNCIPE
Príncipe
Ciudad de la Paz
Cong
São Tomé
São Tomé
Libreville
Mbandaka
DEMOCRA
OF THE
GABON
Port-Gentil
REPUBLIC OF THE CONGO
Lake Mai-Ndombe
Brazzaville
Bandundu
Kasai
Loubomo
Pointe-Noire
Kinshasa
Kikwit
Matadi
Kwilu
Tshika
Kwango
Luanda
Cuanza
Saurimo
Casse
ANGOLA
Luena
Lobito
Benguela
Huambo
Namibe
Lubango
Kwana
Cunene
Cubango
Cuito
ETOSHA PAN
Cape Fria
Grootfontein
NAMIBIA
BO
NAMIB DESERT
Windhoek
Swakopmund
Walvis Bay
KALAHARI DESERT
Rehoboth
Lüderitz
Keetmanshoop
Alexander Bay
SOU
Kenhardt
Carnarvon
Calvinia
Beaufort Wes
Great Karoo
Worcest
Cape Town
Cape of Good Hope
Mosselbaa
False Bay

THE DISTANCE to the bottom of South Africa's deepest gold mine is 3777 m – this would take four minutes in a high-speed lift.

In the next ...South Africa will mine 226 g of gold – enough for 75 18ct-gold wedding rings. minute...

Search and Find

Angola
- Luanda E6

Botswana
- Gaborone H8

Cameroon
- Yaoundé C5

Central African Republic
- Bangui B7

Comoros
- Moroni F12

Democratic Republic of the Congo
- Kinshasa D6

Equatorial Guinea
- Ciudad de la Paz C5
- Malabo C5

Eswatini
- Lobamba I9
- Mbabane I9

Gabon
- Libreville C5

Lesotho
- Maseru I8

Madagascar
- Antananarivo. .G12

Malawi
- Lilongwe F10

Mauritius
- Port Louis. . . H14

Mozambique
- Maputo I9

Namibia
- Windhoek H7

Republic of the Congo
- Brazzaville. . . . D6

São Tomé and Príncipe
- São Tomé C4

Seychelles
- Victoria D14

South Africa
- Cape Town J7
- Pretoria H9

Zambia
- Lusaka F9

Zimbabwe
- Harare G9

Victoria

SEYCHELLES

SOUTH SUDAN

Bakouma

Bondo

Uele

Watsa

Mount Ngaliema
5109 m

Basoko

Kisangani

UGANDA

Lake Edward

RWANDA

Lake Kivu

Bukavu

BURUNDI

Lake Tanganyika

TANZANIA

kenie

Lomami

Congo

IC REPUBLIC CONGO

kenie

nanga

Mbuji-Mayi

Kalemie

Lake Mweru

Kamina

Mbala

Lubilash

Kolwezi

Kasama

Likasi

Lubumbashi

Lake Bangweulu

Mufulira

Kitwe Ndola

Kafue

Kabwe Chipata

Kafue

ZAMBIA

Lusaka

Lake Cahora Bassa

Zomba

Tete

Zambezi

MALAWI

Lake Malawi

Lilongwe

Lúrio

Nacala

Nampula

Blantyre

Moçambique

Cape Delgado

COMOROS

Moroni

MAYOTTE (FRANCE)

Antsiranana

Mahajanga

INDIAN OCEAN

Livingstone

Lake Kariba

Harare

Chitungwiza

Chimoio

Quelimane

MOZAMBIQUE

Zambezi

MOZAMBIQUE CHANNEL

MADAGASCAR

avango Delta

Victoria Falls

Maun

ZIMBABWE

Bulawayo

Beira

Save

Antananarivo

SWANA

Francistown

Selebi-Phikwe

Messina

Inhambane

MAURITIUS

Fianarantsoa

Molepolole

Pietersburg

Gaborone

Pretoria

obatse

Johannesburg

Soweto

Vereeniging

Vaal

Limpopo

Mbabane

Maputo

ESWATINI

Lobamba

RÉUNION (FRANCE)

Port Louis

H AFRICA

Kimberley

Maseru

loemfontein

LESOTHO

Pietermaritzburg

Durban

Orange

Middelburg

Umtata

DRAKENSBERG MOUNTAINS

Port Shepstone

East London

Port Elizabeth

0 100 200 300 400 500 mi
0 200 400 600 800 km

African elephants live in herds of females, led by a matriarch – normally the oldest female. They work together to keep the herd safe. When they walk in file, the youngsters stay close to the adults so they are protected from predators.

Asia

ARCTIC OCEAN

RUSSIA

KAZAKHSTAN

MONGOLIA

UZBEKISTAN

KYRGYZSTAN

1

TURKEY

TURKMENISTAN

TAJIKISTAN

NORTH KOREA

CHINA

SOUTH KOREA

JAPAN

SYRIA

2

IRAQ

AFGHANISTAN

3 4

5

IRAN

PAKISTAN

NEPAL

9

SAUDI ARABIA

6 7

8

BANGLADESH

TAIWAN

OMAN

INDIA

BURMA (MYANMAR)

LAOS

YEMEN

THAILAND

VIETNAM

PACIFIC OCEAN

CAMBODIA

PHILIPPINES

SRI LANKA

10

12

MALAYSIA

11

INDONESIA

INDIAN OCEAN

EAST TIMOR (TIMOR-LESTE)

KEY
1 AZERBAIJAN
2 LEBANON
3 ISRAEL
4 JORDAN
5 KUWAIT
6 BAHRAIN
7 QATAR
8 UNITED ARAB EMIRATES
9 BHUTAN
10 BRUNEI
11 SINGAPORE
12 MALDIVES

COUNTRY FACTFILE

Country	Life expectancy	Population to nearest thousand	Population growth %	Population as urban %	Area km²	Population density per km²	Capital city	Currency	Languages
Afghanistan	52	28,224,000	2.4	27	645,807	43.2	Kabul	Afghani	Dari, Pashto
Azerbaijan*	73	9,828,000	0.9	57	86,600	110.8	Baku	Manat	Azeri
Bahrain	79	1,490,000	2.3	92	716	1836.6	Manama	Bahraini Dinar	Arabic, Urdu, English
Bangladesh	73	166,221,000	1	37	147,570	1126.4	Dhaka	Taka	Bangla, English
Bhutan	71	727,000	1.1	41	46,500	18.9	Thimphu	Ngultrum	Dzongkha, Nepali
Brunei	77	423,000	1.6	78	5765	73.4	Bandar Seri Begawan	Bruneian Dollar	Malay
Burma (Myanmar)	68	53,370,000	0.9	34	676,577	78.9	Naypyidaw	Kyat	Burmese, Shan
Cambodia	65	18,849,000	1.8	22	181,035	87.5	Phnom Penh	Riel	Khmer
China	76	1,391,700,000	0.4	59	9,559,686	148.5	Beijing	Yuan	Chinese (Guoyo), Wu, Yuëh
Cyprus†	79	1,141,000	1.3	70	9251	123.3	Nicosia	Euro	Greek, Turkish, English
East Timor (Timor-Leste)	68	1,184,000	2.1	33	14,874	79.6	Dili	US Dollar	Tetum, Portuguese
India	69	1,339,000,000	1.2	34	3,287,263	407.4	New Delhi	Indian Rupee	Hindi, English, Telegu, Bengali
Indonesia	73	263,990,000	0.9	55	1,904,413	138.6	Jakarta	Indonesian Rupiah	Bahasa Indonesian, Javanese, Sudanese
Iran	74	79,926,000	1.2	75	1,641,918	48.7	Tehran	Iranian Rial	Farsi (Persian), Azeri
Iraq	75	38,270,000	2.6	76	434,128	88	Baghdad	New Iraqi Dinar	Arabic, Kurdish
Israel	83	8,627,000	1.5	92	20,400	398.6	Jerusalem	Israeli Shekel	Hebrew, Arabic
Japan	85	127,095,000	-0.1	92	377,819	336.4	Tokyo	Yen	Japanese
Jordan	75	9,798,000	2.1	91	89,342	110.3	Amman	Jordanian Dinar	Arabic
Kazakhstan	71	18,157,000	1	64	2,717,300	6.7	Astana	Tenge	Kazakh, Russian
Korea, North	71	25,490,000	0.5	62	122,762	207.6	Pyongyang	North Korean Won	Korean
Korea, South	83	52,858,000	0.5	83	99,461	527.4	Seoul, Sejong	South Korean Won	Korean
Kuwait	78	4,438,000	1.5	98	17,818	261.5	Kuwait City	Kuwaiti Dinar	Arabic, Farsi, English
Kyrgyzstan	71	6,257,000	1.1	36	198,500	31.3	Bishkek	Som	Kyrgyz, Russian
Laos	65	6,850,000	1.5	39	236,800	28.6	Vientiane	Kip	Lao
Lebanon	78	6,106,000	3	90	10,201	486.8	Beirut	Lebanese Pound	Arabic
Malaysia	75	32,050,000	1.4	76	329,847	97	Kuala Lumpur, Putrajaya	Ringgit	Bahasa Melayu (Malay), Chinese, English
Maldives	76	435,000	1	46	298	1459.7	Male	Rufiyaa	Dhivehi (Maldivian)
Mongolia	70	3,132,000	1.2	72	1,564,100	2	Ulaanbaatar	Tugrik	Khalkha Mongol
Nepal	71	29,300,000	1.2	20	147,181	199	Kathmandu	Nepalese Rupee	Nepali, Maithali
Oman	76	4,414,000	2	85	309,500	14.3	Muscat	Omani Rial	Arabic, Baluchi
Pakistan	68	213,123,000	1.4	39	880,254	242.1	Islamabad	Pakistani Rupee	Urdu, Punjabi, Sindhi
Philippines	69	104,920,000	1.6	65	300,076	349.6	Manila	Philippine Peso	Filipino (Tagalog), Cebuano, English
Qatar	79	2,640,000	2.3	99	11,427	231	Doha	Qatari Rial	Arabic, Hindi, Malayalam
Russia	71	144,530,000	0	78	17,075,400	8.5	Moscow	Rouble	Russian, Tatar, Ukrainian
Saudi Arabia	76	32,950,000	1.5	86	2,149,803	15.3	Riyadh	Saudi Riyal	Arabic, Malayalam, Tagalog
Singapore	85	5,612,000	1.8	100	720	7794.4	Singapore	Singapore Dollar	Chinese, Malay, English
Sri Lanka	77	21,444,000	0.8	23	65,613	326.8	Colombo, Kotte	Sri Lankan Rupee	Sinhala, Tamil
Syria	75	18,270,000	0	58	185,180	98.7	Damascus	Syrian Pound	Arabic
Taiwan	80	23,540,000	0.2	78	36,179	650.7	Taipei	Taiwan dollar	Chinese (Mandarin), Min
Tajikistan	68	8,551,000	1.6	28	143,100	59.8	Dushanbe	Somoni	Tajik, Uzbek
Thailand	75	67,653,000	0.3	50	514,000	137.8	Bangkok	Baht	Thai, Chinese
Turkey	75	80,811,000	0.5	75	780,580	108.6	Ankara	Turkish Lira	Turkish, Kurdish
Turkmenistan	70	5,750,000	1.1	52	488,100	11.8	Ashgabat	Turkmen Manat	Turkmen, Uzbek
United Arab Emirates	78	9,121,000	2.4	90	83,600	112.4	Abu Dhabi	Emirati Dirham	Arabic, Hindu, Urdu
Uzbekistan	74	32,121,000	0.9	51	444,103	72.3	Tashkent	Uzbek Soum	Uzbek, Russian
Vietnam	74	92,695,000	0.9	36	329,315	281.5	Hanoi	Dong	Vietnamese
Yemen	66	28,250,000	2.3	37	527,970	53.5	Sana'a	Yemeni Rial	Arabic

* Although Azerbaijan is a member of some European organizations, it is historically and culturally part of western Asia.
† Cyprus is part of Europe, but the mapping can be found in this section.

The Near East

Mostly a poor, mountainous region, Turkey has a beautiful coastline and thriving tourist industry. The country is being transformed by the Great Anatolian project – reservoirs will be built along the Tigris and Euphrates rivers, to irrigate 16,000 km² of land. Although geographically closer to Asia, Turkey is internationally recognized as part of Europe. Israel was created in 1948. Land was taken from the Palestinians resulting in conflict with Syria, Jordan and Lebanon. Syria has been in civil conflict since 2011 as political power has been contested. Sheep and goats are the main livestock. Where irrigation is possible, vegetables and fruit are grown, much of which is exported to Europe.

BULGARIA
GREECE
Edirne
Tekirdag
Istanbul
Bosporus Strait
Sea of Marmara
Izmit
Bursa
Sakarya
Balikesir
Eskisehir
Kütahya
A N A T O
P L A T
Manisa
Usak
Izmir
Ephesus
Nazilli
Aydin
Denizli
Isparta
Bodrum
T A U
Antalya

The **Temple Mount** in Jerusalem [I9] is an important religious site. The Dome of the Rock is a Muslim shrine. The Western Wall dates back to 500 BC and is used by Jews for prayer.

THE DISTANCE from Europe to Asia across the Bosporus Strait [B6] is only 700 m and takes one minute by car across a bridge.

Search and Find

Cyprus
- Nicosia F8

Israel
- Jerusalem I9

Jordan
- Amman H10

Lebanon
- Beirut G9

Syria
- Damascus . . H10

Turkey
- Ankara C8

Did You Know?

Cyprus is the third largest island in the Mediterranean. The northern area of the island is Turkish Cypriot and the southern area is Greek Cypriot. Although geographically closer to Asia, Cyprus joined the EU in 2004.

Facts and Stats

- Turkey's area of 769,604 km² is 7.5 times the area of Iceland.
- Mount Ararat [D14] is the highest mountain at 5137 m – 16 times higher than the Eiffel Tower.
- The life expectancy of people in Israel is 83 years, compared to 75 years in Jordan and a world average of 69 years.

Pamukkale, which means 'cotton castle' in Turkish, was formed from the water of a very hot spring. The water contains a lot of chalk, which results in the limestone cliffs that can be seen today.

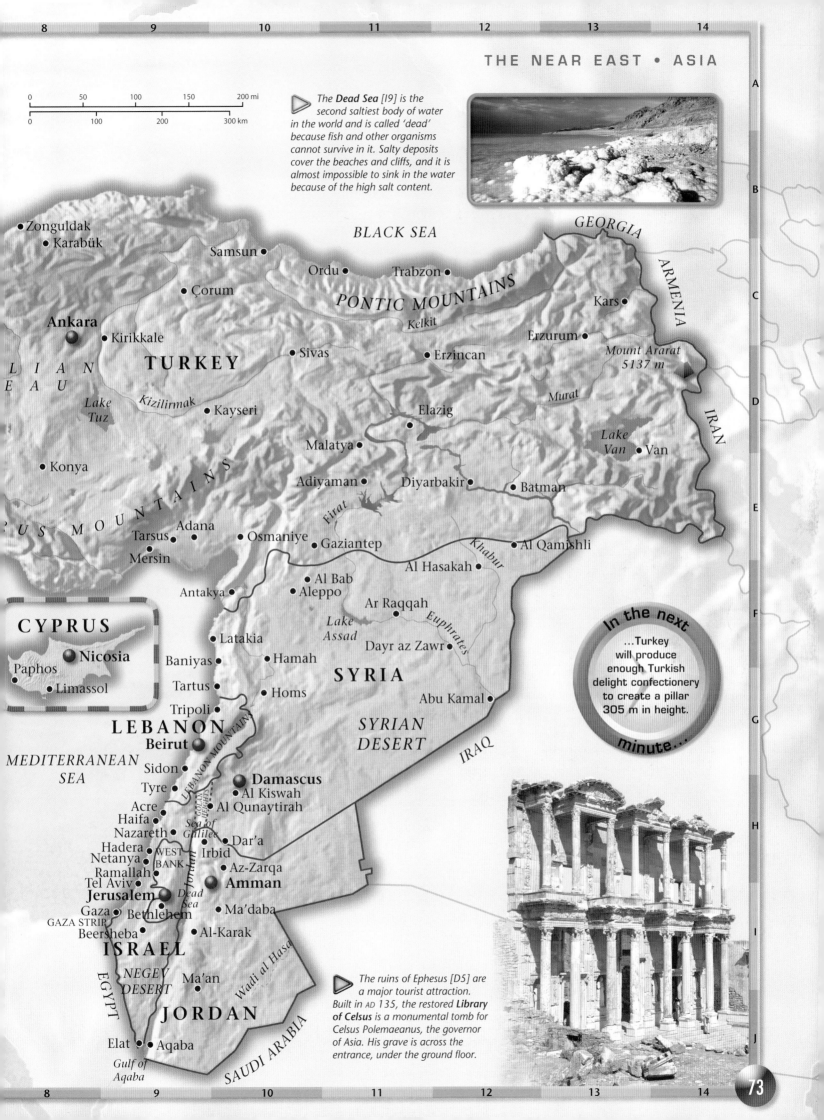

0 50 100 150 200 mi
0 100 200 300 km

The **Dead Sea** [I9] is the second saltiest body of water in the world and is called 'dead' because fish and other organisms cannot survive in it. Salty deposits cover the beaches and cliffs, and it is almost impossible to sink in the water because of the high salt content.

BLACK SEA

GEORGIA
ARMENIA

• Zonguldak
• Karabük

Samsun •

Ordu •   Trabzon •

Çorum •

PONTIC MOUNTAINS

Kars •

Kelkit

Ankara   Erzurum •

• Kirikkale

Erzincan •

Mount Ararat
5137 m

TURKEY

Sivas •

Murat

Lake
Tuz

Kizilirmak

Elazig •

• Kayseri

Lake
Van   • Van

IRAN

• Konya

Malatya •

Diyarbakir •

• Batman

Adiyaman •

MOUNTAINS

Firat

Adana   Osmaniye •   Gaziantep •

Khabur   • Al Qamishli

Tarsus •

Al Hasakah •

Mersin •

• Al Bab

Antakya •   • Aleppo

Ar Raqqah •

Euphrates

CYPRUS

Latakia •

Lake
Assad

Dayr az Zawr •

Nicosia

Baniyas •   • Hamah

SYRIA

Paphos •

Tartus •   • Homs

• Limassol

Abu Kamal •

Tripoli •

LEBANON

SYRIAN
DESERT

Beirut

IRAQ

**MEDITERRANEAN
SEA**

Sidon •

Tyre •   **Damascus**

LEBANON MOUNTAINS

• Al Kiswah

Acre •   GOLAN HEIGHTS   Al Qunaytirah •

Haifa •

Sea of
Galilee

Nazareth •   Dar'a •

Hadera •   WEST   Irbid •

Netanya •   BANK

Ramallah •   Jordan   Az-Zarqa •

Tel Aviv •   **Amman**

Jerusalem   Dead
Sea

Gaza •   Bethlehem •   Ma'daba •

GAZA STRIP

Beersheba •   Al-Karak •

ISRAEL

EGYPT   NEGEV   Ma'an •
DESERT   Wadi al Hasa

JORDAN

Elat • • Aqaba

SAUDI ARABIA

Gulf of
Aqaba

...Turkey will produce enough Turkish delight confectionery to create a pillar 305 m in height.

In the next minute...

The ruins of Ephesus [D5] are a major tourist attraction. Built in AD 135, the restored **Library of Celsus** is a monumental tomb for Celsus Polemaeanus, the governor of Asia. His grave is across the entrance, under the ground floor.

The Middle East

Vast oil and gas reserves have made several countries in the Middle East some of the wealthiest in the world. However, before oil was discovered, this was a poor region of desert tribes and coastal fishing. The area between the Euphrates and Tigris rivers was once home to the great civilization of Mesopotamia. Conflict and sanctions have damaged the economies of Iraq and Iran, but other countries such as the UAE are investing in tourism and other forms of industry. The city of Dubai now has the largest indoor ski slope in the world.

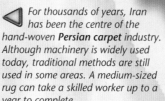

*For thousands of years, Iran has been the centre of the hand-woven **Persian carpet** industry. Although machinery is widely used today, traditional methods are still used in some areas. A medium-sized rug can take a skilled worker up to a year to complete.*

Extreme Weather

Midday temperatures can reach 50°C in the desert areas, but snow is common in the mountains of Iran and Iraq.

Did You Know?

The United Arab Emirates obtains more than 80 percent of its water supply by desalinating sea water.

*Millions of Muslims have made a pilgrimage, or Hajj, to Mecca [G5]. The holiest place in Islam is the **Kaaba**. Non-Muslims cannot enter Mecca.*

ARMENIA

TURKEY

Tabr

Mosul • Arbil
Kirkuk •

IRAQ

SYRIA

Bakhtara

Baghdad

Tigris

S Y R I A N
D E S E R T
Karbala •
Najaf •
Euphrates

An Nasiriyah •

JORDAN

Al Jawf • • Sakakah

EGYPT

N A F U D
D E S E R T

H I J A Z

Buraydah •

Shaqra •

Riyadh •

Medina
• Yanbu

RED SEA

S A U D I

Jeddah
• • Mecca
• Taif

As-Sulayyil •

A S I R

• Abha

• Jizan
• Harad

Sana'a
• Al-Hudaydah

• Ta'izz

• Aden

Baku

AZERBAIJAN

CASPIAN SEA

Rasht

TURKMENISTAN

Babol · Gorgan
ELBURZ MOUNTAINS
Mashhad

Karaj · **Tehran**

Qom

Hamadan

Kashan

IRAN

AFGHANISTAN

ZAGROS MOUNTAINS

Esfahan

Yazd

Ahvaz

Basra

Kerman

Abadan

UWAIT

Zahedan

PAKISTAN

Kuwait City

Shiraz

Busheher

PERSIAN GULF

Bandar-e Lengeh · Bandar 'Abbas

Al Qatif · BAHRAIN

Strait of Hormuz

Ad-Dammam · **Manama**

OMAN

Jask

QATAR · Sharjah

Al-Hufuf · Doha

Dubai

GULF OF OMAN

Abu Dhabi

Suhar

UNITED ARAB

Jabal ash Sham
3035 m

Matrah

ARABIAN SEA

EMIRATES

Muscat

ARABIA

Nizwa · Sur

EMPTY QUARTER

OMAN

Khaluf

YEMEN

Salalah

Al Mukalla

GULF OF ADEN

SOCOTRA
(YEMEN)

THE DISTANCE from Yemen to Africa is only 30 km across the Red Sea and takes four hours by canoe.

Facts and Stats

• The average income per person in Qatar is £48,308, compared to a world average of £8196.

• Saudi Arabia has an area of 2.1 million km² and is 21 times the area of Iceland.

• The longest river is the Euphrates [C7]. At 2800 km in length, it is nearly 2.5 times shorter than the Nile river.

In the next
...Qatar will produce 391,000 m³ of natural gas – enough to power a house for 151 years.
minute...

0 100 200 300 400 mi
0 200 400 600 km

Built in the 2009, the **Burj Khalifa** [F10], in the UAE city of Dubai, is the tallest building in the world. At 829.8 m in height, it has 163 floors and is a mix of office, residential and hotel space. Its New Deck observatory, on the 148th floor, is the highest observation deck in the world.

Indian subcontinent

With ice-covered mountains, tropical lowlands and hot deserts, this region is one of contrasts. Afghanistan is a war-torn, semi-desert nation that is in the process of rebuilding amidst ongoing conflicts. India has one of the most rapidly growing economies in the world. A highly educated, English-speaking workforce has resulted in many European and American companies establishing various support operations in India. The 'Bollywood' film studios are a worldwide success and cities are rapidly expanding. However, out of India's 1.34 billion population, two thirds remain poor, rural farmers. Pakistan, Bangladesh and the Himalayan states of Nepal and Bhutan remain relatively undeveloped.

The **Taj Mahal** in Agra [D9], India, was built for Mumtaz Mahal, the wife of Emperor Shah Jahan. When she died in 1629, the Emperor ordered the most beautiful tomb in the world to be built. It took 20,000 workers about 20 years to build. The Emperor and his wife are buried beneath the 60-m-high white dome.

Search and Find

Afghanistan
- Kabul B7

Bangladesh
- Dhaka E11

Bhutan
- Thimphu D11

India
- New Delhi D9

Nepal
- Kathmandu . . D10

Pakistan
- Islamabad B8

Sri Lanka
- Colombo J9
- Kotte J9

Did You Know?

Great Britain ruled India from 1858 until 1947. This is why English is widely spoken and cricket is the national sport.

THE DISTANCE from the Everest base camp to the summit is 10 km. In 2000, it was climbed in less than 17 hours.

World Record

In 1985, Mawsynram [E12] recorded the world's highest yearly rainfall – over 26,000 mm.

Many Hindus go to a mandir, or **temple**, to say prayers and to make offerings of food to the gods. The temples are beautifully decorated with carvings of gods and spirits.

TURKMENISTAN

Sheberghan

Mazar-e Shari

Herat

AFGHANISTAN

IRAN

Farah

Kabul

Helmand

Qandahar

RIGESTAN DESERT

Quetta

SULAIMAN

PAKISTAN

Larkana

Sukku

Gwadar

Indus

Hyderabad

Karachi

Mirpur Kha

Gulf of Kachchh

RANN OF KACHCHH

Ahmadabad

Jamnagar

ARABIAN SEA

Bhavnagar

Sura

Gulf of Khambhat

Mumbai (Bombay)

WESTERN GH

INDIAN OCEAN

8 9 10 11 12 13 14

A
B
C
D
E
F
G
H
I
J

TAJIKISTAN

K2
8611 m

SIGIRIYA, or Lion's Mouth, was the
fortress of Sri Lankan King Kashyapa
(AD 477–495). Only the two giant
paws of the lion remain.

Facts and Stats

• The longest river in the region is
the Brahmaputra [D12]. At 2900 km
in length, it is almost half the length
of the Nile river.

• The highest mountain in the world
is Mount Everest [D11] at 8848 m
in height – 28 times higher than the
Eiffel Tower.

• The life expectancy of people in
Afghanistan is 52 years, compared
to 76 years in Sri Lanka and a world
average of 69 years.

Extreme Weather

The heaviest recorded
hailstones, weighing up to
one kilogram killed 92 people in
Bangladesh on 14 April 1986.

Mardan
Islamabad
shawar
walpindi
Srinagar
aisalabad Gujranwala
Lahore Amritsar
Multan Sahiwal Ludhiana
Sutlej
Bahawalpur Chandigarh

Meerut
Delhi
New Delhi

HIMALAYAS

CHINA

NEPAL

Ganges
Jaipur Agra
Jodhpur Ajmer
Yamuna
Pokhara
Kathmandu
Lucknow
Kanpur
Mount Everest
8848 m
Thimphu
BHUTAN
Biratnagar
Jorhat
Brahmaputra
Guwahati
Rangpur
NAGA HILLS
Mawsynram
Udaipur
Lalitpur
Allahabad Varanasi
Patna
Rajshahi
Sylhet Imphal
Bhopal
adodara
Narmada
Dhanbad
BANGLADESH
Agartala
Indore
Dhaka
INDIA
Jamshedpur
Khulna
Chittagong
Kolkata
(Calcutta)
Nagpur Raipur

BURMA (MYANMAR)

Cuttack
BAY OF
BENGAL
Pune
(Poona)
Godavari
EASTERN GHATS
Solapur
Hyderabad
Kolhapur
Krishna
Vishakhapatnam
Hubli-Dhawar
Vijayawada
Kurnool

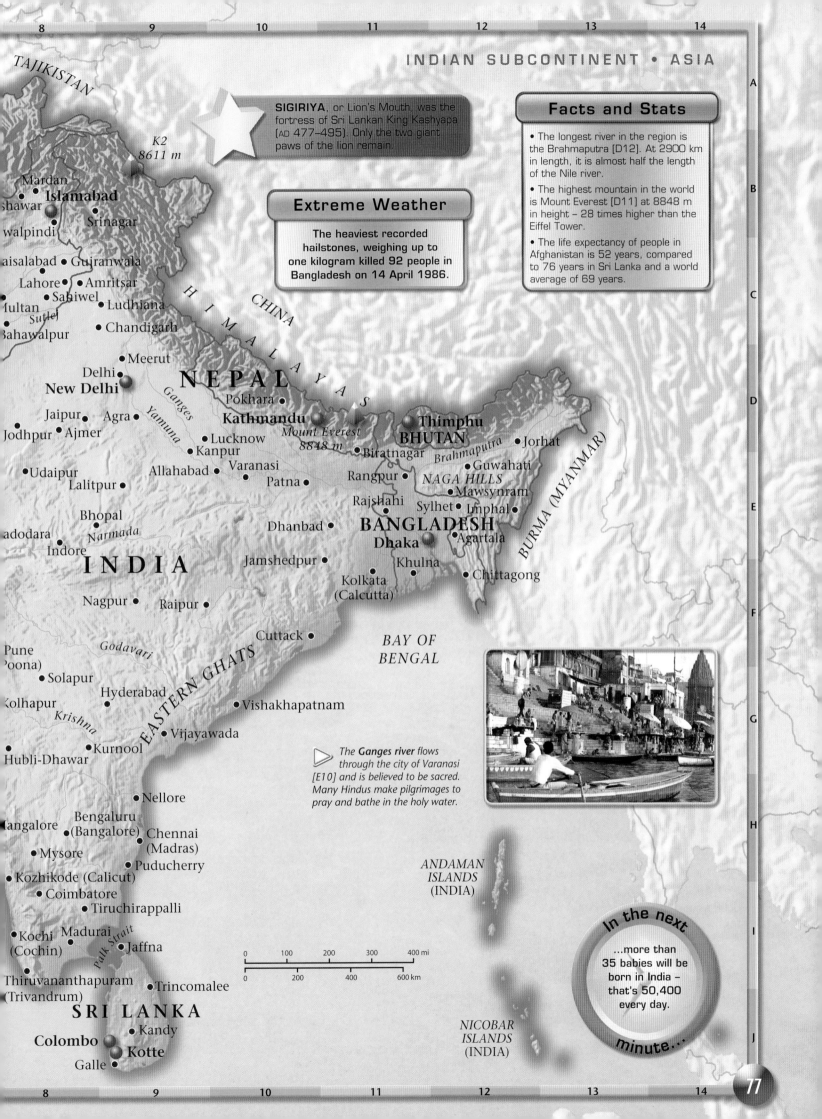

The **Ganges river** flows
through the city of Varanasi
[E10] and is believed to be sacred.
Many Hindus make pilgrimages to
pray and bathe in the holy water.

Nellore
angalore
Bengaluru
(Bangalore)
Chennai
(Madras)
Mysore
Puducherry
Kozhikode (Calicut)
Coimbatore
Tiruchirappalli

ANDAMAN
ISLANDS
(INDIA)

Kochi
(Cochin)
Madurai
Palk Strait
Jaffna
Thiruvananthapuram
(Trivandrum)
Trincomalee

SRI LANKA

Colombo
Kandy
Kotte
Galle

NICOBAR
ISLANDS
(INDIA)

0 100 200 300 400 mi
0 200 400 600 km

In the next
...more than
35 babies will be
born in India –
that's 50,400
every day.
minute...

Vietnam and the Philippines

Lush tropical rainforests lead to wonderful sandy beaches and warm seas. Rice fields and remote villages give way to sprawling cities. Despite the growth of tourism in Thailand and Vietnam, most of this area is poor. Many people live near the coast and they are still mainly dependent on fishing and farming. Rice is the main crop, grown in the river valleys in wet paddy fields. Vietnam has recovered from wars in the 20th century and is now a major coffee producer.

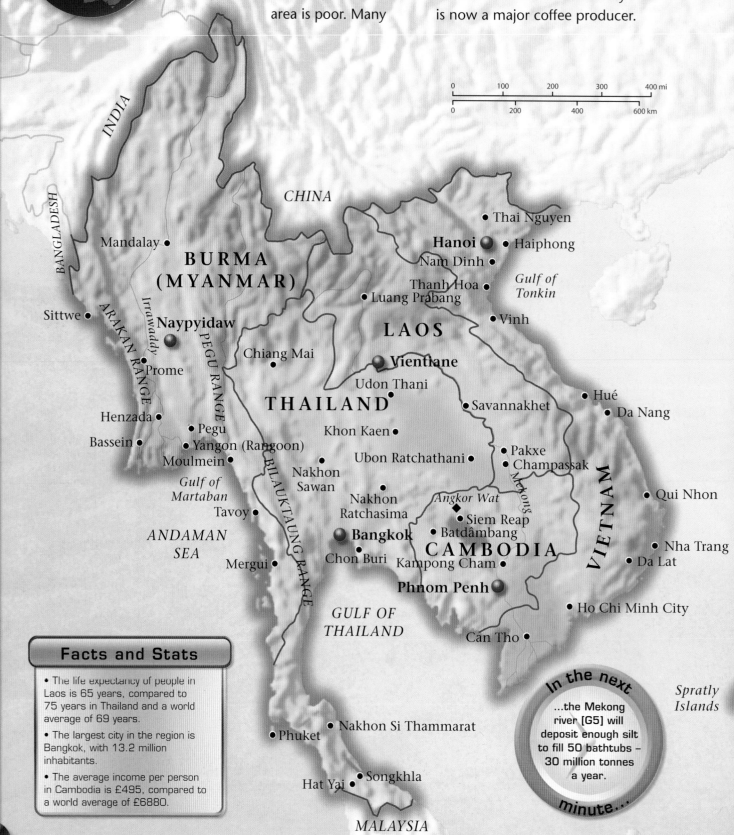

0 100 200 300 400 mi
0 200 400 600 km

CHINA

INDIA

BANGLADESH

Sittwe

Mandalay

BURMA (MYANMAR)

ARAKAN RANGE

Irrawaddy

Naypyidaw

Prome

PEGU RANGE

Chiang Mai

Thai Nguyen

Hanoi • Haiphong

Nam Dinh

Thanh Hoa

Gulf of Tonkin

Luang Prabang

Vinh

LAOS

Vientiane

Udon Thani

Hué

Da Nang

THAILAND

Henzada

Pegu

Bassein

Yangon (Rangoon)

Moulmein

Khon Kaen

Savannakhet

Gulf of Martaban

BILAUKTAUNG RANGE

Nakhon Sawan

Ubon Ratchathani

Pakxe

Champassak

Mekong

Qui Nhon

Tavoy

Nakhon Ratchasima

Angkor Wat

Siem Reap

VIETNAM

ANDAMAN SEA

Bangkok

Batdâmbang

Nha Trang

Mergui

Chon Buri

CAMBODIA

Kampong Cham

Da Lat

Phnom Penh

GULF OF THAILAND

Ho Chi Minh City

Can Tho

Facts and Stats

• The life expectancy of people in Laos is 65 years, compared to 75 years in Thailand and a world average of 69 years.

• The largest city in the region is Bangkok, with 13.2 million inhabitants.

• The average income per person in Cambodia is £495, compared to a world average of £6880.

Nakhon Si Thammarat

Phuket

In the next
...the Mekong river [G5] will deposit enough silt to fill 50 bathtubs – 30 million tonnes a year.
minute...

Spratly Islands

Hat Yai • Songkhla

MALAYSIA

Many young men in Thailand temporarily become **Buddhist monks** to learn more about their faith. They shave their heads and beards and wear robes to show commitment to the holy life.

Search and Find

Cambodia
- Phnom Penh . . H5

Laos
- Vientiane F4

Burma (Myanmar)
- Naypyidaw F2

Philippines
- Manila F10

Thailand
- Bangkok H4

Vietnam
- Hanoi E5

THE DISTANCE from Yangon [G2] to Bangkok [H4] is 640 km and would take an elephant three days of non-stop walking.

The canals in Bangkok [H4] are used for **floating markets** where fresh produce, such as fruit, vegetables and flowers, is sold from boats.

Luzon Strait

Babuyan Islands

Laoag •

• Tuguegarao

Luzon

PHILIPPINES

PACIFIC OCEAN

Angeles • • Cabanatuan

Manila ◉ • Quezon City

Batangas •

Mindoro

• Calbayog
Samar

SOUTH CHINA SEA

Mindoro Strait

• Ormoc
Leyte

Panay Bacolod

Iloilo • • Cebu

Negros

Butuan •

Palawan Passage

Cagayan de Oro •

• Puerto Princesa

Mindanao

Palawan

Pagadian • Davao •

SULU SEA

General Santos

Moro Gulf

Zamboanga

CELEBES SEA

Balabac Strait

SULU ARCHIPELAGO

Did You Know?

The ruins of the ancient city of Angkor Wat [G5], complete with Hindu temples and royal palaces, were discovered in the Cambodian rainforest 150 years ago.

Extreme Weather

In July, the monsoon rains bring the city of Yangon [G2] as much rain as London gets in a year.

Many tropical countries suffer from rainy seasons called monsoons, which result in serious flooding. In some parts of Asia, **houses are built on stilts** over bodies of water to protect them against water damage.

Indonesia, Malaysia and Singapore

Situated on the Equator, this region has a hot, wet climate. Malaysia is part of the Asian mainland and the large island of Borneo. It is developing rapidly with car and shipbuilding industries. Singapore is the richest country in this region, based on its technology industry, banking and high educational standards. A safe, law-abiding nation, laws against all types of crime, even dropping litter, are strictly enforced. Indonesia consists of over 13,000 islands. Natural disasters, poor communications and corruption have restricted economic growth. Although East Timor became independent from Indonesia in 2002, it remains impoverished.

THAILAND

George Town
Kuala Terengganu
Ipoh • MALAY
Medan •　PENINSULA
Kelang • **Kuala Lumpur**
　　　　Putrajaya　M A L A Y S I A
　　　　Johor Baharu
Pekanbaru •　**Singapore**
　　　　　　SINGAPORE
Padang •　*Sumatra*
　　　　Bangka
Jambi •
Palembang •　*Belitung*

Kota Kinabalu
Bandar Seri Begawan　• Sandakan
BRUNEI　*SABAH*

Natuna Island

SARAWAK
• Kuching

CELEBES SEA

Manado •

Pontianak • *Kapuas*
KALIMANTAN
Balikpapan •
Borneo
Banjarmasin •

Palu •
Sulawesi
Makassar Strait
MOLUCCA SEA

Strait of Malacca
Barito

I N D O N E S I A

Tanjungkarang •
Telukbetung
　　Jakarta
Bandung •　*Java*
　　Surakarta •
Malang •

JAVA SEA
• Semarang
• Surabaya

• Makasar

FLORES SEA

Komodo Flores
Bali Mataram •　• Ende
Lombok　*Sumbawa*
Sumba　Kupang •

Di
Timo

▷ More than 450 m in height, the **Petronas Towers** in Kuala Lumpur [E2] contain 88 floors of offices, a shopping mall, a concert hall and parking for 4500 cars.

Extreme Weather

At the Equator, the climate is the same throughout the year – hot and very wet. Singapore's temperature averages at 27°C.

...seven new cars will be made in this region – that's 3.7 million a year.

Tea has been grown throughout Indonesia for more than 200 years, especially in Java and Sumatra. These small islands now produce 7 percent of the world's tea exports. The shoots are picked by hand, packed and exported.

Did You Know?

The 2004 tsunami in southeast Asia was caused by an undersea earthquake. The waves travelled at speeds of up to 800 km/h – 230,000 people were killed and five million were made homeless.

Search and Find

Brunei
- Bandar Seri Begawan E5

East Timor
- Dili. H7

Indonesia
- Jakarta H3

Malaysia
- Kuala Lumpur . .E2
- Putrajaya E2

Singapore
- Singapore. F2

THE DISTANCE from Singapore to Malaysia is only 1056 m and the Joho–Singapore Causeway can be crossed by car in one minute.

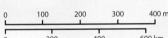

0   100   200   300   400 mi

0   200   400   600 km

Halmahera

• Sorong

SERAM SEA

Seram

• Ambon

New Guinea

Jayapura •

ru

ANDA SEA

Aru Islands

etar

Tanimbar Island

ARAFURA SEA

Bacau

AST TIMOR

*The **Batak people** live in Sumatra, Indonesia. Easily recognizable, their houses are built on stilts and have high, thatched roofs. Often ornaments and paintings are placed on the outside to ward away evil spirits.*

Facts and Stats

- The average income per person in Singapore is £43,899 compared to £1734 in East Timor and a world average of £8196.

- The life expectancy of people in Singapore is 85 years, compared to 68 years in East Timor and a world average of 69 years.

- Indonesia's area of 1.9 million km² is 18 times the area of Iceland.

Japan

Japan consists of four main islands – Kyushu, Hokkaido, Honshu and Shikoku. More than 70 percent of the country is covered with forested volcanic mountains such as Mount Fuji. Most of Japan's population lives on the flatlands along the coast, resulting in a very high population density. People live in high-rise flats or small houses, but frequent earthquakes can cause immense damage. Agriculture, industry, and urban development are concentrated on the main island of Honshu in the area between Osaka and Tokyo. Japan is one of the richest nations in the world, with well-known brands such as Toyota, Honda, Nissan, Sony, Panasonic and JVC.

▷ **The Golden Pavilion**, Kyoto [G8], was originally built in the 14th century for a samurai general. The temple has been destroyed many times, and was most recently rebuilt in the 1950s. The pavilion, except the basement floor, is covered in pure gold leaf.

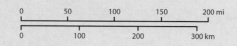

0   50   100   150   200 mi
0   100   200   300 km

SEA OF JAPAN

MOUNT FUJI [G9] is an active volcano, but last erupted in 1707. More than 200,000 people walk to its snow-capped summit each year.

THE DISTANCE from Tokyo [G10] to Osaka [H8] is 515 km. It only takes 2.5 hours by high-speed train, travelling at 206 km/h.

Oki Island

Matsue • • Yonago • Tottori

Tsushima Hiroshima Okayama • Kobe

Shimonoseki Kure • Takamatsu • Wakayan

Kitakyushu • Hofu Tokushima •

Fukuoka • Matsuyama • Kochi

Kii Channel

Sasebo • Oita • *Shikoku*

Kumamoto • Saiki •

Nagasaki • *Bungo Channel*

Amakusa Island Nobeoka •

Koshiki Island *Kyushu*

Miyazaki •

Miyakonojo •

Kagoshima •

Korea Strait

▷ **Sumo wrestling** is a popular sport in Japan. Competitors have a body weight of up to 270 kg and their aim is to push their opponent out of the ring. Sumo is more than 2000 years old, and has strict rules and ceremonies.

Tanega Island

Yaku Island

Map Labels

Soya Strait

Rebun Island
• Wakkanai

Rishiri Island

• Abashiri

Ishikari
• Asahikawa
Hokkaido

Otaru • • Ebetsu
• Kushiro
Sapporo • • Chitose
• Obihiro
Tomakomai •

• Muroran

Uchiura Bay

Hakodate •

Cape Erimo

Tsugaru Strait

• Aomori • Hachinohe
Hirosaki •

Akita • • Miyako
Hanamaki • • Kamaishi

Sakata • • Kesennuma

Yamagata • • Ishinomaki
• Sendai

Sado Island
• Niigata • Fukushima

Nagaoka • Aizu • • Koriyama

Shinano
Honshu • Iwaki

Toyama • Utsunomiya • • Hitachi
Nagano • • Mito
anazawa • • Takasaki
Komatsu • Matsumoto • Saitama •
ukui • **JAPAN** Kofu **Tokyo** •
• Chiba
Mount Fuji • Kawasaki
3776 m Yokohama
Gifu • • Fuji
Kyoto • Shizuoka
Nagoya • • Toyota
Osaka • Toyohashi • Hamamatsu
Sakai

PACIFIC OCEAN

Miyake Island

Hachijo Island

▷ **Geisha** are female Japanese entertainers who are skilled in many traditional arts, such as music, singing and dancing. Although the make-up and clothing of geisha change throughout their career, they generally wear a white base, red lipstick and black outlines to their eyes.

In the next ...Japan will manufacture 15 cars and 50 computer consoles. **minute...**

Did You Know?

People in Japan often wear face masks to protect themselves from fumes, pollution and germs.

Extreme Weather

The mountains of the northern island of Hokkaido have some of the heaviest snowfall in the world. The 1972 Winter Olympics were held there.

Facts and Stats

• The highest mountain is Mount Fuji [G9] at 3776 m. It is 12 times higher than the Eiffel Tower.

• The life expectancy of people in Japan is 85 years, compared to a world average of 69 years.

• The average income per person in Japan is £29,232, compared to a world average of £8196.

▷ With so many people, cars and businesses crammed into a small area, **Tokyo** [G10] is one of the most congested cities in the world. Tokyo Tower is based on the Eiffel Tower, Paris, although it is actually more than 8 m taller.

China and Korea

One fifth of the world's population lives in China. Once a poor, rural nation, China has the fastest-growing economy in the world. Each year, millions of farm workers move to the cities to work in factories. A new power station has to be built every week, making China the biggest user of coal and oil in the world. In contrast, Mongolia has a small, mainly rural population. North Korea is a Communist state with a low standard of living, but South Korea is much richer due to its shipbuilding, electronic and car industries.

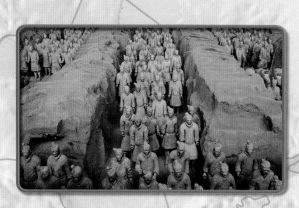

In 210–209 BC, thousands of **terracotta soldiers** were buried with the first emperor of China, Qin Shi Huangdi, as it was believed to make him powerful in heaven. The tomb was discovered in 1974 near Xi'an [F10].

Search and Find

China	South Korea
• Beijing E11	• Sejong E13
Mongolia	• Seoul E13
• Ulaanbaatar . . .C9	**Taiwan**
North Korea	• Taipei H13
• Pyongyang . . D12	

LHASA [H7] in the Himalayas is the capital of Tibet and home to many Buddhist monasteries and ancient palaces.

THE DISTANCE from one end of The Great Wall of China to the other is 8850 km. With all its branches the wall is over 21,000 km long.

Facts and Stats

• China has a population of 1391 million, which would fill 13,917 Olympic stadiums. Mongolia's population of 3.1 million would only fill 31 stadiums.

• China's area of 9.6 million km² is 93 times the area of Iceland.

• The Chang Jiang (Yangtze) [G10] is the longest river at 6300 km in length. The Nile river is nearly twice as long.

One of China's largest cities, **Shanghai** [F12] has a population of 20.9 million. The skyline is dominated by high-rise office buildings and the city is rapidly becoming one of the most important financial centres in the world. The Oriental Pearl Tower is the fifth highest tower in the world at 468 m.

ALTAI MOUNTAINS

• Ulaangom

Uliastay

KAZAKHSTAN

• Tacheng

• Yining

• Urumqi

• Turpan

Korla •

Bosten Hu

TARIM BASIN

• Kashi

SINKIANG

TAKLIMAKAN DESERT

ALTUN SHAN

• Shache

• Hotan

Golmud •

KUNLUN SHAN

KYRGYZSTAN

TAJIKISTAN

AFGHANISTAN

PAKISTAN

INDIA

TIBET

• Gar

Amdo •

HIMALAYAS

NEPAL

PLATEAU OF

Mount Everest 8848 m

• Lhasa

• Gyangzê

INDI

BHUTAN

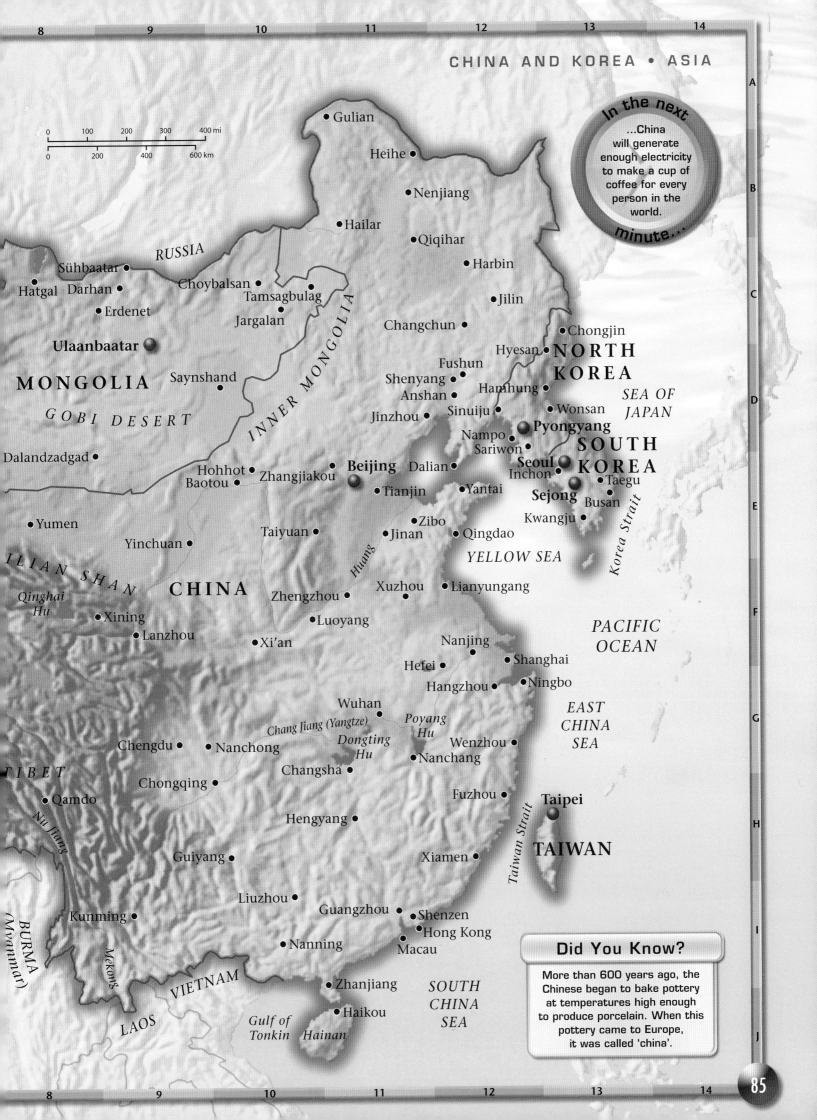

In the next ...China will generate enough electricity to make a cup of coffee for every person in the world. minute...

0 100 200 300 400 mi
0 200 400 600 km

• Gulian

Heihe •

• Nenjiang

RUSSIA

• Hailar

• Qiqihar

Sühbaatar •

• Harbin

Hatgal • Darhan •

Choybalsan •

Tamsagbulag •

• Jilin

• Chongjin

Changchun •

NORTH KOREA

Erdenet •

Jargalan •

Hyesan •

Ulaanbaatar •

Fushun •

MONGOLIA

Saynshand •

INNER MONGOLIA

Shenyang •

Hamhung •

SEA OF JAPAN

GOBI DESERT

Anshan •

Wonsan •

Jinzhou •

Sinuiju •

Nampo •

Pyongyang •

SOUTH KOREA

Dalandzadgad •

Hohhot •

Zhangjiakou •

Beijing •

Dalian •

Sariwon •

Seoul •

Inchon •

Taegu •

Baotou •

Tianjin •

Yantai •

Sejong •

Busan •

Yumen •

Yinchuan •

Taiyuan •

Zibo •

Jinan •

Qingdao •

Kwangju •

Korea Strait

QILIAN SHAN

CHINA

Huang

YELLOW SEA

Qinghai Hu

Xining •

Zhengzhou •

Xuzhou •

Lianyungang •

Lanzhou •

Luoyang •

PACIFIC OCEAN

Xi'an •

Nanjing •

Hefei •

Shanghai •

Hangzhou •

Ningbo •

Wuhan •

EAST CHINA SEA

Chang Jiang (Yangtze)

Poyang Hu

Chengdu •

Nanchong •

Dongting Hu

Wenzhou •

Chongqing •

Changsha •

Nanchang •

TIBET

Qamdo •

Fuzhou •

Hengyang •

Taipei •

Nu Jiang

TAIWAN

Guiyang •

Xiamen •

Taiwan Strait

Liuzhou •

Kunming •

Guangzhou •

Shenzen •

Hong Kong •

Nanning •

Macau •

BURMA (Myanmar)

Mekong

Zhanjiang •

SOUTH CHINA SEA

LAOS

VIETNAM

Gulf of Tonkin

Haikou •

Hainan

Did You Know?

More than 600 years ago, the Chinese began to bake pottery at temperatures high enough to produce porcelain. When this pottery came to Europe, it was called 'china'.

Central Asia and east Russia

Russia is the largest country in the world. However, eastern Russia contains large areas that are unpopulated. Vast areas north of the Arctic Circle suffer freezing conditions that make farming impossible. To the south, much is covered by forest or grassland. Towns are found only where there are natural resources, such as coal, oil, gas, iron and uranium. Kazakhstan is rapidly becoming wealthy due to selling oil, gas and metals to Europe and China, but Turkmenistan, Uzbekistan, Tajikistan and Kyrgyzstan remain underdeveloped.

Extreme Weather

In January 1926, Oymyakon [F10] recorded the lowest temperature for any permanently inhabited location on Earth at −71.2°C.

In the next minute... ...11,000 Russians will be playing chess, making it the nation's most popular sport.

SEVERNAYA ZEMLYA

ARCTIC OCEAN

KARA SEA

• Noril'sk

SIBERIA

• Vorkuta

Yenisey

Tunguska

• Serov

• Surgut   • Nizhnevartovsk

Ob

RUSSIA

Angara   *Lena*

• Yekaterinburg
   • Kurgan
• Chelyabinsk

Tomsk •   Krasnoyarsk •   • Ust'Ilimsk

• Kansk

• Kemerovo   • Bratsk

YABLO MOUN

Semey •   Omsk •   • Novosibirsk
Kokshetau •   Novokuznetsk •   • Abakan

Lake Baikal

Pavlodar •   Barnaul •   Usol'ye-Sibirskoye •

Orenburg •

Ural

Astana

Angarsk •

Chita •

Irkutsk •   • Ulan-Ude

• Aqtobe

Oskemen •

MONGOLIA

Qaraghandy •

Lake Balkhash

• Atyrau   Zhezkazgan •

KAZAKHSTAN

Ustyurt Plateau *Aral Sea*   Qyzylorda •   Taldyqorgan •

CHINA

• Aktau   **UZBEKISTAN**   Almaty •

Tashkent   • **Bishkek**

KYRGYZSTAN

Turkmenabat •   Namangen •

TURKMENISTAN

Balkanabat •

Dushanbe

Ashgabat   **TAJIKISTAN**

IRAN

AFGHANISTAN   PAKISTAN

URAL MOUNTAINS

CASPIAN SEA

Search and Find

Kazakhstan	Tajikistan
• Astana H3	• Dushanbe J3
Kyrgyzstan	**Turkmenistan**
• Bishkek I4	• Ashgabat J3
Russian Federation	**Uzbekistan**
• Moscow (see page 45)	• Tashkent I3

▷ **Lake Baikal** [H7] is the oldest and deepest lake in the world at 1637 m in depth. It holds more than 20 percent of the world's fresh water.

Facts and Stats

• Turkmenistan's population of 5.75 million would fill 58 Olympic stadiums.

• The life expectancy in Russia is 71 years, compared to a world average of 69 years.

• The average income per person in Russia is £8172, compared to £609 in Tajikistan and a world average of £8196.

THE DISTANCE from Moscow in European Russia to the far east of Russia takes six days and four hours to travel by train at 62 km/h.

Did You Know?

Russia has 11 time zones. When it is 12 p.m. in Moscow, it is 3 p.m. in Novosibirsk [H5] and 7 p.m. in Vladivostok [I9].

LAPTEV SEA

EAST SIBERIAN SEA

CHUKCHI SEA

Lena

VERKHOYANSK MOUNTAINS

CHERSKIY MOUNTAINS

Kolyma

Yakutsk

Oymyakon

Magadan

BERING SEA

| 0 | 250 | 500 | 750 | 1000 mi |
| 0 | 400 | 800 | 1200 | 1600 km |

SEA OF OKHOTSK

NOVYY TAINS

Amur

Petropavlovsk-Kamchatskiy

VLADIVOSTOK [I9] is home to the Russian navy's Pacific fleet. Until 1991, foreigners were not allowed into the city in case they were spies.

CHINA

Blagoveshchensk

Komsomol'sk-na-Amure

Khabarovsk

PACIFIC OCEAN

SIKHOTE-ALIN MOUNTAINS

Yuzhno-Sakhalinsk

Vladivostok

NORTH KOREA

▷ The **Aral Sea** [I3] has shrunk by 90 percent since 1960. The remaining water has become very salty, killing off so many fish that the commercial fishing industry stopped and many boats have been abandoned.

Oceania

PACIFIC
OCEAN

MARSHALL
ISLANDS

PALAU

MICRONESIA

NAURU

KIRIBATI

PAPUA
NEW GUINEA

SOLOMON
ISLANDS

TUVALU

SAMOA

COOK ISLANDS

VANUATU

FIJI

TONGA NIUE

INDIAN
OCEAN

PACIFIC
OCEAN

AUSTRALIA

NEW
ZEALAND

SOUTHERN OCEAN

COUNTRY FACTFILE

Country	Life expectancy	Population to nearest thousand	Population growth %	Population as urban %	Area km²	Population density per km²	Capital city	Currency	Languages
Australia	82	24,599,000	1	90	7,702,315	3.2	Canberra	Australian Dollar	English
Cook Islands*	76	13,700	−2.7	75	237	57.8	Avarua	New Zealand Dollar	Cook Island Maori, English
Fiji	73	885,000	0.6	56	18,272	48.4	Suva	Fijian Dollar	English, Fijian
Kiribati	67	116,000	1.1	54	811	143	Bairiki	Australian Dollar	I-Kiribati, English
Marshall Islands	73	53,000	0	77	181	292.8	Majuro	US Dollar	Marshallese, English
Micronesia	73	106,000	0	26	701	151.2	Palikir	US Dollar	English, Chuukese, Pohnpeain
Nauru	67	11,000	0.5	N/A	21	523.8	Yaren	Australian Dollar	Nauruan
New Zealand	81	4,693,000	0.8	87	265,910	17.6	Wellington	New Zealand Dollar	English, Maori
Niue*	75	1400	−0.03	45	259	5.4	Alofi	New Zealand Dollar	Niuean, English
Palau	73	18,000	0	87	458	38.6	Ngerulmud-Melekeok	US Dollar	Palauan, English
Papua New Guinea	67	8,250,000	1.7	17	462,840	17.8	Port Moresby	Kina	Tok Pisin (Pidgin English), English
Samoa	74	192,000	0.6	34	2831	67.8	Apia	Tala	Samoan
Solomon Islands	76	653,000	1.9	24	28,370	23	Honiara	Solmon Islands Dollar	Melanesian languages
Tonga	76	101,000	−0.1	43	748	133.7	Nuku'alofa	Pa'anga	Tongan
Tuvalu	67	11,000	0.9	62	24	458.3	Vaiaku (Funafuti)	Australian Dollar	Mela
Vanuatu	74	272,000	1.9	26	12,190	22.3	Port-Vila	Vatu	Bislama, English, French

* Both the Cook Islands and Niue are self-governing states, but in free association with New Zealand, which is responsible for the aspects of foreign relations and defence that these countries agree to.

Australia

Much of Australia's inland is desert, known as the outback. Most people live in the eastern fertile land between Adelaide and Brisbane, and the capital, Canberra, is in the mountains of the Great Dividing Range. Many lakes in Australia vary in extent and some dry out in drought. Aboriginal people have lived in Australia for more than 40,000 years. In 1787, British settlers began to arrive and immigration has continued ever since. Aboriginals now make up just 2 percent of the population. Rich in gold, iron ore and coal, Australia is one of the wealthiest nations in the world.

Extreme Weather

To fight the effects of long periods of drought, Toowoomba [F13] may use recycled sewage in the water supply.

Did You Know?

The Great Barrier Reef [D12] stretches for more than 2000 km off the coast of Queensland.

SYDNEY [H12] is the largest city and has two of the most famous sights in the world – the Opera House and Sydney Harbour Bridge.

THE DISTANCE from the east coast to the west coast is 3000 km – the same as from London to Boston, USA.

Facts and Stats

• Australia's area of 7.7 million km² is 75 times the area of Iceland.

• The Murray–Darling [H11] is the longest river. At 3750 km, it is more than half the length of the Nile river.

• Mount Kosciuszko [H11] is the highest mountain at 2229 m in height – seven times higher than the Eiffel Tower.

INDIAN OCEAN

Melvill Island
Bathurst Island
Darwin

Joseph Bonaparte Gulf

Daly

Drysdale

Wyndham

Victoria

KIMBERLEY PLATEAU

Broome
Derby
Fitzroy
Halls Creek

Port Hedland
GREAT SANDY DESERT

NOR

Dampier
De Grey

MAC

Onslow
Exmouth

Ashburton

WESTERN AUSTRALIA

Uluru (Ayers Rock)

Carnarvon

GIBSON DESERT

Denham
Murchison

Meekatharra

Laverton

Geraldton

GREAT VICTORIA DESERT

Kalgoorlie

Perth
Freemantle
Mandurah
Balladonia
Norseman

Great Australian

Bunbury
Wagin

Augusta
Esperance

Albany
SOUTHERN OCEAN

At almost 50 m in width **Sydney Harbour Bridge** [H12] is one of the widest bridges in the world. It is 503 m in length, and has two railway tracks, eight lanes for cars, a bicycle path and a pedestrian path. About 160,000 vehicles cross the bridge each day.

Kangaroos can reach speeds of up to 50 km/h. They can be a danger on the roads, causing damage to vehicles in accidents as they weigh up to 90 kg. Therefore 'kangaroo crossing' signs are found throughout Australia.

RNHEM LAND

Groote
Eylandt

Roper

therine

Gulf of
Carpentaria

Wellesley
Islands

Cape
York
Peninsula

Mitchell

• Cooktown

• Port Doulgas
Cairns •
Atherton • • Innisfail

• Normanton
Burketown •

Flinders

GREAT BARRIER REEF

ANAMI
ESERT

• Tennant Creek

Norman

• Townsville
Bowen •

PACIFIC
OCEAN

HERN TERRITORY

Georgina

• Mount Isa

• Mackay

QUEENSLAND

GREAT DIVIDING RANGE

Diamantina

Thomson

Barcoo

• Rockhampton
• Gladstone

DONNELL RANGES

• Alice Springs

AUSTRALIA

• Charleville

Warrego

Bundaberg

Fraser
Island

Marla •

Toowoomba •

• Sunshine Coast
• Brisbane
• Gold Coast

Coober Pedy •

SOUTH AUSTRALIA
Tarcoola •

• Marree

Bourke •

Tamworth •

• Grafton
• Coffs Harbour
• Port Macquarie

Ceduna •

NEW SOUTH WALES

GREAT DIVIDING RANGE

Port Augusta •
Whyalla • • Port Pirie

Darling

Dubbo •

• Newcastle
• Gosford
• Sydney
• Wollongong

Bight

Port Lincoln •

• Mildura

• Adelaide •

Murray

Wagga Wagga

Canberra
AUSTRALIAN
CAPITAL
TERRITORY

Kangaroo
Island

VICTORIA

Mount Kosciuszko
2229 m

Bendigo •

TASMAN
SEA

Mount Gambier •

Ballarat •
Geelong •

• Melbourne
Sale •

King Island

Bass Strait

Flinders Island

Cape Barren Island

0   100   200   300   400   500 mi

0   200   400   600   800 km

Burnie • • Devonport
• Launceston

Queenstown •

TASMANIA

• Hobart

South East Cape

...six kangaroos will be born in Australia. There are twice as many kangaroos than humans.

In the next

minute...

91

New Zealand and the Pacific Islands

New Zealand consists of two main islands and has a population of 4.7 million. The country generates a wealthy economy, mainly by selling its farm produce worldwide. English is the national language due to the many immigrants who started commercial farms and industries. The area of the Pacific Ocean east of Australia contains thousands of tropical islands including the Solomon Islands, Fiji, Vanuatu, Samoa, Kiribati, Tonga, Micronesia, Palau, the Marshall Islands, Papua New Guinea, Nauru and Tuvalu. Many people are leaving the Pacific Islands for education and work in Australia, New Zealand and the USA.

Bora-Bora is a small island in French Polynesia [I14] with a population of only 8000 people. The biggest industry is tourism as people are attracted to the stunning clear waters and tranquil atmosphere. Resorts with bungalows on stilts are a common feature.

In the next ...New Zealand's wine growers will make more than 230 bottles of wine for export. **minute...**

THE DISTANCE from the top to the bottom of the Nevis Highwire, New Zealand's highest bungee jump, is 135 m.

OTAGO PENINSULA [I7] is home to albatrosses, penguins, seals, whales and dolphins.

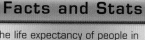

Facts and Stats

• The life expectancy of people in New Zealand is 81 years, compared to a world average of 69 years.

• There are 31 doctors per 10,000 people compared to a world average of 15 doctors.

• Aoraki/Mount Cook [H7] is the highest mountain at 3724 m – nearly 12 times higher than the Eiffel Tower.

The Maori were the first settlers in New Zealand, as they sailed from Polynesia 1000 years ago. Maori tikis are large carvings that are believed to protect sacred sites against evil.

TASMAN SEA

Cape Foulwind

Westport

Greymouth

South

Aoraki/Mount Cook 3724 m

SOUTHERN ALPS

Timaru

Waitaki

Oamar

Otago Peninsula

Dunedin

Cape Providence

Clutha

Foveaux Strait

Invercargill

Codfish Island

Ruapuke Island

Stewart Island

NEW ZEALAND AND THE PACIFIC ISLANDS • OCEANIA

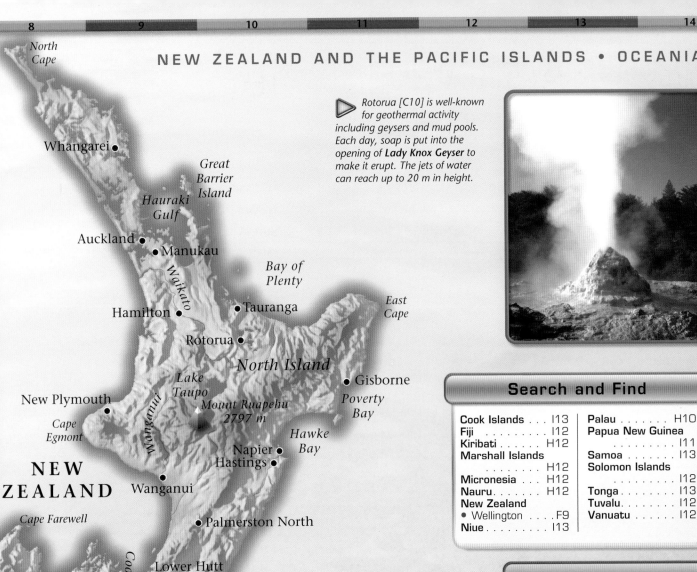

North Cape

Whangarei

Great Barrier Island

Hauraki Gulf

Auckland
Manukau

Bay of Plenty

Waikato

Hamilton
Tauranga

East Cape

Rotorua

North Island

Lake Taupo

Gisborne

Mount Ruapehu 2797 m

Poverty Bay

New Plymouth

Cape Egmont

Wanganui

Hawke Bay

Napier
Hastings

NEW ZEALAND

Wanganui

Cape Farewell

Palmerston North

Cook Strait

Lower Hutt
Wellington

Nelson

Blenheim

Cape Palliser

Island

Christchurch

Canterbury Bight

SOUTH PACIFIC OCEAN

Rotorua [C10] is well-known for geothermal activity including geysers and mud pools. Each day, soap is put into the opening of **Lady Knox Geyser** to make it erupt. The jets of water can reach up to 20 m in height.

Search and Find

Cook Islands . . . I13		Palau H10	
Fiji I12		Papua New Guinea	
Kiribati H12		. . . . I11	
Marshall Islands		Samoa I13	
. . . . H12		Solomon Islands	
Micronesia . . . H12		. . . . I12	
Nauru H12		Tonga I13	
New Zealand		Tuvalu I12	
● Wellington F9		Vanuatu I12	
Niue I13			

Extreme Weather

The mountains of South Island have hurricane winds of more than 250 km/h.

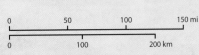

0   50   100   150 mi

0   100   200 km

PACIFIC OCEAN

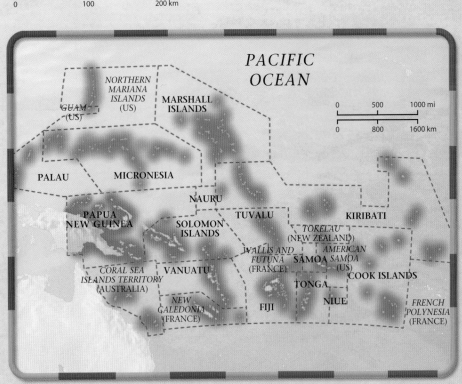

NORTHERN MARIANA ISLANDS (US)

GUAM (US)

MARSHALL ISLANDS

0   500   1000 mi

0   800   1600 km

PALAU

MICRONESIA

NAURU

PAPUA NEW GUINEA

TUVALU

KIRIBATI

SOLOMON ISLANDS

TOKELAU (NEW ZEALAND)

WALLIS AND FUTUNA (FRANCE)

SAMOA

AMERICAN SAMOA (US)

CORAL SEA ISLANDS TERRITORY (AUSTRALIA)

VANUATU

COOK ISLANDS

TONGA

NEW CALEDONIA (FRANCE)

FIJI

NIUE

FRENCH POLYNESIA (FRANCE)

Did You Know?

The sea level is rising due to global warming. Two South Pacific islands in Kiribati, Tebua Tarawa and Abanuea, have already disappeared.

Countries of the world

Gazetteer

The gazetteer helps you to find towns and features on the maps. For example, **New York City** *Town* New York, USA 21 F12 shows that New York City is a town in the state of New York, USA. The town is on page 21 and can be found in square F12 by using the grid, or graticule. The letters run on the left and right, and the numbers run along the top and bottom. Trace where F and 21 meet to find New York City.

KEY: DRC – Democratic Republic of the Congo, UAE – United Arab Emirates, CAR – Central African Republic, RS – Research station

Aachen *Town* Germany 50 F6
Aalst *Town* Belgium 50 E5
Abadan *Town* Iran 75 D8
Abakan *Town* Russia 86 H5
Abéché *Town* Chad 65 G13
Aberdeen *Town* Scotland, UK 41 D9
Aberdeen *Town* S Dakota, USA 25 F13
Aberystwyth *Town* Wales, UK 41 H8
Abha *Town* Saudi Arabia 74 H6
Abidjan *Capital* Côte d'Ivoire 64 I6
Abilene *Town* Texas, USA 27 G12
Abkhazia *State* Georgia 58 I7
Abu Dhabi *Capital* UAE 75 F10
Abuja *Capital* Nigeria 65 H10
Abu Kamal *Town* Syria 73 G12
Acapulco *Town* Mexico 31 I9
Accra *Capital* Ghana 64 I7
Aconcagua, Cerro *Mountain* Argentina 36 G7
Adana *Town* Turkey 73 E9
Ad-Dammam *Town* Saudi Arabia 75 E8
Addis Ababa *Capital* Ethiopia 67 E9
Adelaide *Town* Australia 91 H9
Aden, Gulf of 67 C12, 74 J7
Aden *Town* Yemen 74 J7
Adirondack Mountains USA 21 E11
Adiyaman *Town* Turkey 73 E11
Adrar *Town* Algeria 62 F4
Adriatic Sea 49 E8
Afghanistan *Country* 76
Agadir *Town* Morocco 62 E2
Agen *Town* France 46 G7
Agra *Town* India 77 D9
Agrigento *Town* Sicily, Italy 48 H6
Aguascalientes *Town* Mexico 31 G8
Ahaggar *Mountain range* Algeria 62 G6
Ahmadabad *Town* India 76 E7
Ahvaz *Town* Iran 75 D8
Aïr Mountains Niger 65 F10
Aix-en-Provence *Town* France 47 H10
Aizu *Town* Japan 83 F10
Ajaccio *Town* France 47 J12
Akita *Town* Japan 83 D10
Akron *Town* Ohio, USA 21 G8
Aktau *Town* Kazakhstan 86 I2
Alabama *River* Alabama, USA 23 F8
Alabama *State* USA 23
Åland Island Finland 43 G9
Alaska, Gulf of 25 C11, 28 F4

Alaska *State* USA 25
Albacete *Town* Spain 45 F10
Alba Iulia *Town* Romania 55 E9
Albania *Country* 49
Albany *River* Ontario, Canada 29 H10
Albany *State capital* New York, USA 21 E12
Albany *Town* Australia 90 H5
Albany *Town* Georgia, USA 23 F9
Albert, Lake DRC/Uganda 66 F7
Alberta *Province* Canada 28
Albuquerque *Town* New Mexico, USA 27 F9
Alcoy *Town* Spain 45 G11
Aleppo *Town* Syria 73 F10
Alessandria *Town* Italy 48 C5
Aleutian Islands Alaska, USA 25 C9
Alexandria *Town* Egypt 63 E12
Alexandria *Town* Louisiana, USA 22 G5
Alexandroúpolis *Town* Greece 49 F13
Algeciras *Town* Spain 44 I7
Algeria *Country* 62
Algiers *Capital* Algeria 62 C6
Al Hasakah *Town* Syria 73 F12
Al-Hudaydah *Town* Yemen 74 I6
Al-Hufuf *Town* Saudi Arabia 75 F8
Alicante *Town* Spain 45 G11
Alice Springs *Town* Australia 91 E8
Al Jawf *Town* Saudi Arabia 74 D5
Al-Karak *Town* Jordan 73 I9
Alkmaar *Town* Netherlands 50 C6
Allahabad *Town* India 77 E9
Allegheny *River* Pennsylvania, USA 21 G9
Allentown *Town* Pennsylvania, USA 21 G11
Almaty *Town* Kazakhstan 86 I4
Almería *Town* Spain 45 H9
Al Mukalla *Town* Yemen 75 I8
Alps *Mountain range* France/Italy/Switzerland 47 G10
Al Qamishli *Town* Syria 73 E12
Al Qunaytirah *Town* Syria 73 H9
Altai Mountains Mongolia/Russia 84 D7
Altamaha *River* Georgia, USA 23 F10
Altamira *Town* Brazil 37 B9
Altun Shan *Mountain range* China 84 F6
Amarillo *Town* Texas, USA 27 F11

Amazon *River* Brazil 36 B7, 37 B9
Amazon Basin Brazil 36 B7
Ambato *Town* Ecuador 36 B5
Ambon *Town* Indonesia 81 G8
American Samoa *Dep. territory* USA 93 I13
Amiens *Town* France 47 B9
Amman *Capital* Jordan 73 H10
Amritsar *Town* India 77 C8
Amsterdam *Capital* Netherlands 50 D6
Amu Dar'ya *River* Uzbekistan 86 J3
Amundsen Gulf 17 D9
Amundsen-Scott (US) *RS* Antarctica 16 F4
Amundsen Sea 16 F1
Amur *River* China/Russia 87 H8
Anaheim *Town* California, USA 26 F5
Anápolis *Town* Brazil 37 D9
Anatolian Plateau Turkey 72 D7
Anchorage *Town* Alaska, USA 25 C11
Ancona *Town* Italy 48 D7
Andaman Islands India 77 H12
Andaman Sea 78 H2
Anderson *Town* Indiana, USA 20 H7
Andes *Mountain range* 36 F7
Andorra *Country* 45
Andorra la Vella *Capital* Andorra 45 C12
Andreanof Islands Alaska, USA 25 C9
Angarsk *Town* Russia 86 H6
Angeles *Town* Philippines 79 F10
Angers *Town* France 46 C7
Angola *Country* 68
Angoulême *Town* France 46 E7
Anguilla *Dep. territory* UK 35 D12
Ankara *Capital* Turkey 73 C8
Annaba *Town* Algeria 62 D7
Annapolis *State capital* Maryland, USA 21 H11
Ann Arbor *Town* Michigan, USA 20 F7
An Nasiriyah *Town* Iraq 74 D7
Anshan *Town* China 85 D12
Antakya *Town* Turkey 73 F10
Antalya *Town* Turkey 72 E7
Antananarivo *Capital* Madagascar 69 G12
Antarctica 16
Antarctic Peninsula Antarctica 16 E2

Antibes *Town* France 47 H11
Anticosti Island Quebec, Canada 29 H13
Antigua and Barbuda *Country* 35
Antofagasta *Town* Chile 36 E6
Antsiranana *Town* Madagascar 69 F13
Antwerp *Town* Belgium 50 E5
Aomori *Town* Japan 83 D10
Aoraki/Mount Cook New Zealand 92 G7
Aosta *Town* Italy 48 B4
Apeldoorn *Town* Netherlands 50 D7
Appalachian Mountains USA 21 H10, 23 C10
Appleton *Town* Wisconsin, USA 20 F5
Aqaba *Town* Jordan 73 J9
Aqtobe *Town* Russia 86 H2
Arabian Sea 75 F12, 76 E6
Aracaju *Town* Brazil 37 C11
Arad *Town* Romania 54 D7
Arafura Sea 81 H9
Araguaína *Town* Brazil 37 C10
Arakan Range *Mountain range* Burma (Myanmar) 78 F2
Aral Sea Kazakhstan/Uzbekistan 86 I3
Ararat, Mount Turkey 73 D14
Arbil *Town* Iraq 74 B7
Arctic Ocean 17, 28, 43, 59, 86
Arequipa *Town* Peru 36 D6
Arezzo *Town* Italy 48 D6
Argentina *Country* 36
Århus *Town* Denmark 42 I6
Arica *Town* Chile 36 D6
Arizona *State* USA 26
Arkansas *State* USA 22
Arkhangelsk *Town* Russia 59 D8
Arles *Town* France 47 H9
Arlington *Town* Texas, USA 27 G13
Armenia *Country* 59
Armenia *Town* Colombia 35 H8
Arnhem *Town* Netherlands 50 D6
Arnhem Land Australia 91 B8
Ar Raqqah *Town* Syria 73 F11
Arua *Town* Uganda 66 F7
Aruba *Dep. territory* Netherlands 35 E9
Aru Islands Indonesia 81 G9
Arusha *Town* Tanzania 67 H9
Asahikawa *Town* Japan 83 B10

Ashgabat *Capital* Turkmenistan 86 J3

Asmara *Capital* Eritrea 67 C9

Assad, Lake Syria 73 F11

Assen *Town* Netherlands 50 C7

As-Sulayyil *Town* Saudi Arabia 74 G7

Astana *Capital* Kazakhstan 86 H3

Astrakhan *Town* Russia 59 H8

Asunción *Capital* Paraguay 37 E8

Aswan *Town* Egypt 63 H13

Asyut *Town* Egypt 63 G13

Atacama Desert Chile 36 E7

Atbara *Town* Sudan 67 B8

Athens *Capital* Greece 49 H12

Atlanta *State capital* Georgia, USA 23 E9

Atlantic City *Town* New Jersey, USA 21 G12

Atlantic Ocean 21, 23, 29, 37, 40, 42, 43, 44, 62, 64

Atlas Mountains Morocco 62 E3

Atyrau *Town* Kazakhstan 86 I2

Auckland *Town* New Zealand 93 C9

Augsburg *Town* Germany 51 I9

Augusta *Town* Georgia, USA 23 E10

Augusta *State capital* Maine, USA 21 D13

Aurora *Town* Illinois, USA 20 G6

Austin *State capital* Texas, USA 27 H13

Australia *Country* 90

Australian Capital Territory *State* Australia 91

Austria *Country* 40

Auxerre *Town* France 47 D9

Aveiro *Town* Portugal 44 E5

Avignon *Town* France 47 G9

Ávila *Town* Spain 45 E8

Axel Heiberg Island Nunavut, Canada 29 C9

Ayacucho *Town* Peru 36 D6

Aydin *Town* Turkey 72 D6

Azerbaijan *Country* 75

Azov, Sea of 58 I7

Az-Zarqa *Town* Jordan 73 H10

Az-Zawiyah *Town* Libya 73 H10

Bacău *Town* Romania 55 D12

Bacolod *Town* Philippines 79 G11

Badajoz *Town* Spain 44 F6

Baden-Baden *Town* Germany 50 H7

Baffin Bay Canada 17 G9, 29 D10

Baffin Island Canada 17 G8, 29 E10

Baghdad *Capital* Iraq 74 C7

Bahamas *Country* 35

Bahawalpur *Town* Pakistan 77 C8

Bahía Blanca *Town* Argentina 37 G8

Bahrain *Country* 75

Baikal, Lake Russia 86 H7

Bakersfield *Town* California, USA 26 E5

Bakhtaran *Town* Iran 74 C7

Baku *Capital* Azerbaijan 75 A8

Balaton, Lake Hungary 54 D5

Balearic Islands Spain 45

Bali *Island* Indonesia 80 H5

Balikesir *Town* Turkey 72 C6

Balikpapan *Town* Indonesia 80 F5

Balkanabat *Town* Turkmenistan 86 J2

Balkan Mountains Bulgaria 55 H10

Balkhash, Lake Kazakhstan 86 I4

Ballarat *Town* Australia 91 I10

Baltic Sea 43 H9, 56 B6, 58 F5

Baltimore *Town* Maryland, USA 21 H11

Bamako *Capital* Mali 64 G5

Bambari *Town* CAR 68 B7

Bamberg *Town* Germany 51 G9

Bamenda *Town* Cameroon 68 B5

Bandar 'Abbas *Town* Iran 75 E10

Bandar Seri Begawan *Capital* Brunei 80 E5

Banda Sea 81 G8

Bandundu *Town* DRC 68 D7

Bandung *Town* Indonesia 80 H3

Bangalore *See* Bengaluru

Bangkok *Capital* Thailand 78 H4

Bangladesh *Country* 77

Bangor *Town* Maine, USA 21 C13

Bangui *Capital* CAR 68 B7

Baniyas *Town* Syria 73 F10

Banja Luka *Town* Bosnia and Herz. 49 C8

Banjarmasin *Town* Indonesia 80 G5

Banjul *Capital* Gambia 64 G3

Banská Bystrica *Town* Slovakia 57 I8

Baotou *Town* China 85 E10

Bar *Town* Montenegro 49 E9

Barbados *Country* 35

Barcelona *Town* Spain 45 D13

Barcelona *Town* Venezuela 35 F11

Barents Sea 17 G13, 58 B7

Bari *Town* Italy 49 F8

Barinas *Town* Venezuela 35 F9

Barnaul *Town* Russia 86 H5

Barquisimeto *Town* Venezuela 35 F9

Barrancabermeja *Town* Colombia 35 G8

Barranquilla *Town* Colombia 35 F8

Basel *Town* Switzerland 52 E3

Basra *Town* Iraq 75 D8

Bassein *Town* Burma (Myanmar) 78 G2

Basseterre *Capital* St. Kitts and Nevis 35 D12

Bass Strait Australia 91 I11

Batangas *Town* Philippines 79 F10

Batdâmbang *Town* Cambodia 78 G5

Batman *Town* Turkey 73 E12

Batna *Town* Algeria 62 D6

Baton Rouge *State capital* Louisiana, USA 22 G6

Bayamo *Town* Cuba 35 C8

Bayreuth *Town* Germany 51 G10

Beaufort Sea 17 C9, 28 D6

Beaumont *Town* Texas, USA 27 H14

Béchar *Town* Algeria 62 E4

Beersheba *Town* Israel 73 I9

Beijing *Capital* China 85 E11

Beira *Town* Mozambique 69 G10

Beirut *Capital* Lebanon 73 G9

Beja *Town* Portugal 44 G5

Belarus *Country* 58

Belém *Town* Brazil 37 B10

Belfast *Capital* Northern Ireland, UK 40 F7

Belgium *Country* 50

Belgrade *Capital* Serbia 49 C10

Belgrano II (Argentina) *RS* Antarctica 16 E3

Belize *Country* 34

Belize City *Town* Belize 34 C5

Bellingham *Town* Washington, USA 24 C4

Belmopan *Capital* Belize 34 C5

Belo Horizonte *Town* Brazil 37 E10

Bendigo *Town* Australia 91 H11

Benevento *Town* Italy 48 F7

Bengal, Bay of 77 F11

Bengaluru (Bangalore) *Town* India 77 H8

Benghazi *Town* Libya 63 E10

Benguela *Town* Angola 68 F6

Benidorm *Town* Spain 45 G11

Benin *Country* 65

Benin City *Town* Nigeria 65 I9

Ben Nevis *Mountain* Scotland, UK 41 D8

Benue *River* Nigeria 65 I10

Berbera *Town* Somalia 67 D11

Bergamo *Town* Italy 48 B5

Bergen *Town* Norway 42 F5

Bergerac *Town* France 46 F7

Bering Sea 25 B9, 87 G13

Berlin *Capital* Germany 51 D11

Bern *Capital* Switzerland 52 F3

Besançon *Town* France 47 E10

Bethlehem *Town* Israel 73 I9

Béziers *Town* France 47 H8

Bhavnagar *Town* India 76 E7

Bhopal *Town* India 77 E8

Bhutan *Country* 77

Bialystok *Town* Poland 57 D11

Biel *Town* Switzerland 52 F3

Bielefeld *Town* Germany 51 D8

Bielsko-Biala *Town* Poland 57 H8

Bighorn Mountains Wyoming, USA 25 G9

Bihac *Town* Bosnia and Herz. 49 C8

Bilauktaung Range Thailand 78 G3

Bilbao *Town* Spain 45 B9

Billings *Town* Montana, USA 25 F9

Biloxi *Town* Mississippi, USA 22 G7

Biratnagar *Town* Nepal 77 D11

Birmingham *Town* Alabama, USA 23 E8

Birmingham *Town* England, UK 41 H9

Biscay, Bay of 45 A9, 46 E5

Bishkek *Capital* Kyrgyzstan 86 I4

Bismarck *State capital* N Dakota, USA 25 F12

Bissau *Capital* Guinea-Bissau 64 G3

Bitola *Town* Macedonia 49 F11

Bizerte *Town* Tunisia 62 C7

Black Forest Germany 50 I7

Blackpool *Town* England, UK 41 F8

Black Sea 55 H14, 58 I6, 73 B11

Blagoevgrad *Town* Bulgaria 55 I9

Blagoveshchensk *Town* Russia 87 H8

Blantyre *Town* Malawi 69 G10

Blida *Town* Algeria 62 D6

Bloemfontein *Town* South Africa 69 I8

Bloomington *Town* Indiana, USA 20 I6

Bloomington *Town* Minnesota, USA 20 E3

Blue Nile *River* Ethiopia/Sudan 67 D8

Bo *Town* Sierra Leone 64 I4

Boa Vista *Town* Brazil 37 A8

Bobo Dioulasso *Town* Burkina Faso 64 H6

Bodrum *Town* Turkey 72 E5

Bogotá *Capital* Colombia 35 H8

Bohemian Forest Czech Republic/ Germany 51 H11, 56 H4

Boise *State capital* Idaho, USA 24 G5

Bolivia *Country* 36

Bologna *Town* Italy 48 C6

Bolzano *Town* Italy 48 B6

Bombay *See* Mumbai

Bonaire *Dep. territory* Netherlands 35 F10

Bonifacio, Strait of 47 J12

Bonn *Town* Germany 50 F7

Borås *Town* Sweden 42 H7

Bordeaux *Town* France 46 F6

Borgholm *Town* Sweden 43 I8

Borneo *Island* Indonesia 80 G4

Bornholm *Dep. territory* Denmark 42 J7

Bosnia and Herzegovina *Country* 49

Boston *State capital* Massachusetts, USA 21 E13
Botswana *Country* 69
Bouar *Town* CAR 68 B6
Boulder *Town* Colorado, USA 27 C10
Boulogne *Town* France 47 A9
Bourges *Town* France 47 D9
Bourke *Town* Australia 91 F11
Bournemouth *Town* England, UK 41 I9
Bozeman *Town* Montana, USA 25 F8
Brahmaputra *River* Asia 77 E12
Braila *Town* Romania 55 E12
Brandenburg *Town* Germany 51 D11
Brasília *Capital* Brazil 37 D10
Brasov *Town* Romania 55 E10
Bratislava *Capital* Slovakia 56 J7
Bratsk *Town* Russia 86 G6
Braunschweig *Town* Germany 51 D10
Brazil *Country* 37
Brazzaville *Capital* Republic of the Congo 68 D6
Breda *Town* Netherlands 50 D5
Bremen *Town* Germany 51 C9
Bremerhaven *Town* Germany 51 C8
Brescia *Town* Italy 48 B5
Brest *Town* France 46 B5
Bridgeport *Town* Connecticut, USA 21 F12
Bridgetown *Capital* Barbados 35 E12
Brig *Town* Switzerland 52 G3
Brighton *Town* England, UK 41 I10
Brindisi *Town* Italy 49 F9
Brisbane *Town* Australia 91 F13
Bristol *Town* England, UK 41 H9
British Columbia *Province* Canada 28
Brive *Town* France 47 F8
Brno *Town* Czech Republic 56 H6
Broome *Town* Australia 90 C5
Brownsville *Town* Texas, USA 27 J13
Bruges *Town* Belgium 50 E4
Brunei *Country* 80
Brussels *Capital* Belgium 50 E5
Bryansk *Town* Russia 58 G6
Bucaramanga *Town* Colombia 35 G8
Bucharest *Capital* Romania 55 F11
Budapest *Capital* Hungary 54 C6
Buenaventura *Town* Colombia 34 H7
Buenos Aires *Capital* Argentina 37 G8
Buffalo *Town* New York, USA 21 F9
Bug *River* Poland 57 D10
Bujumbura *Capital* Burundi 66 H7

Bukavu *Town* DRC 69 D9
Bulawayo *Town* Zimbabwe 69 G9
Bulgaria *Country* 55
Buraydah *Town* Saudi Arabia 74 E7
Burgas *Town* Bulgaria 55 H12
Burgos *Town* Spain 45 C8
Burketown *Town* Australia 91 C10
Burkina Faso *Country* 64
Burlington *Town* Vermont, USA 21 D12
Burma (Myanmar) *Country* 78
Burns *Town* Oregon, USA 24 G4
Burnsville *Town* Minnesota, USA 20 E3
Bursa *Town* Turkey 72 C6
Burundi *Country* 66
Butuan *Town* Philippines 79 G12
Bydgoszcz *Town* Poland 57 D8
Bytom *Town* Poland 57 G8

Cabanatuan *Town* Philippines 79 E10
Cáceres *Town* Spain 44 F6
Cádiz *Town* Spain 44 I7
Caen *Town* France 47 B8
Cagayan de Oro *Town* Philippines 79 G11
Cagliari *Town* Sardinia, Italy 48 G4
Cairns *Town* Australia 91 C11
Cairo *Capital* Egypt 63 F13
Calais *Town* France 47 A9
Calama *Town* Chile 36 E7
Calarasi *Town* Romania 55 F12
Calbayog *Town* Philippines 79 F11
Calcutta *See Kolkata*
Calgary *Town* Alberta, Canada 28 H7
Cali *Town* Colombia 34 H7
Calicut *See Kozhikode*
California, Gulf of 30 D5
California *State* USA 26
Callao *Town* Peru 36 D5
Caltanissetta *Town* Sicily, Italy 48 H7
Camagüey *Town* Cuba 35 C8
Cambodia *Country* 78
Cambrian Mountains Wales, UK 41 H8
Cambridge *Town* England, UK 41 H10
Cameroon *Country* 68
Campeche, Bay of Mexico 31 H11
Campina Grande *Town* Brazil 37 C12
Campinas *Town* Brazil 37 E10
Campobasso *Town* Italy 48 E7
Campo Grande *Town* Brazil 37 E9
Canada *Country* 28
Canary Islands Spain 64 B4
Canberra *Capital* Australia 91 H12
Cancún *Town* Mexico 31 G14
Cannes *Town* France 47 H11

Cantabrian Mountains Spain 44 B7
Can Tho *Town* Vietnam 78 H5
Canton *Town* Ohio, USA 21 G9
Cape Horn *Chile* 37 J8
Cape Town *Capital* South Africa 68 J7
Cape Verde (Cabo Verde) *Country* 64
Cap-Haïtien *Town* Haiti 35 C9
Caracas *Capital* Venezuela 35 F10
Cárdenas *Town* Cuba 34 B7
Cardiff *Capital* Wales, UK 41 H8
Caribbean Sea 35 E9
Carlisle *Town* England, UK 41 F9
Carlsbad *Town* New Mexico, USA 27 G10
Carnarvon *Town* Australia 90 E3
Carpathian Mountains Poland/ Romania/Slovakia 55 D11
Carrara *Town* Italy 48 C5
Carson City *State capital* Nevada, USA 26 C5
Cartagena *Town* Colombia 35 F8
Cartagena *Town* Spain 45 H11
Casablanca *Town* Morocco 62 D3
Casey (Australia) *RS* Antarctica 16 G7
Casper *Town* Wyoming, USA 25 H9
Caspian Sea 59 I9, 75 B8, 86 I2
Cassai (Kasai) *River* Angola/DRC 68 E7
Castellón de la Plana *Town* Spain 45 E11
Castries *Capital* St. Lucia 35 E12
Catania *Town* Sicily, Italy 48 H7
Catanzaro *Town* Italy 49 G8
Cayman Islands *Dep. territory* UK 34 C7
Cebu *Town* Philippines 79 G11
Cedar City *Town* Utah, USA 26 D7
Cedar Rapids *Town* Iowa, USA 20 G4
Celebes Sea 79 H11, 80 E6
Celje *Town* Slovenia 49 B8
Central African Republic (CAR) *Country* 68
Ceské Budejovice *Town* Czech Republic 56 H5
Ceuta *Town* Spain 44 J7, 62 D3
Chad, Lake Chad 65 G12
Chad *Country* 65
Châlons-en-Champagne *Town* France 47 C10
Chalon-sur-Saône *Town* France 47 E10
Chambéry *Town* France 47 F10
Champaign *Town* Illinois, USA 20 H6
Chandigarh *Town* India 77 C8

Chang Cheng (China) *RS* Antarctica 16 D1
Changchun *Town* China 85 C12
Chang Jiang (Yangtze) *River* China 85 G10
Changsha *Town* China 85 G11
Channel Islands *Dep. territory* UK 41 J9
Charleroi *Town* Belgium 50 F5
Charleston *State capital* West Virginia, USA 21 I9
Charleston *Town* S Carolina, USA 23 E11
Charleville Mézières *Town* France 47 B10
Charlotte *Town* N Carolina, USA 23 C10
Charlottetown *Province capital* Prince Edward Islands, Canada 29 I13
Châteauroux *Town* France 47 D8
Chattanooga *Town* Tennessee, USA 23 D8
Cheb *Town* Czech Republic 56 G3
Chelm *Town* Poland 57 F11
Chelyabinsk *Town* Russia 86 G3
Chemnitz *Town* Germany 51 F11
Chengdu *Town* China 85 G9
Chennai (Madras) *Town* India 77 H9
Chester *Town* England, UK 41 G9
Chetumal *Town* Mexico 31 H13
Cheyenne *State capital* Wyoming, USA 25 I10
Chiang Mai *Town* Thailand 78 F3
Chiba *Town* Japan 83 G10
Chicago *Town* Illinois, USA 20 G6
Chichén Itzá Mexico 31 G13
Chiclayo *Town* Peru 36 C5
Chicoutimi *Town* Quebec, Canada 29 I12
Chihuahua *Town* Mexico 30 D7
Chile *Country* 36
Chillan *Town* Chile 36 G6
Chilpancingo *Town* Mexico 31 I9
Chimbote *Town* Peru 36 C5
Chimoio *Town* Mozambique 69 G10
China *Country* 85
Chinandega *Town* Nicaragua 34 E5
Chioggia *Town* Italy 48 C6
Chipata *Town* Zambia 69 F9
Chirripó Grande, Cerro *Mountain* Costa Rica 34 F5
Chisinau *Capital* Moldova 58 H6
Chita *Town* Russia 86 H7
Chitose *Town* Japan 83 B10
Chittagong *Town* Bangladesh 77 F12
Chitungwiza *Town* Zimbabwe 69 G9
Chon Buri *Town* Thailand 78 H4
Chongjin *Town* North Korea 85 C13

Chongqing *Town* China 85 H10

Choybalsan *Town* Mongolia 85 C10

Christchurch *Town* New Zealand 93 G8

Chukchi Sea 17 C11, 25 A10, 87 E13

Churchill *Town* Manitoba, Canada 29 G9

Cienfuegos *Town* Cuba 34 B7

Cincinnati *Town* Ohio, USA 21 H7

Ciudad Bolívar *Town* Venezuela 35 G11

Ciudad de la Paz *Capital* Equatorial Guinea 68 C5

Ciudad del Este *Town* Paraguay 37 F9

Ciudad Guayana *Town* Venezuela 35 G11

Ciudad Juárez *Town* Mexico 30 C7

Ciudad Madero *Town* Mexico 31 F10

Ciudad Obregón *Town* Mexico 30 D6

Ciudad Real *Town* Spain 45 F8

Ciudid Victoria *Town* Mexico 31 F9

Civitavecchia *Town* Italy 48 E6

Clarksville *Town* Tennessee, USA 22 C7

Clearwater *Town* Florida, USA 23 H10

Clermont-Ferrand *Town* France 47 E9

Cleveland *Town* Ohio, USA 21 G8

Clovis *Town* New Mexico, USA 27 F11

Cluj-Napoca *Town* Romania 55 D9

Coast Ranges California/Oregon, USA 24 F2, 26 B4

Coatzacoalcos *Town* Mexico 31 H11

Cochin *See Kochi*

Cognac *Town* France 46 E7

Coimbatore *Town* India 77 I8

Coimbra *Town* Portugal 44 E5

Colchester *Town* England, UK 41 H10

Colima *Town* Mexico 31 H8

Cologne *Town* Germany 50 E7

Colombia *Country* 35

Colombo *Capital* Sri Lanka 77 J9

Colón *Town* Panama 34 F7

Colorado *River* Mexico/USA 27 D8

Colorado *State* USA 27

Colorado Springs *Town* Colorado, USA 27 D10

Columbia *State capital* S Carolina, USA 23 D10

Columbia *Town* Missouri, USA 22 B5

Columbus *State capital* Ohio, USA 21 H8

Columbus *Town* Georgia, USA 23 F9

Como *Town* Italy 48 B5

Comodoro Rivadavia *Town* Argentina 36 H7

Comoros *Country* 69

Conakry *Capital* Guinea 64 H4

Concepción *Town* Chile 36 G6

Concord *State capital* New Hampshire, USA 21 E13

Congo *River* Western Central Africa 68 C7, 69 D8

Congo, Democratic Republic of the (DRC) *Country* 68

Congo, Republic of the *Country* 68

Connecticut *State* USA 21

Constanta *Town* Romania 55 F13

Constantine *Town* Algeria 62 D6

Coober Pedy *Town* Australia 91 F8

Cook Islands *Dep. territory* New Zealand 93 I13

Cook Strait New Zealand 93 F9

Cooktown *Town* Australia 91 B11

Copenhagen *Capital* Denmark 42 I7

Coquimbo *Town* Chile 36 F6

Coral Sea Islands Territory *Dep. territory* Australia 93 I11

Cordillera Central *Mountain range* Colombia/Panama 34 F6, 35 H8

Córdoba *Town* Argentina 36 F7

Córdoba *Town* Spain 45 G8

Corfu *Island* Greece 49 G10

Cork *Town* Republic of Ireland 40 H6

Corpus Christi *Town* Texas, USA 27 I13

Corrientes *Town* Argentina 37 F8

Corsica *Island* France 47 I12

Çorum *Town* Turkey 73 C9

Corvallis *Town* Oregon, USA 24 F3

Cosenza *Town* Italy 49 G8

Costa Rica *Country* 34

Côte d'Ivoire *Country* 64

Cotonou *Capital* Benin 65 I8

Cottbus *Town* Germany 51 E12

Council Bluffs *Town* Iowa, USA 20 H2

Coventry *Town* England, UK 41 H9

Craiova *Town* Romania 55 G9

Cremona *Town* Italy 48 C5

Crete, Sea of Greece 49 I12

Crete *Island* Greece 49 J12

Crimea Ukraine 58 I7

Croatia *Country* 49

Crotone *Town* Italy 49 G8

Cuba *Country* 34

Cúcuta *Town* Colombia 35 G8

Cuernavaca *Town* Mexico 31 H9

Cuito *River* Angola 68 G7

Culiacán *Town* Mexico 30 E6

Cumaná *Town* Venezuela 35 F11

Curaçao *Dep. territory* Netherlands 35 E10

Curitiba *Town* Brazil 37 F9

Cusco *Town* Peru 36 D6

Cuttack *Town* India 77 F10

Cuxhaven *Town* Germany 51 B9

Cyprus *Country* 73

Czech Republic Country 56

Czestochowa *Town* Poland 57 F8

Dakar *Capital* Senegal 64 F3

Dalandzadgad *Town* Mongolia 85 D8

Da Lat *Town* Vietnam 78 H6

Dalian *Town* China 85 E12

Dallas *Town* Texas, USA 27 G13

Damascus *Capital* Syria 73 H10

Dampier *Town* Australia 90 D4

Da Nang *Town* Vietnam 78 F6

Danube *River* Europe 51 I8, 40 E12, 54 D5, 55 G10, 57 J8

Danzig, Gulf of 57 B8

Dar'a *Town* Syria 73 H10

Dar es Salaam *Capital* Tanzania 67 I9

Darfur Sudan 66 D6

Darhan *Town* Mongolia 85 C9

Darien, Gulf of 34 F7

Darling *River* Australia 91 G10

Darmstadt *Town* Germany 51 G8

Darnah *Town* Libya 63 E10

Darwin *Town* Australia 90 B7

Davao *Town* Philippines 79 H12

Davenport *Town* Iowa, USA 20 G5

David *Town* Panama 34 F6

Dayr az Zawr *Town* Syria 73 F12

Dayton *Town* Ohio, USA 21 H8

Daytona Beach *Town* Florida, USA 23 G11

Dead Sea Jordan 73 I9

Death Valley California, USA 26 E6

Debrecen *Town* Hungary 55 C8

Decatur *Town* Illinois, USA 20 H6

Delaware *State* USA 21

Delft *Town* Netherlands 50 D5

Delhi *Town* India 77 D9

Del Rio *Town* Texas, USA 27 I11

Democratic Republic of the Congo (DRC) *See* Congo, Republic of the

Denali Alaska, USA 25 B11

Den Helder *Town* Netherlands 50 C6

Denizli *Town* Turkey 72 D6

Denmark *Country* 42

Denver *State capital* Colorado, USA 27 C10

Derby *Town* England, UK 41 G9

Des Moines *State capital* Iowa, USA 20 G3

Dessau *Town* Germany 51 E11

Detroit *Town* Michigan, USA 20 F8

Devon Island Nunavut, Canada 29 D9

Dhaka *Capital* Bangladesh 77 E11

Dhanbad *Town* India 77 E10

Dieppe *Town* France 47 B8

Dijon *Town* France 47 D10

Dili *Capital* East Timor (Timor-Leste) 80 H7

Dimitrovgrad *Town* Bulgaria 55 I11

Dire Dawa *Town* Ethiopia 67 D10

Diyarbakir *Town* Turkey 73 E12

Djibouti *Capital* Djibouti 67 D11

Djibouti *Country* 67

Dnieper *River* Ukraine 58 H6

Dniester *River* Ukraine 58 H6

Dnipropetrovsik *Town* Ukraine 58 H7

Dobrich *Town* Bulgaria 55 G13

Dodge City *Town* Kansas, USA 27 E12

Dodoma *Capital* Tanzania 67 I9

Doha *Capital* Qatar 75 F9

Dominica *Country* 35

Dominican Republic *Country* 35

Don *River* Russia 59 H8

Donetsk *Town* Ukraine 58 H7

Dordogne *River* France 46 F7

Dordrecht *Town* Netherlands 50 D5

Dortmund *Town* Germany 50 E7

Douala *Town* Cameroon 68 B5

Douglas *Town* Arizona, USA 27 G8

Dover *State capital* Delaware, USA 21 G12

Dover *Town* England, UK 41 I11

Drakensberg Mountains South Africa 69 J8

Drama *Town* Greece 49 F12

Drammen *Town* Norway 42 G6

Dresden *Town* Germany 51 F12

Drobeta-Turnu Severin *Town* Romania 55 F8

Drogheda *Town* Republic of Ireland 40 F7

Dubai *Town* UAE 75 F10

Dublin *Capital* Republic of Ireland 40 G7

Dubrovnik *Town* Croatia 49 E9

Duisburg *Town* Germany 50 E7

Duluth *Town* Minnesota, USA 20 D3

Dumont d'Urville (France) *RS* Antarctica 16 H5

Dunaujvaros *Town* Hungary 54 D6

Dundee *Town* Scotland, UK 41 D9

Dunedin *Town* New Zealand 92 I7

Dunkerque *Town* France 47 A9

Durango *Town* Colorado, USA 27 E9

Durango *Town* Mexico 30 F7

Durban *Town* South Africa 69 I9

Durham *Town* N Carolina, USA 23 C11

Durrës *Town* Albania 49 F9

Dushanbe *Capital* Tajikistan 86 J3
Düsseldorf *Town* Germany 50 E7

East Cape New Zealand 93 C11
East China Sea Pacific Ocean 85 G13
Eastern Ghats *Mountain range* India 77 G9
East London *Town* South Africa 69 J8
East Siberian Sea Arctic Ocean 17 C13, 87 E11
East Timor (Timor-Leste) *Country* 81
Eau Claire *Town* Wisconsin, USA 20 E4
Ebetsu *Town* Japan 83 B10
Ebro *River* Spain 45 C10
Ecuador *Country* 36
Edinburgh *Capital* Scotland, UK 41 E8
Edirne *Town* Turkey 72 B5
Edmonton *Province capital* Alberta, Canada 28 H7
Edward, Lake DRC/Uganda 66 G7, 69 C9
Edwards Plateau Texas, USA 27 H12
Egypt *Country* 63
Eindhoven *Town* Netherlands 50 E6
El Aaiún *Capital* Western Sahara 64 C5
Elat *Town* Israel 73 J9
Elazig *Town* Turkey 73 D11
Elbasan *Town* Albania 49 F10
Elbe *River* Czech Republic/Germany 51 E11, 56 G6
Elblag *Town* Poland 57 B8
Elbrus, Mount Russia 59 I8
Elche *Town* Spain 45 G11
El Fasher *Town* Sudan 66 C6
Elgin *Town* Illinois, USA 20 G6
Ellesmere Island Canada 17 F10, 29 C9
Ellsworth Land Antarctica 16 F2
El Minya *Town* Egypt 63 F13
El Obeid *Town* Sudan 66 D7
El Paso *Town* Texas, USA 27 G9
El Progreso *Town* Honduras 34 D5
El Salvador *Country* 34
Emmen *Town* Netherlands 50 C7
Empty Quarter *Desert* Saudi Arabia 75 H9
Ende *Town* Indonesia 80 H6
England *Country* UK 41
English Channel France/UK 41 I9, 46 A6
Enid *Town* Oklahoma, USA 27 E13
Enschede *Town* Netherlands 50 D7
Ensenada *Town* Mexico 30 B4
Enugu *Town* Nigeria 65 I10

Equatorial Guinea *Country* 68
Erdenet *Town* Mongolia 85 C9
Erfurt *Town* Germany 51 F10
Erie, Lake USA 21 F9
Erie *Town* Pennsylvania, USA 21 F9
Eritrea *Country* 67
Erzincan *Town* Turkey 73 D11
Erzurum *Town* Turkey 73 C13
Esbjerg *Town* Denmark 42 I5
Escuintla *Town* Guatemala 34 D4
Esfahan *Town* Iran 75 C9
Eskisehir *Town* Turkey 72 C7
Esmeraldas *Town* Ecuador 36 A5
Esperance *Town* Australia 90 H6
Esperanza (Argentina) *RS* Antarctica 16 D1
Espoo *Town* Finland 43 G10
Essen *Town* Germany 50 E7
Estonia *Country* 58
Eswatini *Country* 69
Ethiopia *Country* 67
Etna, Mount Italy 48 H7
Eugene *Town* Oregon, USA 24 F3
Euphrates *River* Iraq/Syria/Turkey 73 F12, 74 C8
Evansville *Town* Indiana, USA 20 J6
Everest, Mount China/Nepal 77 D11, 84 H6
Everett *Town* Washington, USA 24 D4
Everglades, The Florida, USA 23 J11
Évora *Town* Portugal 44 G5
Exeter *Town* England, UK 41 I8

Fairbanks *Town* Alaska, USA 25 B11
Faisalabad *Town* Pakistan 77 C8
Falkland Islands *Dep. territory* UK 37 J8
Fargo *Town* N Dakota, USA 25 F13
Fayetteville *Town* N Carolina, USA 23 C11
Feira de Santana *Town* Brazil 37 D11
Ferrara *Town* Italy 48 C6
Fes *Town* Morocco 62 D3
Feuilles *River* Quebec, Canada 29 G11
Fianarantsoa *Town* Madagascar 69 H12
Fiji *Country* 93 I12
Finland, Gulf of 58 E5
Finland *Country* 43
Firat *River* Turkey 73 E11
Fitzroy *River* Australia 90 C6
Flagstaff *Town* Arizona, USA 27 F8
Flensburg *Town* Germany 51 A9
Flint *Town* Michigan, USA 20 F7
Florence *Town* Italy 48 D6
Flores Sea 80 H6
Florianópolio *Town* Brazil 37 F9

Florida *State* USA 23
Florida Keys *Island group* Florida, USA 23 J11
Focsani *Town* Romania 55 E12
Foggia *Town* Italy 49 E8
Fontainebleau *Town* France 47 C9
Forli *Town* Italy 48 C6
Fort Albany *Town* Ontario, Canada 29 H10
Fortaleza *Town* Brazil 37 B11
Fort Collins *Town* Colorado, USA 27 C10
Fort Lauderdale *Town* Florida, USA 23 I12
Fort Myers *Town* Florida, USA 23 I11
Fort Smith *Town* Arkansas, USA 22 D4
Fort Wayne *Town* Indiana, USA 20 G7
Fort Worth *Town* Texas, USA 27 G13
Foveaux Strait New Zealand 92 J5
Fox Islands Alaska, USA 25 C9
France *Country* 46
Francistown *Town* Botswana 69 H8
Frankfurt am Main *Town* Germany 51 G8
Frankfurt an der Oder *Town* Germany 51 D12
Fraser Island Australia 91 E13
Fredericton *Province capital* New Brunswick, Canada 29 I13
Fredrikstad *Town* Norway 42 G6
Freemantle *Town* Australia 90 G4
Freetown *Capital* Sierra Leone 64 H4
Freiburg im Breisgau *Town* Germany 50 I7
French Guiana *Dep. territory* France 35 H14
French Polynesia *Dep. territory* France 93 I14
Fresno *Town* California, USA 26 D5
Fuji, Mount Japan 83 G9
Fuji *Town* Japan 83 G9
Fukui *Town* Japan 83 G8
Fukuoka *Town* Japan 82 H5
Fukushima *Town* Japan 83 F10
Fulda *Town* Germany 51 F9
Fürth *Town* Germany 51 H9
Fushun *Town* China 85 D12
Fuzhou *Town* China 85 H12

Gabon *Country* 68
Gaborone *Capital* Botswana 69 H8
Gabrovo *Town* Bulgaria 55 H11
Gainesville *Town* Florida, USA 23 G10
Gallup *Town* New Mexico, USA 27 E9
Galveston *Town* Texas, USA 27 I14

Galway *Town* Republic of Ireland 40 G6
Gambia *Country* 64
Gander *Town* Newfoundland and Labrador, Canada 29 H14
Ganges *River* India 77 D9
Gao *Town* Mali 65 F8
Gar *Town* China 84 G5
Garland *Town* Texas, USA 27 G13
Garonne *River* France 46 F7
Garoua *Town* Cameroon 68 A6
Gary *Town* Indiana, USA 20 G6
Gaspé *Town* Quebec, Canada 29 H13
Gävle *Town* Sweden 43 G8
Gaza *Town* Israel 73 I9
Gaza Strip *Disputed region* Near East 73 I9
Gaziantep *Town* Turkey 73 E10
Gbarnga *Town* Liberia 64 I5
Gdansk *Town* Poland 57 B8
Gdynia *Town* Poland 57 B8
Geelong *Town* Australia 91 I11
General Santos *Town* Philippines 79 H12
Geneva, Lake Switzerland 52 G1
Geneva *Town* Switzerland 52 G1
Genk *Town* Belgium 50 E6
Genoa *Town* Italy 48 C5
Georgetown *Capital* Guyana 35 G13
George Town *Town* Malaysia 80 E2
Georgia *Country* 59
Georgia *State* USA 23
Gera *Town* Germany 51 F10
Germany *Country* 50
Ghana *Country* 64
Ghardaïa *Town* Algeria 62 E6
Ghent *Town* Belgium 50 E5
Gibraltar *Dep. territory* UK 44 I7
Gibraltar, Strait of Morocco/Spain 44 I7, 62 C3
Gibson Desert Australia 90 E5
Giessen *Town* Germany 51 F8
Gifu *Town* Japan 83 G8
Gijón *Town* Spain 44 B7
Gillette *Town* Wyoming, USA 25 G10
Girona *Town* Spain 45 C13
Gisborne *Town* New Zealand 93 D11
Giurgiu *Town* Romania 55 G11
Gjakove *Town* Kosovo 49 E10
Glasgow *Town* Scotland, UK 41 E8
Gliwice *Town* Poland 57 G8
Gloucester *Town* England, UK 41 H9
Gobi Desert Mongolia 85 D9
Godavari *River* India 77 F9
Godoy Cruz *Town* Argentina 36 G7
Goiânia *Town* Brazil 37 D9

Golan Heights *Mountain range* Syria 73 H9

Golmud *Town* China 84 F7

Gómez Palacio *Town* Mexico 31 E8

Gonaïves *Town* Haiti 35 C9

Gonder *Town* Ethiopia 67 D9

Gore *Town* Ethiopia 67 E9

Gorgan *Town* Iran 75 B9

Görlitz *Town* Germany 51 F12

Gorzow Wielkopolski *Town* Poland 56 D6

Gosford *Town* Australia 91 G12

Göteborg *Town* Sweden 42 H6

Gotland *Island* Sweden 43 H8

Göttingen *Town* Germany 51 E9

Gouda *Town* Netherlands 50 D6

Governador Valadares *Town* Brazil 37 E10

Grafton *Town* Australia 91 F13

Grampian Mountains Scotland, UK 41 D8

Granada *Town* Spain 45 H9

Gran Chaco Argentina 36 F7

Grand Canyon Arizona, USA 26 E7

Grand Forks *Town* N Dakota, USA 25 E13

Grand Rapids *Town* Michigan, USA 20 F7

Graz *Town* Austria 40 G12

Great Australian Bight Australia 90 G7

Great Barrier Island New Zealand 93 B9

Great Barrier Reef Australia 91 C12

Great Basin Nevada, USA 26 D6

Great Dividing Range Australia 91 D12

Great Falls *Town* Montana, USA 25 E8

Great Karoo South Africa 68 J7

Great Rift Valley Kenya 67 F9

Great Sandy Desert Australia 90 D6

Great Victoria Desert Australia 90 G5

Greece *Country* 49

Greeley *Town* Colorado, USA 27 C10

Green Bay *Town* Wisconsin, USA 20 E5

Greenland Sea 17 H11, 43 G12

Greensboro *Town* N Carolina, USA 23 C11

Greenville *Town* Mississippi, USA 22 E6

Greenville *Town* S Carolina, USA 23 D10

Greifswald *Town* Germany 51 B12

Grenada *Country* 35

Grenoble *Town* France 47 F10

Greymouth *Town* New Zealand 92 G7

Groningen *Town* Netherlands 50 C7

Grootfontein *Town* Namibia 68 G7

Grosseto *Town* Italy 48 D6

Grozny *Town* Russia 59 I8

Guadalajara *Town* Mexico 31 G8

Guadalajara *Town* Spain 45 E9

Guadeloupe *Dep. territory* France 35 D12

Guam *Dep. territory* USA 93 H11

Guanabacoa *Town* Cuba 34 B7

Guanare *Town* Venezuela 35 F9

Guangzhou *Town* China 85 I11

Guantánamo *Town* Cuba 35 C8

Guatemala *Country* 34

Guatemala City *Capital* Guatemala 34 D4

Guayaquil *Town* Ecuador 36 B5

Guaymas *Town* Mexico 30 D5

Guernsey *Island* Channel Islands, UK 41 J9

Guiana Highlands *Mountain range* Guyana/Venezuela 35 G12

Guinea, Gulf of 64 J7

Guinea *Country* 64

Guinea-Bissau *Country* 64

Guiyang *Town* China 85 H10

Gujranwala *Town* Pakistan 77 C8

Guwahati *Town* India 77 E12

Guyana *Country* 35

Gwadar *Town* Pakistan 76 D5

Gyor *Town* Hungary 54 C5

Haarlem *Town* Netherlands 50 D6

Hachinohe *Town* Japan 83 D10

Hadera *Town* Israel 73 H9

Haifa *Town* Israel 73 H9

Haikou *Town* China 85 J11

Hailar *Town* China 85 B11

Haiphong *Town* Vietnam 78 E5

Haiti *Country* 35

Hakodate *Town* Japan 83 C10

Halifax *Province capital* Nova Scotia, Canada 29 I13

Halle *Town* Germany 51 E10

Halley (UK) *RS* Antarctica 16 D3

Halmstad *Town* Sweden 42 I7

Hamadan *Town* Iran 75 C8

Hamah *Town* Syria 73 F10

Hamamatsu *Town* Japan 83 G9

Hamar *Town* Norway 42 G6

Hamburg *Town* Germany 51 C9

Hamhung *Town* North Korea 85 D13

Hamilton *Town* New Zealand 93 C9

Hamilton *Town* Ontario, Canada 29 J11

Hamm *Town* Germany 51 E8

Hanamaki *Town* Japan 83 E10

Hangzhou *Town* China 85 G12

Hannover *Town* Germany 51 D9

Hanoi *Capital* Vietnam 78 E5

Harare *Capital* Zimbabwe 69 G9

Harbel *Town* Liberia 64 I5

Harbin *Town* China 85 C12

Harer *Town* Ethiopia 67 E10

Hargeisa *Town* Somalia 67 D11

Harrisburg *State capital* Pennsylvania, USA 21 G11

Hartford *State capital* Connecticut, USA 21 F12

Hasselt *Town* Belgium 50 E6

Hastings *Town* New Zealand 93 E10

Hat Yai *Town* Thailand 78 J4

Haugesund *Town* Norway 42 G5

Havana *Capital* Cuba 34 B7

Hawaii *State* USA 26

Hefei *Town* China 85 F12

Heidelberg *Town* Germany 51 G8

Heilbronn *Town* Germany 51 H8

Helena *State capital* Montana, USA 24 E7

Helsingborg *Town* Sweden 42 I7

Helsinki *Capital* Finland 43 G10

Hengyang *Town* China 85 H11

Henzada *Town* Burrma (Myanmar) 78 F2

Herat *Town* Afghanistan 76 A6

Heredia *Town* Costa Rica 34 F5

Hermosillo *Town* Mexico 30 D5

Hilversum *Town* Netherlands 50 D6

Himalayas Asia 77 D10, 84 H6

Hims *Town* Syria 73 G10

Hirosaki *Town* Japan 83 D10

Hiroshima *Town* Japan 82 H6

Hitachi *Town* Japan 83 F10

Hobart *Town* Australia 91 J11

Ho Chi Minh City *Town* Vietnam 78 H6

Hofu *Town* Japan 82 H6

Hohhot *Town* China 85 E10

Hokkaido *Island* Japan 83 B11

Holguín *Town* Cuba 35 C8

Homyel *Town* Belarus 58 G6

Honduras *Country* 34

Hong Kong *Town* China 85 I11

Honolulu *State capital* Hawaii, USA 26 H3

Honshu *Island* Japan 83 F9

Hormuz, Strait of Iran/Oman 75 E10

Houston *Town* Texas, USA 27 H14

Hradec Kralove *Town* Czech Republic 56 G6

Hrodna *Town* Belarus 58 G5

Huacho *Town* Peru 36 C5

Huambo *Town* Angola 68 F6

Huancayo *Town* Peru 36 D6

Huang *River* China 85 F11

Hudson Bay Canada 29 G10

Hué *Town* Vietnam 78 F6

Huelva *Town* Spain 44 H6

Hull *Town* England, UK 41 F10

Hungary *Country* 54

Huntington *Town* West Virginia, USA 21 I9

Huntsville *Town* Alabama, USA 23 D8

Huron, Lake USA 20 E8

Hyderabad *Town* India 77 G8

Hyderabad *Town* Pakistan 76 D7

Hyesan *Town* North Korea 85 D13

Iasi *Town* Romania 55 C12

Ibadan *Town* Nigeria 65 I9

Ibagué *Town* Colombia 35 H8

Ibarra *Town* Ecuador 36 A5

Ibiza Balearic Islands, Spain 45 F12

Ibiza *Town* Ibiza, Spain 45 F12

Ica *Town* Peru 36 D5

Iceland *Country* 43

Idaho *State* USA 24

Idaho Falls *Town* Idaho, USA 24 G7

Illinois *River* Illinois, USA 20 H5

Illinois *State* USA 20

Iloilo *Town* Philippines 79 G11

Ilorin *Town* Nigeria 65 I9

Imperatriz *Town* Brazil 37 B10

Imphal *Town* India 77 E12

Inchon *Town* South Korea 85 E13

Independence *Town* Missouri, USA 22 B4

India *Country* 77

Indiana *State* USA 20

Indianapolis *State capital* Indiana, USA 20 H7

Indian Ocean 67, 69, 76, 90

Indonesia *Country* 80

Indore *Town* India 77 E8

Indus *River* Pakistan 76 D7

Ingolstadt *Town* Germany 51 H10

Inhambane *Town* Mozambique 69 H10

Innsbruck *Town* Austria 52 F7

In Salah *Town* Algeria 62 F5

Invercargill *Town* New Zealand 92 J6

Inverness *Town* Scotland, UK 41 C8

Ioánnina *Town* Greece 49 G10

Ionian Sea 49 H9

Iowa *State* USA 20

Ipoh *Town* Malaysia 80 E2

Ipswich *Town* England, UK 41 H10

Iqaluit *Province capital* Nunavut, Canada 29 F11

Iquique *Town* Chile 36 E6

Iquitos *Town* Peru 36 B6

Iráklion *Town* Crete, Greece 49 I12

Iran *Country* 75

Iraq *Country* 74

Irbid *Town* Jordan 73 H9

Ireland, Republic of *Country* 40

Iringa *Town* Tanzania 67 I9
Irish Sea 40 F7
Irkutsk *Town* Russia 86 H6
Irrawaddy *River* Burma (Myanmar) 78 F2
Ishinomaki *Town* Japan 83 E10
Islamabad *Capital* Pakistan 77 B8
Isle of Man *Dep. territory* UK 41 F8
Isparta *Town* Turkey 72 E7
Israel *Country* 73
Istanbul *Town* Turkey 72 B6
Itabuna *Town* Brazil 37 D11
Italy *Country* 48
Iwaki *Town* Japan 83 F10
Izhevsk *Town* Russia 59 F9
Izmir *Town* Turkey 72 D5
Izmit *Town* Turkey 72 C7

Jackson *State capital* Mississippi, USA 22 F6
Jacksonville *Town* Florida, USA 23 G10
Jaén *Town* Spain 45 H8
Jaffna *Town* Sri Lanka 77 I9
Jaipur *Town* India 77 D8
Jakarta *Capital* Indonesia 80 H3
Jamaica *Country* 35
Jambi *Town* Indonesia 80 F2
Jamnagar *Town* India 76 E7
Jamshedpur *Town* India 77 E10
Janesville *Town* Wisconsin, USA 20 G5
Jangbono (South Korea) *RS* Antarctica 16 H5
Japan, Sea of 82 F7, 85 D13
Japan *Country* 82
Java *Island* Indonesia 80 H4
Java Sea 80 H4
Jayapura *Town* Indonesia 81 F11
Jefferson City *State capital* Missouri, USA 22 B5
Jena *Town* Germany 51 F10
Jersey *Island* Channel Islands, UK 41 J9
Jerusalem *Capital* Israel 73 I9
Jiddah *Town* Saudi Arabia 74 G5
Jihlava *Town* Czech Republic 56 H6
Jilin *Town* China 85 C12
Jima *Town* Ethiopia 67 E9
Jinan *Town* China 85 E11
Jinzhou *Town* China 85 D11
João Pessoa *Town* Brazil 37 C12
Jodhpur *Town* India 77 D8
Johannesburg *Town* South Africa 69 J9
John o'Groats *Town* Scotland, UK 41 C9
Johor Baharu *Town* Malaysia 80 F2
Joliet *Town* Illinois, USA 20 G6
Jönköping *Town* Sweden 42 H7

Jordan *Country* 73
Jordan *River* Jordan 73 H9
Jorhat *Town* India 77 D12
Joseph Bonaparte Gulf 90 B7
Juazeiro *Town* Brazil 37 C11
Juazeiro do Norte *Town* Brazil 37 C11
Juba *Capital* South Sudan 67 F8
Judenburg *Town* Austria 40 G11
Juliaca *Town* Peru 36 D6
Juneau *State capital* Alaska, USA 25 C11
Jyväskylä *Town* Finland 43 F10

K2 *Mountain* China/Pakistan 77 B9
Kabul *Capital* Afghanistan 76 B7
Kabwe *Town* Zambia 69 F9
Kachchh, Rann of India 76 E7
Kaduna *Town* Nigeria 65 H10
Kagoshima *Town* Japan 82 I5
Kairouan *Town* Tunisia 62 D7
Kaiserslautern *Town* Germany 50 G7
Kalahari Desert Namibia 68 H7
Kalamata *Town* Peleponnese, Greece 49 I11
Kalamazoo *Town* Michigan, USA 20 G7
Kalemie *Town* DRC 69 E9
Kalgoorlie *Town* Australia 90 G5
Kaliningrad *Town* Russia 58 G5
Kalisz *Town* Poland 56 E7
Kamina *Town* DRC 69 E8
Kamloops *Town* British Columbia, Canada 28 H6
Kampala *Capital* Uganda 67 G8
Kampong Cham *Town* Cambodia 78 H5
Kananga *Town* DRC 69 E8
Kanazawa *Town* Japan 83 F8
Kandy *Town* Sri Lanka 77 J9
Kankan *Town* Guinea 64 H5
Kano *Town* Nigeria 65 G10
Kanpur *Town* India 77 D9
Kansas *River* Kansas, USA 27 D13
Kansas *State* USA 27
Kansas City *Town* Missouri, USA 22 B4
Kansk *Town* Russia 86 G6
Kaposvár *Town* Hungary 54 D5
Karabük *Town* Turkey 73 B8
Karachi *Town* Pakistan 76 D6
Kara Sea 17 G14, 59 B10, 86 D4
Karbala *Town* Iraq 74 C7
Kardhitsa *Town* Greece 49 G11
Karlovac *Town* Croatia 49 C8
Karlovy Vary *Town* Czech Republic 56 G4
Karlskrona *Town* Sweden 42 I7
Karlsruhe *Town* Germany 50 H7

Karlstad *Town* Sweden 42 G7
Kars *Town* Turkey 73 C13
Kasai (Cassai) *River* Angola/DRC 68 D7
Kashi *Town* China 84 E4
Kassala *Town* Sudan 67 C9
Kassel *Town* Germany 51 E9
Katherine *Town* Australia 91 B8
Kathmandu *Capital* Nepal 77 D10
Katowice *Town* Poland 57 G8
Katsina *Town* Nigeria 65 G10
Kattegat *Sea* 42 H6
Kaunas *Town* Lithuania 58 G5
Kaválla *Town* Greece 49 F12
Kawasaki *Town* Japan 83 G10
Kayseri *Town* Turkey 73 D9
Kazakhstan *Country* 86
Kazan *Town* Russia 59 F9
Kecskemét *Town* Hungary 54 D6
Kelang *Town* Malaysia 80 E2
Kemerovo *Town* Russia 86 G5
Kemi *Town* Finland 43 D9
Kénitra *Town* Morocco 62 D3
Kentucky *State* USA 23
Kenya *Country* 67
Kerman *Town* Iran 75 D10
Kesennuma *Town* Japan 83 E10
Kettering *Town* Ohio, USA 21 H8
Key West *Town* Florida, USA 23 J11
Khabarovsk *Town* Russia 87 H9
Kharkiv *Town* Ukraine 58 H7
Khartoum *Capital* Sudan 67 C8
Khaskovo *Town* Bulgaria I11
Khon Kaen *Town* Thailand 78 G4
Khulna *Town* Bangladesh 77 F11
Kiel *Town* Germany 51 B10
Kiev *Capital* Ukraine 58 G6
Kigali *Capital* Rwanda 66 G7
Kigoma *Town* Tanzania 66 H7
Kikwit *Town* DRC 68 D7
Kilimanjaro, Mount Tanzania 67 H9
Kimberley *Town* South Africa 69 I8
Kimberley Plateau Australia 90 C6
Kingston *Capital* Jamaica 35 D8
Kingstown *Capital* St. Vincent 35 E12
Kinshasa *Capital* DRC 68 D6
Kiribati *Country* 93 I13
Kirikkale *Town* Turkey 73 C9
Kirkuk *Town* Iraq 74 B7
Kirov *Town* Russia 58 G6
Kiruna *Town* Sweden 43 C8
Kisangani *Town* DRC 69 C8
Kismaayo *Town* Somalia 67 G10
Kisumu *Town* Kenya 67 G8
Kitakyushu *Town* Japan 82 H5
Kitchener *Town* Ontario, Canada 29 J11

Kitwe *Town* Zambia 69 F9
Kivu, Lake DRC/Rwanda 66 H7, 69 D9
Klagenfurt *Town* Austria 40 H11
Klamath Falls *Town* Oregon, USA 24 G3
Knoxville *Town* Tennessee, USA 23 C9
Kobe *Town* Japan 82 H7
Koblenz *Town* Germany 50 F7
Kochi (Cochin) *Town* India 77 I8
Kochi *Town* Japan 82 H7
Kodiak *Town* Alaska, USA 25 C10
Kofu *Town* Japan 83 G9
Kokshetau *Town* Kazakhstan 86 H3
Kolhapur *Town* India 76 G7
Kolkata (Calcutta) *Town* India 77 F11
Kolwezi *Town* DRC 69 E8
Komatsu *Town* Japan 83 F8
Komsomol'sk-na-Amure *Town* Russian Fed. 87 H9
Konya *Town* Turkey 73 E8
Koper *Town* Slovenia 48 B7
Korçë *Town* Albania 49 F10
Korea, North *Country* 85
Korea, South *Country* 85
Korea Strait Japan/South Korea 82 H4, 85 E13
Koriyama *Town* Japan 83 F10
Korla *Town* China 84 E6
Kortrijk *Town* Belgium 50 E4
Kosice *Town* Slovakia 57 I10
Kosovo *Country* 49
Kosovska Mitrovica *Town* Kosovo 49 D10
Koszalin *Town* Poland 56 B6
Kotka *Town* Finland 43 G10
Kotte *Capital* Sri Lanka 77 J9
Kotto *River* CAR 68 B7
Kozáni *Town* Greece 49 F11
Kozhikode (Calicut) *Town* India 77 H8
Kragujevac *Town* Serbia 49 D10
Kraków *Town* Poland 57 G9
Krasnodar *Town* Russia 58 I7
Krasnoyarsk *Town* Russia 86 G5
Krefeld *Town* Germany 50 E7
Kristiansand *Town* Norway 42 H5
Krusevac *Town* Serbia 49 D11
Kryvyy Rih *Town* Ukraine 58 H6
Kuala Lumpur *Capital* Malaysia 80 E2
Kuala Terengganu *Town* Malaysia 80 E2
Kuching *Town* Malaysia 80 F4
Kugluktuk *Town* Nunavut, Canada 28 E7
Kumamoto *Town* Japan 82 I5
Kumanovo *Town* Macedonia 49 E11

Kumasi *Town* Ghana 64 I7

Kunlun Shan *Mountain range* China 84 F6

Kunming *Town* China 85 I9

Kuopio *Town* Finland 43 E10

Kupang *Town* Indonesia 80 H7

Kure *Town* Japan 82 H6

Kushiro *Town* Japan 83 B11

Kütahya *Town* Turkey 72 D7

Kuwait *Country* 75

Kuwait City *Capital* Kuwait 75 E8

Kwangju *Town* South Korea 85 E13

Kwango *River* DRC 68 E6

Kwilu *River* DRC 68 D7

Kyoto *Town* Japan 83 G8

Kyrgyzstan *Country* 86

Kyushu *Island* Japan 82 I5

Kyustendil *Town* Bulgaria 55 I9

Labrador Sea 29 F12

La Ceiba *Town* Honduras 34 D5

La Coruña *Town* Spain 44 B5

La Crosse *Town* Wisconsin, USA 20 F4

Ladoga, Lake *Russia* 58 E6

Lafayette *Town* Louisiana, USA 22 H5

Lagos *Town* Nigeria 65 I8

Lagos *Town* Portugal 44 H5

Lahore *Town* Pakistan 77 C8

Lahti *Town* Finland 43 F10

Lake Charles *Town* Louisiana, USA 22 H5

Lakewood *Town* Colorado, USA 27 D10

Lalitpur *Town* India 77 E9

Lamía *Town* Greece 49 G11

Lansing *State capital* Michigan, USA 20 F7

Lanzhou *Town* China 85 F9

Laoag *Town* Philippines 79 D10

Laos *Country* 78

La Paz *Capital* Bolivia 36 D7

La Paz *Town* Mexico 30 F5

La Plata *Town* Argentina 37 G8

Laptev Sea 17 D13, 87 D8

Laredo *Town* Texas, USA 27 I12

Larissa *Town* Greece 49 G11

Larkana *Town* Pakistan 76 C7

La Rochelle *Town* France 46 E6

La Romana *Town* Dominican Republic 35 D10

Las Cruces *Town* New Mexico, USA 27 G9

La Serena *Town* Chile 36 F6

La Spezia *Town* Italy 48 C5

Las Vegas *Town* Nevada, USA 26 E6

Latina *Town* Italy 48 E6

Latvia *Country* 58

Launceston *Town* Australia 91 J11

Lausanne *Town* Switzerland 52 G1

Laval *Town* France 46 C7

Lawton *Town* Oklahoma, USA 27 F12

Lebanon *Country* 73

Lecce *Town* Italy 49 F9

Leeds *Town* England, UK 41 F9

Leeuwarden *Town* Netherlands 50 C7

Legnica *Town* Poland 56 F6

Le Havre *Town* France 47 B8

Leicester *Town* England, UK 41 G9

Leiden *Town* Netherlands 50 D6

Leipzig *Town* Germany 51 F11

Le Mans *Town* France 47 C8

Lena *River* Russia 86 G7

León *Town* Mexico 31 G8

León *Town* Nicaragua 34 E5

León *Town* Spain 44 C7

Lerwick *Town* Scotland, UK 41 A9

Leskovac *Town* Serbia 49 D11

Lesotho *Country* 69

Lethbridge *Town* Alberta, Canada 28 I7

Leuven *Town* Belgium 50 E5

Lewis *Island* Scotland, UK 40 C7

Lewiston *Town* Idaho, USA 24 E5

Lewiston *Town* Maine, USA 21 D13

Lexington *Town* Kentucky, USA 23 B8

Lhasa *Town* China 84 H7

Lianyungang *Town* China 85 F12

Liberec *Town* Czech Republic 56 F5

Liberia *Country* 64

Libreville *Capital* Gabon 68 C5

Libya *Country* 63

Libyan Desert *Egypt/Libya/Sudan* 63 G11, 66 A6

Liechtenstein *Country* 52

Liège *Town* Belgium 50 F6

Liepaja *Town* Latvia 58 F5

Likasi *Town* DRC 69 F8

Lille *Town* France 47 A10

Lillehammer *Town* Norway 42 F6

Lilongwe *Capital* Malawi 69 F10

Lima *Capital* Peru 36 D5

Limassol *Town* Cyprus 73 G8

Limerick *Town* Republic of Ireland 40 G6

Limoges *Town* France 47 E8

Limpopo *River* South Africa 69 H9

Linares *Town* Spain 45 G9

Lincoln *State capital* Nebraska, USA 25 I14

Lincoln Sea 17 G11

Lindi *Town* Tanzania 67 J10

Linköping *Town* Sweden 42 H7

Linz *Town* Austria 40 E11

Lipetsk *Town* Russia 58 G7

Lisbon *Capital* Portugal 44 G4

Lithuania *Country* 58

Little Rock *State capital* Arkansas, USA 22 E5

Liuzhou *Town* China 85 I10

Liverpool *Town* England, UK 41 G8

Livingstone *Town* Zambia 69 G8

Livorno *Town* Italy 48 D5

Ljubljana *Capital* Slovenia 48 B7

Lleida *Town* Spain 45 C11

Lobamba *Capital* Eswatini 69 I9

Lobito *Town* Angola 68 F6

Lodz *Town* Poland 57 E8

Logroño *Town* Spain 45 C9

Loire *River* France 46 D7

Lomami *River* DRC 69 D8

Lomas de Zamora *Town* Argentina 37 G8

Lomé *Capital* Togo 65 I8

London *Capital* England, UK 41 H10

London *Town* Ontario, Canada 29 J11

Londonderry *Town* Northern Ireland, UK 40 E7

Long Beach *Town* California, USA 26 F5

Long Island *New York, USA* 21 F12

Longview *Town* Texas, USA 27 G14

Lorca *Town* Spain 45 H10

Lorient *Town* France 46 C6

Los Angeles *Town* California, USA 26 F5

Los Angeles *Town* Chile 36 H6

Los Mochis *Town* Mexico 30 E6

Louisiana *State* USA 22

Louisville *Town* Kentucky, USA 23 B8

Lowell *Town* Massachusetts, USA 21 E13

Lower Hutt *Town* New Zealand 93 F9

Luanda *Capital* Angola 68 E6

Lubango *Town* Angola 68 F6

Lubbock *Town* Texas, USA 27 F11

Lübeck *Town* Germany 51 B10

Lublin *Town* Poland 57 F11

Lubumbashi *Town* DRC 69 F9

Lucknow *Town* India 77 D9

Lüderitz *Town* Namibia 68 I6

Ludhiana *Town* India 77 C8

Ludwigshafen *Town* Germany 51 G7

Luena *Town* Angola 68 F7

Lugano *Town* Switzerland 52 H4

Lugo *Town* Spain 44 B6

Luleå *Town* Sweden 43 D9

Lund *Town* Sweden 42 I7

Lüneburg *Town* Germany 51 C10

Luoyang *Town* China 85 F10

Lusaka *Capital* Zambia 69 F9

Luxembourg *Capital* Luxembourg 50 G6

Luxembourg *Country* 50 G6

Luxor *Town* Egypt 63 G13

Luzon *Island* Philippines 79 E10

Lviv *Town* Ukraine 58 H5

Lynchburg *Town* Virgina, USA 23 B11

Lyon *Town* France 47 F10

Maas (Meuse) *River* Belgium/ France/Netherlands 50 E6

Maastricht *Town* Netherlands 50 E6

Macapá *Town* Brazil 37 B9

Macau *Town* China 85 I11

Macdonnell Ranges *Australia* 91 E8

Macedonia *Country* 49

Maceio *Town* Brazil 37 C11

Mackay *Town* Australia 91 D12

Macon *Town* Georgia, USA 23 E9

Ma'daba *Town* Jordan 73 I10

Madagascar *Country* 69

Madeira *River* Brazil 37 B8

Madison *State capital* Wisconsin, USA 20 F5

Madras *See Chennai*

Madrid *Capital* Spain 45 E8

Madurai *Town* India 77 I8

Magadan *Town* Russia 87 G11

Magdeburg *Town* Germany 51 D10

Magnitogorsk *Town* Russia 59 G10

Mahajanga *Town* Madagascar 69 G12

Maiduguri *Town* Nigeria 65 H11

Main *River* Germany 51 G10

Maine, Gulf of 21 D14

Maine *State* USA 21

Mainz *Town* Germany 51 G8

Maitri (India) *RS* Antarctica 16 C5

Malabo *Capital* Equatorial Guinea 68 C5

Málaga *Town* Spain 45 I8

Malakal *Town* South Sudan 67 D8

Malang *Town* Indonesia 80 H4

Malatya *Town* Turkey 73 D11

Malawi *Country* 69

Malaysia *Country* 80

Mali *Country* 64

Mallorca *Balearic Islands, Spain* 45 E13

Malmö *Town* Sweden 42 I7

Malta *Country* 48

Manado *Town* Indonesia 80 F7

Managua *Capital* Nicaragua 34 E5

Manama *Capital* Bahrain 75 F8

Manaus *Town* Brazil 37 B8

Manchester *Town* England, UK
41 G9

Manchester *Town* New Hampshire,
USA 21 E13

Mandalay *Town* Burma (Myanmar)
78 E2

Mangalore *Town* India 76 H7

Manila *Capital* Philippines 79 F10

Manisa *Town* Turkey 72 D5

Manitoba *Province* Canada 29

Manizales *Town* Colombia 35 H8

Mankato *Town* Minnesota, USA
20 F3

Mannheim *Town* Germany 51 G8

Manta *Town* Ecuador 36 B5

Maputo *Capital* Mozambique 69 I9

Marabá *Town* Brazil 37 B9

Maracaibo *Town* Venezuela 35 F9

Maracay *Town* Venezuela 35 F10

Maradi *Town* Niger 65 G10

Marajo Island Brazil 37 B9

Marambio (Argentina) *RS* Antarctica
16 D1

Marbella *Town* Spain 45 I8

Mardan *Town* Pakistan 77 B8

Mar del Plata *Town* Argentina 37 G8

Maribor *Town* Slovenia 49 B8

Marie Byrd Land Antarctica 16 F3

Marka *Town* Somalia 67 G11

Marmara, Sea of 72 C6

Marquette *Town* Michigan, USA
20 D5

Marrakech *Town* Morocco 62 E2

Marseille *Town* France 47 H10

Marshall Islands *Country* 93 H12

Martin *Town* Slovakia 57 H8

Martinique *Dep. territory* France
35 E12

Maryland *State* USA 21

Masaka *Town* Uganda 67 G8

Maseru *Capital* Lesotho 69 I8

Mashhad *Town* Iran 75 B11

Massa *Town* Italy 48 C5

Massachusetts *State* USA 21

Massawa *Town* Eritrea 67 C9

Massif Central France 47 F9

Matadi *Town* DRC 68 D6

Matamoros *Town* Mexico 31 E10

Mataram *Town* Indonesia 80 H5

Mataró *Town* Spain 45 C13

Matsue *Town* Japan 82 G6

Matsumoto *Town* Japan 83 G9

Matsuyama *Town* Japan 82 H6

Matterhorn, Mount Switzerland
52 H2

Maun *Town* Botswana 69 G8

Mauritania *Country* 64

Mauritius *Country* 69

Mawson (Australia) *RS* Antarctica
16 E6

Mayotte *Dep. territory* France
69 F12

Mazar-e Sharif *Town* Afghanistan
76 A7

Mazatlán *Town* Mexico 30 F7

Mbabane *Capital* Eswatini 69 I9

Mbandaka *Town* DRC 68 C7

Mbeya *Town* Tanzania 67 I9

Mbuji-Mayi *Town* DRC 69 E8

McMurdo (US) *RS* Antarctica
16 H5

Mecca *Town* Saudi Arabia 74 G5

Mechelen *Town* Belgium 50 E5

Medan *Town* Indonesia 80 E1

Medellín *Town* Colombia 35 G8

Medicine Hat *Town* Alberta, Canada
28 I7

Medina *Town* Saudi Arabia 74 F5

Mediterranean Sea 45, 47, 62, 73

Meerut *Town* India 77 D9

Mekong *River* Asia 78 G5, 85 I9

Melbourne *Town* Australia 91 I11

Melilla *Town* Spain 45 J9, 62 D4

Melville Island Canada 17 E9

Memphis *Town* Tennessee, USA
22 D6

Mendoza *Town* Argentina 36 G7

Menorca Balearic Islands, Spain
45 E14

Mérida *Town* Mexico 31 G13, 44 F7

Mérida *Town* Spain 44 F7

Mesa *Town* Arizona, USA 26 F7

Messina *Town* Sicily, Italy 48 H7

Metairie *Town* Louisiana, USA 22 H6

Metz *Town* France 47 C11

Meuse (Maas) *River* Belgium/
France/Netherlands 50 F5

Mexicali *Town* Mexico 30 B4

Mexico, Gulf of 23 H8, 27 J14,
31 F11

Mexico *Country* 30

Mexico City *Capital* Mexico 31 H9

Miami *Town* Florida, USA 23 I12

Michigan, Lake USA 20 E6

Michigan *State* USA 20

Micronesia *Country* 93 H11

Middlesbrough *Town* England, UK
41 F9

Midland *Town* Texas, USA 27 G11

Milan *Town* Italy 48 B5

Miles City *Town* Montana, USA
25 F10

Milwaukee *Town* Wisconsin, USA
20 F6

Mindanao *Island* Philippines 79 G12

Mindoro Strait South China Sea
79 G10

Minneapolis *Town* Minnesota, USA
20 E3

Minnesota *State* USA 20

Minot *Town* N Dakota, USA
25 E12

Minsk *Capital* Belarus 58 G6

Mirny (Russian Federation) *RS*
Antarctica 16 F7

Mirpur Khas *Town* Pakistan 76 D7

Miskolc *Town* Hungary 54 B7

Mississippi *River* USA 20 F4, 22 E6

Mississippi *State* USA 22

Missouri *River* Montana, USA 25 E10

Missouri *State* USA 22

Mito *Town* Japan 83 F10

Miyako *Town* Japan 83 D10

Miyakonojo *Town* Japan 82 I5

Miyazaki *Town* Japan 82 I6

Mobile *Town* Alabama, USA 22 G7

Modesto *Town* California, USA
26 C4

Mogadishu *Capital* Somalia 67 F11

Moldova *Country* 58

Molucca Sea 80 F7

Mombasa *Town* Kenya 67 H10

Monaco *Capital* Monaco 47 H11

Monaco *Country* 47

Monclova *Town* Mexico 31 E9

Mongolia *Country* 85

Monroe *Town* Louisiana, USA 22 F5

Monrovia *Capital* Liberia 64 I4

Mons *Town* Belgium 50 F5

Montana *State* USA 25

Montana *Town* Bulgaria 55 H9

Montauban *Town* France 46 G7

Mont Blanc *Mountain* France 47 F11

Mont-de-Marsan *Town* France
46 F7

Montego Bay *Town* Jamaica
35 C8

Montélimar *Town* France 47 G10

Montenegro *Country* 49

Monterey *Town* California, USA
26 D4

Montería *Town* Colombia 35 F8

Monterrey *Town* Mexico 31 E9

Montevideo *Capital* Uruguay 37 G8

Montgomery *State capital* Alabama,
USA 23 F8

Montluçon *Town* France 47 E9

Montpelier *State capital* Vermont,
USA 21 D12

Montpellier *Town* France 47 H9

Montreal *Town* Quebec, Canada
29 I12

Montserrat *Dep. territory* UK 35 D12

Monza *Town* Italy 48 B5

Moorhead *Town* Minnesota, USA
20 D2

Mopti *Town* Mali 64 G6

Morelia *Town* Mexico 31 H8

Morocco *Country* 62

Moroni *Capital* Comoros 69 F12

Moscow *Capital* Russia 58 F7

Mosselbaai *Town* South Africa 68 J7

Mossoró *Town* Brazil 37 B11

Mostar *Town* Bosnia and Herz.
49 D9

Mosul *Town* Iraq 74 B6

Moulmein *Town* Burma (Myanmar)
78 G3

Moundou *Town* Chad 65 I12

Mount Isa *Town* Australia 91 D10

Mozambique *Country* 69

Mufulira *Town* Zambia 69 F9

Mulhouse *Town* France 47 D12

Multan *Town* Pakistan 77 C8

Mumbai (Bombay) *Town* India
76 F7

Muncie *Town* Indiana, USA 20 H7

Munich *Town* Germany 51 I10

Münster *Town* Germany 50 D7

Murcia *Town* Spain 45 G10

Murmansk *Town* Russia 58 C7

Muroran *Town* Japan 83 C10

Murray *River* Australia 91 H11

Muscat *Capital* Oman 75 F11

Mwanza *Town* Tanzania 67 H8

Mweru, Lake DRC 69 E9

Myanmar *See Burma*

Myrtle Beach *Town* S Carolina, USA
23 D11

Mysore *Town* India 77 H8

Myvatn *Lake* Iceland 43 H13

Nacala *Town* Mozambique
69 F11

Nagano *Town* Japan 83 F9

Nagaoka *Town* Japan 83 F9

Nagasaki *Town* Japan 82 I5

Nagoya *Town* Japan 83 G8

Nagpur *Town* India 77 F9

Nain *Town* Newfoundland and
Labrador, Canada 29 G12

Nairobi *Capital* Kenya 67 G9

Nakhon Ratchasima *Town* Thailand
78 G4

Nakhon Sawan *Town* Thailand
78 G4

Nakhon Si Thammarat *Town*
Thailand 78 I4

Nakuru *Town* Kenya 67 G9

Namangan *Town* Uzbekistan 86 I4

Nam Dinh *Town* Vietnam 78 E5

Namib Desert Namibia 68 H6

Namibe *Town* Angola 68 F6

Namibia *Country* 68

Nampula *Town* Mozambique 69 F11

Namur *Town* Belgium 50 F5

Nanchang *Town* China 85 G11

Nanchong *Town* China 85 G9

Nancy *Town* France 47 C11

Nanjing *Town* China 85 F12

Nanning *Town* China 85 I10

Nantes *Town* France 46 D6
Napier *Town* New Zealand 93 D10
Naples *Town* Italy 48 F7
Narvik *Town* Norway 43 C8
Nashville *State capital* Tennessee, USA 23 C8
Nassau *Capital* Bahamas 35 A8
Nasser, Lake Egypt 63 H13
Natal *Town* Brazil 37 C12
Nauru *Country* 93 H12
Naypyidaw *Capital* Burma (Myanmar) 78 F2
Nazareth *Town* Israel 73 H9
Nazilli *Town* Turkey 72 D6
Nazret *Town* Ethiopia 67 E10
N'Djamena *Capital* Chad 65 H12
Ndola *Town* Zambia 69 F9
Neápolis *Town* Greece 49 I11
Near Islands Alaska, USA 25 B8
Nebraska *State* USA 25
Negev Desert Israel 73 I9
Negotin *Town* Serbia 49 C11
Negro *River* Brazil 36 B7
Nellore *Town* India 77 H9
Nelson *Town* New Zealand 93 F8
Nepal *Country* 77
Netanya *Town* Israel 73 H9
Netherlands *Country* 50
Neubrandenburg *Town* Germany 51 C11
Neuchâtel *Town* Switzerland 52 F2
Neumayer III (Germany) *RS* Antarctica 16 C4
Neuquén *Town* Argentina 36 H7
Nevada *State* USA 26
Newark *Town* New Jersey, USA 21 F12
New Brunswick *Province* Canada 29
New Caledonia *Dep. territory* France 93 J12
Newcastle *Town* Australia 91 G12
Newcastle upon Tyne *Town* England, UK 41 E9
New Delhi *Capital* India 77 D9
Newfoundland and Labrador *Province* Canada 29
New Guinea *Island* Indonesia 81 G10
New Hampshire *State* USA 21
New Haven *Town* Connecticut, USA 21 F12
New Jersey *State* USA 21
New Mexico *State* USA 27
New Orleans *Town* Louisiana, USA 22 H6
New Plymouth *Town* New Zealand 93 D9
Newport *Town* Vermont, USA 21 C12
Newport *Town* Wales, UK 41 H8

Newport News *Town* Virginia, USA 23 B12
New South Wales *State* Australia 91
New York *State* USA 21
New York City *Town* New York, USA 21 F12
New Zealand *Country* 92
Nha Trang *Town* Vietnam 78 H7
Niagara Falls USA 21 F9
Niamey *Capital* Niger 65 G8
Nicaragua *Country* 34
Nice *Town* France 47 H11
Nicobar Islands India 77 J12
Nicosia *Capital* Cyprus 73 F8
Niger *Country* 65
Niger *River* West Africa 65 I9
Nigeria *Country* 65
Niigata *Town* Japan 83 F9
Niksic *Town* Montenegro 49 D9
Nile *River* East Africa 63 F13, 66 B7
Nîmes *Town* France 47 G9
Ningbo *Town* China 85 G12
Nis *Town* Serbia 49 D11
Nitra *Town* Slovakia 57 I8
Niue *Dep. territory* New Zealand 93 I13
Nizhnevartovsk *Town* Russia 86 G4
Nizhniy Novgorod *Town* Russia 59 F8
Nobeoka *Town* Japan 82 I6
Norfolk *Town* Nebraska, USA 25 H13
Norfolk *Town* Virginia, USA 23 B12
Noril'sk *Town* Russia 86 E5
Norman *Town* Oklahoma, USA 27 F13
Norrköping *Town* Sweden 43 H8
Northampton *Town* England, UK 41 H9
North Cape New Zealand 93 A8
North Cape Norway 43 A9
North Carolina *State* USA 23
North Dakota *State* USA 25
Northern Ireland *Country* UK 40
Northern Mariana Islands *Dep. territory* USA 93 G11
Northern Territory *State* Australia 91
North Island New Zealand 93
North Korea *See* Korea, North
North Sea 41, 42, 50
Northwest Territories *Province* Canada 28
Norway *Country* 42
Norwegian Sea 17 I11, 43 J13
Norwich *Town* England, UK 41 G10
Nottingham *Town* England, UK 41 G9

Nouadhibou *Town* Mauritania 64 D3
Nouakchott *Capital* Mauritania 64 E3
Nova Iguaçu *Town* Brazil 37 E10
Novara *Town* Italy 48 B4
Nova Scotia *Province* Canada 29
Novaya Zemlya *Island* Russia 17 G13, 59 B10
Novgorod *Town* Russia 58 F6
Novi Sad *Town* Serbia 49 C10
Novokuznetsk *Town* Russia 86 H5
Novolazervskaya (Russia) *RS* Antarctica 16 C5
Novosibirsk *Town* Russia 86 H5
Nubian Desert Sudan 67 A8
Nueva Gerona *Town* Cuba 34 B6
Nuevo Laredo *Town* Mexico 31 D9
Nunavut *Province* Canada 29
Nuremberg *Town* Germany 51 H10
Nyala *Town* Sudan 66 D6
Nyíregyháza *Town* Hungary 55 C8

Oakland *Town* California, USA 26 C4
Oamaru *Town* New Zealand 92 I7
Oaxaca *Town* Mexico 31 I10
Ob *River* Russia 86 G4
Obihiro *Town* Japan 83 B11
Oceanside *Town* California, USA 26 F5
Odense *Town* Denmark 42 I6
Oder *River* Poland 56 F7
Odessa *Town* Texas, USA 27 G11
Odessa *Town* Ukraine 58 H6
Offenbach *Town* Germany 51 G8
Ogaden Plateau Ethiopia 67 E11
Ogbomosho *Town* Nigeria 65 I9
Ogden *Town* Utah, USA 27 C8
Ohio *State* USA 21
Ohrid, Lake Albania/Macedonia 49 F10
Oita *Town* Japan 82 H6
Okavango Delta Botswana 68 G7
Okayama *Town* Japan 82 H7
Okeechobee, Lake Florida, USA 23 I11
Okhotsk, Sea of 87 G10
Oklahoma *State* USA 27
Oklahoma City *State capital* Oklahoma, USA 27 F13
Öland *Island* Sweden 43 I8
Oldenburg *Town* Germany 51 C8
Olomouc *Town* Czech Republic 56 H7
Olsztyn *Town* Poland 57 C9
Olympia *State capital* Washington, USA 24 D3
Olympus, Mount Greece 49 F11
Omaha *Town* Nebraska, USA 25 I14
Oman, Gulf of 75 F11

Oman *Country* 75
Omdurman *Town* Sudan 67 C8
Omsk *Town* Russia 86 H4
Onega, Lake Russia 58 E7
Onega *Town* Russia 58 D7
Onitsha *Town* Nigeria 65 I9
Ontario, Lake USA 21 E10
Ontario *Province* Canada 29
Opole *Town* Poland 56 F7
Oradea *Town* Romania 55 C8
Oran *Town* Algeria 62 D5
Orange *River* South Africa 69 I8
Orcadas (Argentina) *RS* Antarctica 16 C1
Ordu *Town* Turkey 73 C11
Örebro *Town* Sweden 42 G7
Oregon *State* USA 24
Orenburg *Town* Russia 59 G10, 86 H2
Orense *Town* Spain 44 C6
Orkney Islands Scotland, UK 41 B9
Orlando *Town* Florida, USA 23 H11
Orléans *Town* France 47 D8
Örnsköldsvik *Town* Sweden 43 E8
Orsk *Town* Russia 59 G10
Oruro *Town* Bolivia 36 D7
Osaka *Town* Japan 83 H8
Oshawa *Town* Ontario, Canada 29 J11
Oshkosh *Town* Wisconsin, USA 20 F5
Osijek *Town* Croatia 49 B9
Oslo *Capital* Norway 42 G6
Osmaniye *Town* Turkey 73 E10
Osnabrück *Town* Germany 51 D8
Osorno *Town* Chile 36 H6
Ostend *Town* Belgium 50 E4
Östersund *Town* Sweden 42 E7
Ostrava *Town* Czech Republic 57 H8
Otago Peninsula New Zealand 92 I7
Otaru *Town* Japan 83 B10
Ottawa *Capital* Canada 29 I12
Ouagadougou *Capital* Burkina Faso 64 G7
Oujda *Town* Morocco 62 D4
Oulu *Town* Finland 43 D10
Outer Hebrides *Island group* Scotland, UK 40 C7
Oviedo *Town* Spain 44 B7
Owensboro *Town* Kentucky, USA 22 B7
Oxford *Town* England, UK 41 H9
Oxnard *Town* California, USA 26 E5

Pachuca *Town* Mexico 31 G9
Pacific Ocean 24, 25, 26, 28, 30, 36, 79, 83, 85, 87, 91, 93
Padang *Town* Indonesia 80 F2
Paderborn *Town* Germany 51 E8
Paducah *Town* Kentucky, USA 22 C7

Pakistan *Country* 76

Pakxe *Town* Laos 78 G5

Palau *Country* 93 H10

Palawan Passage South China Sea 79 H9

Palembang *Town* Indonesia 80 G3

Palencia *Town* Spain 45 C8

Palermo *Town* Sicily, Italy 48 H6

Palma *Town* Mallorca, Spain 45 E13

Palmer (US) *RS* Antarctica 16 D1

Palmerston North *Town* New Zealand 93 E9

Palo Alto *Town* California, USA 26 D4

Palu *Town* Indonesia 80 F6

Pamplona *Town* Spain 45 B10

Panama, Gulf of 34 G7

Panama *Country* 34

Panama Canal Panama 34 F6

Panama City *Capital* Panama 34 F7

Pancevo *Town* Serbia 49 C10

Papua New Guinea *Country* 93

Paraguay *Country* 37

Paramaribo *Capital* Suriname 35 G13

Pardubice *Town* Czech Republic 56 G6

Paris *Capital* France 47 C9

Parma *Town* Italy 48 C5

Parnaíba *Town* Brazil 37 B11

Pasadena *Town* California, USA 26 F5

Pasadena *Town* Texas, USA 27 H14

Pasco *Town* Washington, USA 24 E5

Passau *Town* Germany 51 I11

Pasto *Town* Colombia 34 I7

Patagonia Argentina 36 I7

Paterson *Town* New Jersey, USA 21 F12

Patna *Town* India 77 E10

Pátrai *Town* Greece 49 H11

Pau *Town* France 46 G6

Pavlodar *Town* Kazakhstan 86 H4

Pearl *River* Mississippi, USA 22 G6

Pejë *Town* Kosovo 49 E10

Pechora *River* Russia 59 D9

Pécs *Town* Hungary 54 E5

Pedro Juan Caballero *Town* Paraguay 37 E8

Pegu *Town* Burma (Myanmar) 78 G2

Pekanbaru *Town* Indonesia 80 F2

Pennines *Hills* England, UK 41 F9

Pennsylvania *State* USA 21

Penza *Town* Russia 59 G8

Peoria *Town* Illinois, USA 20 H5

Pereira *Town* Colombia 35 H8

Perm *Town* Russia 59 F9

Pernik *Town* Bulgaria 55 I9

Persian Gulf 75 E8

Perth *Town* Australia 90 G4

Perth *Town* Scotland, UK 41 D8

Peru *Country* 36

Perugia *Town* Italy 48 D6

Pescara *Town* Italy 48 E7

Peshawar *Town* Pakistan 77 B8

Peterborough *Town* England, UK 41 G10

Petropavlovsk-Kamchatskiy *Town* Russia 87 H11

Petrozavodsk *Town* Russia 58 E7

Pforzheim *Town* Germany 51 H8

Philadelphia *Town* Pennsylvania, USA 21 G12

Philippines *Country* 79

Phnom Penh *Capital* Cambodia 78 H5

Phoenix *State capital* Arizona, USA 26 F7

Phuket *Town* Thailand 78 I3

Piacenza *Town* Italy 48 C5

Pierre *State capital* S Dakota, USA 25 G12

Pietermaritzburg *Town* South Africa 69 I9

Pietersburg *Town* South Africa 69 H9

Pinar del Río *Town* Cuba 34 B6

Pine Bluff *Town* Arkansas, USA 22 E5

Piraeus *Town* Greece 49 H12

Pisa *Town* Italy 48 D5

Pistoia *Town* Italy 48 C6

Pitesti *Town* Romania 55 F10

Pittsburgh *Town* Pennsylvania, USA 21 G9

Piura *Town* Peru 36 B5

Plano *Town* Texas, USA 27 G13

Platte *River* Nebraska, USA 25 I12

Plauen *Town* Germany 51 F10

Plenty, Bay of New Zealand 93 C10

Pleven *Town* Bulgaria 55 H10

Plock *Town* Poland 57 D9

Ploiesti *Town* Romania 55 F11

Plovdiv *Town* Bulgaria 55 I10

Plymouth *Town* England, UK 41 I8

Plzen *Town* Czech Republic 56 G4

Podgorica *Capital* Montenegro 49 E9

Pointe-Noire *Town* Republic of the Congo 68 D5

Poitiers *Town* France 46 D7

Pokhara *Town* Nepal 77 D10

Poland *Country* 56

Pontianak *Town* Indonesia 80 F4

Poona *See* Pune

Popayán *Town* Colombia 34 H7

Pori *Town* Finland 43 F9

Port Arthur *Town* Texas, USA 27 H14

Port Augusta *Town* Australia 91 G9

Port-au-Prince *Capital* Haiti 35 D9

Port Elizabeth *Town* South Africa 69 J8

Port-Gentil *Town* Gabon 68 C5

Port Harcourt *Town* Nigeria 65 J9

Portland *Town* Maine, USA 21 D13

Portland *Town* Oregon, USA 24 E3

Port Louis *Capital* Mauritius 69 H14

Port Macquarie *Town* Australia 91 G13

Porto *Town* Portugal 44 D5

Porto Alegre *Town* Brazil 37 F9

Port-of-Spain *Capital* Trinidad and Tobago 35 F12

Porto-Novo *Capital* Benin 65 I8

Porto Velho *Town* Brazil 36 C7

Portoviejo *Town* Ecuador 36 B5

Port Said *Town* Egypt 63 E13

Portsmouth *Town* England, UK 41 I9

Portsmouth *Town* New Hampshire, USA 21 D13

Portsmouth *Town* Virginia, USA 23 B12

Port Sudan *Town* Sudan 67 B9

Portugal *Country* 44

Potosí *Town* Bolivia 36 E7

Potsdam *Town* Germany 51 D11

Poznan *Town* Poland 56 E7

Prague *Capital* Czech Republic 56 G5

Praia *Capital* Cape Verde (Cabo Verde) 64 F1

Prato *Town* Italy 48 D6

Presidente Eduardo Frei (Chile) *RS* Antarctica 16 D1

Presov *Town* Slovakia 57 H10

Prespa, Lake Macedonia 49 F10

Presque Isle *Town* Maine, USA 21 B13

Pretoria *Capital* South Africa 69 H9

Préveza *Town* Greece 49 G10

Prichard *Town* Alabama, USA 22 G7

Prilep *Town* Macedonia 49 E11

Prince Edward Island *Province* Canada 29

Princess Elisabeth (Belgium) *RS* Antarctica 16 D5

Prince George *Town* British Columbia, Canada 28 H6

Pristina *Capital* Kosovo 49 D10

Prizren *Town* Kosovo 49 E10

Prome *Town* Burma (Myanmar) 78 F2

Providence *State capital* Rhode Island, USA 21 E13

Provo *Town* Utah, USA 27 C8

Pucallpa *Town* Peru 36 C6

Puducherry *Town* India 77 H9

Puebla *Town* Mexico 31 H10

Pueblo *Town* Colorado, USA 27 D10

Puerto Ayacucho *Town* Venezuela 35 G10

Puerto Montt *Town* Chile 36 H6

Puerto Princesa *Town* Philippines 79 G10

Puerto Rico *Dep. territory* USA 35 D11

Pula *Town* Croatia 48 C7

Pune (Poona) *Town* India 76 F7

Puno *Town* Peru 36 D6

Punta Alta *Town* Argentina 37 H8

Punta Arenas *Town* Chile 36 J7

Puntarenas *Town* Costa Rica 34 F5

Pusan *Town* South Korea 85 E13

Putrajaya *Capital* Malaysia 80 E2

Pyongyang *Capital* North Korea 85 D12

Pyrenees *Mountain range* France/ Spain 45 C11, 46 H7

Qamdo *Town* China 85 H8

Qatar *Country* 75

Qattara Depression Egypt 63 F12

Qena *Town* Egypt 63 G13

Qilian Shan *Mountain range* China 85 F8

Qingdao *Town* China 85 E12

Qom *Town* Iran 75 C8

Quebec *Province* Canada 29

Quebec *Province capital* Quebec, Canada 29 I12

Queen Elizabeth Islands Canada 17 F9

Queensland *State* Australia 91

Queenstown *Town* Australia 91 J11

Quelimane *Town* Mozambique 69 G10

Querétaro *Town* Mexico 31 G9

Quetta *Town* Pakistan 76 C7

Quezaltenango *Town* Guatemala 34 D4

Quibdó *Town* Colombia 34 G7

Quimper *Town* France 46 B5

Qui Nhon *Town* Vietnam 78 G7

Rabat *Capital* Morocco 62 D3

Radom *Town* Poland 57 F10

Ragusa *Town* Sicily, Italy 48 H7

Rainier, Mount Washington, USA 24 D4

Raipur *Town* India 77 F9

Rajshahi *Town* Bangladesh 77 E11

Raleigh *State capital* N Carolina, USA 23 C11

Rancagua *Town* Chile 36 G7

Randers *Town* Denmark 42 I6

Rapid City *Town* S Dakota, USA 25 G11

Rasht *Town* Iran 75 B8
Rat Islands Alaska, USA 25 C8
Ravenna *Town* Italy 48 C6
Rawalpindi *Town* Pakistan 77 B8
Reading *Town* England, UK
  41 H9
Reading *Town* Pennsylvania, USA
  21 G11
Recife *Town* Brazil 37 C12
Red *River* USA 22 G5
Red Deer *Town* Alberta, Canada
  28 H7
Redding *Town* California, USA 26 B4
Red Sea 63 G14, 67 B9, 74 G5
Regensburg *Town* Germany 51 H10
Reggio di Calabria *Town* Italy 49 H8
Reggio nell' Emilia *Town* Italy 48 C5
Regina *Province capital*
  Saskatchewan, Canada 29 I8
Reims *Town* France 47 C10
Rennes *Town* France 46 C7
Reno *Town* Nevada, USA 26 C5
Republic of Ireland *See Ireland,*
  Republic of
Republic of the Congo *See Congo,*
  Republic of
Resistencia *Town* Argentina 37 F8
Resita *Town* Romania 55 E8
Réunion *Dep. territory* France
  69 H14
Reus *Town* Spain 45 D12
Reutlingen *Town* Germany 51 I8
Reykjavik *Capital* Iceland 43 I11
Reynosa *Town* Mexico 31 E10
Rhine *River* Europe 50 F7, 52 E4
Rhode Island *State* USA 21
Rhódes *Town* Rhodes, Greece 49 I14
Rhodope Mountains Bulgaria 55 J10
Rhône *River* France 47 F10
Richmond *State capital* Virginia, USA
  23 B12
Richmond *Town* Kentucky, USA
  23 B9
Riga, Gulf of 58 F5
Ríga *Capital* Latvia 58 F5
Rijeka *Town* Croatia 48 C7
Rimini *Town* Italy 48 C6
Riobamba *Town* Ecuador 36 B5
Río Cuarto *Town* Argentina 37 G7
Rio de Janeiro *Town* Brazil 37 E10
Rio Gallegos *Town* Argentina 36 J7
Rio Grande *Town* Brazil 37 G9
Rivera *Town* Uruguay 37 F8
Riverside *Town* California, USA
  26 F5
Rivne *Town* Ukraine 58 G6
Riyadh *Capital* Saudi Arabia 74 F7
Roanoke *Town* Virginia, USA 23 B11
Rochester *Town* Minnesota, USA
  20 F4

Rochester *Town* New York, USA
  21 E10
Rockford *Town* Illinois, USA 20 G5
Rockhampton *Town* Australia
  91 E12
Rocky Mountains Canada/USA
  24 F7, 27 D9, 28 G6
Roeselare *Town* Belgium 50 E4
Romania *Country* 55
Rome *Capital* Italy 48 E6
Ronne Ice Shelf Antarctica 16 E3
Rosario *Town* Argentina 37 G8
Roseau *Capital* Dominica 35 D12
Ross Ice Shelf Antarctica 16 G4
Ross Sea 16 H4
Rostock *Town* Germany 51 B11
Rostov-na-Donu *Town* Russia 58 H7
Roswell *Town* New Mexico, USA
  27 G10
Rothera (UK) *RS* Antarctica 16 E1
Rotorua *Town* New Zealand
  93 C10
Rotterdam *Town* Netherlands 50 D5
Roubaix *Town* France 47 A10
Rouen *Town* France 47 B8
Rukwa, Lake Tanzania 67 I8
Ruse *Town* Bulgaria 55 G11
Rushmore, Mount S Dakota, USA
  25 H11
Russian Federation *Country* 59,86
Rwanda *Country* 66
Ryazan *Town* Russia 58 G7
Rybinsk *Town* Russia 58 F7
Rzeszow *Town* Poland 57 G11

Saarbrücken *Town* Germany 50 G7
Saba *Dep. territory* Netherlands
  35 D12
Sabac *Town* Serbia 49 C10
Sabah *Region* Malaysia 80 E5
Sabha *Town* Libya 63 F8
Sacramento *State capital* California,
  USA 26 C4
Safi *Town* Morocco 62 E2
Saginaw *Town* Michigan, USA 20 F7
Sagunto *Town* Spain 45 F11
Sahara Desert North Africa 62 H5,
  64 E7
Saiki *Town* Japan 82 I6
St. Augustine *Town* Florida, USA
  23 G11
St. Barthelémy *Dep. territory* France
  35 D12
St. Eustatius *Dep. territory*
  Netherlands 35 D12
St. Étienne *Town* France 47 F9
St. George's *Capital* Grenada 35 E12
St. George's Channel 40 G7
St. John *Town* New Brunswick,
  Canada 29 I13

St. John's *Capital* Antigua and
  Barbuda 35 D12
St. John's *Province capital*
  Newfoundland and Labrador,
  Canada 29 H14
St. Joseph *Town* Missouri, USA
  22 B4
St. Kitts and Nevis *Country* 35
St. Lawrence Island Alaska, USA
  25 B10
St. Louis *Town* Missouri, USA 22 B6
St. Louis *Town* Senegal 64 F3
St. Lucia *Country* 35
St. Malo *Town* France 46 B7
St. Martin/Sint Maarten
  Dep. territory France, Netherlands
  35 D12
St. Moritz *Town* Switzerland 52 G5
St. Nazaire *Town* France 46 C6
St. Paul *State capital* Minnesota,
  USA 20 E3
St. Petersburg *Town* Florida, USA
  23 H10
St. Petersburg *Town* Russia 58 E6
St. Pierre and Miquelon *Dep.*
  territory France 29 H14
St. Quentin *Town* France 47 B10
St. Vincent and the Grenadines
  Country 35
Sakai *Town* Japan 83 H8
Sakata *Town* Japan 83 E10
Salamanca *Town* Spain 44 D7
Salem *State capital* Oregon, USA
  24 F3
Salerno *Town* Italy 48 F7
Salina *Town* Kansas, USA 27 D13
Salinas *Town* California, USA 26 D4
Salta *Town* Argentina 36 E7
Saltillo *Town* Mexico 31 E8
Salt Lake City *State capital* Utah,
  USA 27 C8
Salto *Town* Uruguay 37 F8
Salvador *Town* Brazil 37 D11
Salzburg *Town* Austria 40 F9
Samara *Town* Russia 59 G9
Samarkand *Town* Uzbekistan
  86 J3
Samoa *Country* 93 I13
Samsun *Town* Turkey 73 C10
Sanaa *Capital* Yemen 74 I7
Sanae IV (South Africa) *RS*
  Antarctica 16 C4
San Angelo *Town* Texas, USA
  27 H11
San Antonio *Town* Texas, USA
  27 I12
San Bernardino *Town* California,
  USA 26 F5
San Cristóbal *Town* Venezuela
  35 G9

Sancti Spíritus *Town* Cuba 34 B7
Sandakan *Town* Malaysia 80 E6
Sand Hills Nebraska, USA 25 H12
San Diego *Town* California, USA
  26 F5
San Francisco *Town* California, USA
  26 C4
San Francisco de Macorís *Town*
  Dominican Republic 35 C10
San José *Capital* Costa Rica 34 F5
San Jose *Town* California, USA
  26 D4
San Juan *Town* Argentina 36 F7
Sankt Pölten *Town* Austria 40 E12
San Luis Potosí *Town* Mexico 31 F9
San Marino *Capital* San Marino
  48 D6
San Marino *Country* 48
San Miguel de Tucumán *Town*
  Argentina 36 F7
San Miguelito *Town* Panama 34 F7
San Pedro Sula *Town* Honduras
  34 D5
San Remo *Town* Italy 48 C4
San Salvador *Capital* El Salvador
  34 D4
San Salvador de Jujuy *Town*
  Argentina 36 E7
Santa Barbara *Town* California, USA
  26 E5
Santa Clara *Town* Cuba 34 B7
Santa Cruz *Town* Bolivia 36 D7
Santa Fe *State capital* New Mexico,
  USA 27 E10
Santa Fe *Town* Argentina 37 G8
Santa Marta *Town* Colombia 35 F8
Santander *Town* Spain 45 B8
Santarém *Town* Brazil 37 B9
Santa Rosa *Town* California, USA
  26 C4
Santiago *Capital* Chile 36 G7
Santiago *Town* Dominican Republic
  35 C10
Santiago de Cuba *Town* Cuba 35 C8
Santo Domingo *Capital* Dominican
  Republic 35 D10
Santos *Town* Brazil 37 E10
São Luis *Town* Brazil 37 B10
São Paulo *Town* Brazil 37 E10
São Tomé *Capital* São Tomé and
  Príncipe 68 C4
São Tomé and Príncipe *Country* 68
Sapporo *Town* Japan 83 B10
Sarajevo *Capital* Bosnia and Herz.
  49 D9
Saratov *Town* Russia 59 G8
Sarawak Malaysia 80 F4
Sardinia *Island* Italy 48 F4
Sarh *Town* Chad 65 H13
Sariwon *Town* North Korea 85 D12

Sasebo *Town* Japan 82 H5

Saskatchewan *Province* Canada 29

Saskatoon *Town* Saskatchewan, Canada 29 H8

Sassari *Town* Sardinia, Italy 48 F4

Satu Mare *Town* Romania 55 C8

Saudi Arabia *Country* 74

Savannah *Town* Georgia, USA 23 F11

Savona *Town* Italy 48 C4

Saynshand *Town* Mongolia 85 D10

Scheldt *River* Belgium 50 E4

Schenectady *Town* New York, USA 21 E12

Schwaz *Town* Austria 40 F8

Schwerin *Town* Germany 51 C10

Scotland *Country* UK 41

Scott Base (New Zealand) *RS* Antarctica 16 G4

Scranton *Town* Pennsylvania, USA 21 F11

Seattle *Town* Washington, USA 24 D4

Ségou *Town* Mali 64 G6

Segovia *Town* Spain 45 D8

Seine *River* France 47 B9

Sejong *Town* South Korea 85 E13

Sekondi-Takoradi *Town* Ghana 64 I7

Semarang *Town* Indonesia 80 H4

Sendai *Town* Japan 83 E10

Senegal *Country* 64

Senegal *River* Senegal 64 F4

Seoul *Capital* South Korea 85 E13

Serbia *Country* 49

Serov *Town* Russia 86 G3

Sète *Town* France 47 H9

Setúbal *Town* Portugal 44 G5

Sevastopol *Town* Crimea, Ukraine 58 I7

Severn *River* England, UK 41 H9

Severnaya Zemlya Russia 17 F13, 86 C6

Seville *Town* Spain 44 H7

Seychelles *Country* 69

Sfax *Town* Tunisia 62 D7

Shanghai *Town* China 85 F12

Shannon *River* Republic of Ireland 40 G6

Sheberghan *Town* Afghanistan 76 A7

Sheffield *Town* England, UK 41 G9

Shenyang *Town* China 85 D12

Sherbrooke *Town* Quebec, Canada 29 I12

's-Hertogenbosch *Town* Netherlands 50 D6

Shetland Islands Scotland, UK 41 A9

Shimonoseki *Town* Japan 82 H5

Shinyanga *Town* Tanzania 67 H8

Shiraz *Town* Iran 75 D9

Shizuoka *Town* Japan 83 G9

Shkodër *Town* Albania 49 E10

Showa (Japan) *RS* Antarctica 16 D6

Shreveport *Town* Louisiana, USA 22 F4

Shumen *Town* Bulgaria 55 H12

Sibenik *Town* Croatia 49 D8

Siberia Russia 86 F7

Sibiu *Town* Romania 55 E10

Sicily *Island* Italy 48 H7

Sidi Bel Abbès *Town* Algeria 62 D5

Siegen *Town* Germany 51 F8

Siem Reap *Town* Cambodia 78 G5

Siena *Town* Italy 48 D6

Sierra de Gredos *Mountain range* Spain 44 E7

Sierra Leone *Country* 64

Sierra Nevada *Mountain range* California, USA 26 C5

Sierra Nevada *Mountain range* Spain 45 H9

Signy (UK) *RS* Antarctica 16 C1

Silver City *Town* New Mexico, USA 27 G9

Sincelejo *Town* Colombia 35 F8

Singapore *Capital* Singapore 80 F2

Singapore *Country* 80

Sinuiju *Town* North Korea 85 D12

Sioux City *Town* Iowa, USA 20 G2

Sioux Falls *Town* S Dakota, USA 25 H14

Siracusa *Town* Sicily, Italy 48 H7

Sittwe *Town* Burma (Myanmar) 78 E1

Sivas *Town* Turkey 73 D10

Skagerrak *Sea* Norway 42 H6

Skellefteå *Town* Sweden 43 D9

Skopje *Capital* Macedonia 49 E11

Slavonski Brod *Town* Croatia 49 C9

Sligo *Town* Republic of Ireland 40 F6

Sliven *Town* Bulgaria 55 H12

Slovakia *Country* 57

Slovenia *Country* 48

Smederevo *Town* Serbia 49 C10

Smolensk *Town* Russia 58 F6

Snake *River* Idaho/Oregon, USA 24 H6

Snowdon *Mountain* Wales, UK 41 G8

Socotra *Island* Yemen 75 J10

Søderhamn *Town* Sweden 43 F8

Södertälje *Town* Sweden 43 G8

Sofia *Capital* Bulgaria 55 I9

Soledad *Town* Colombia 35 F8

Solingen *Town* Germany 50 E7

Solomon Islands *Country* 93 I12

Solomon Sea 81 G13

Somalia *Country* 67

Songea *Town* Tanzania 67 J9

Songkhla *Town* Thailand 78 J4

Soria *Town* Spain 45 C9

Sorong *Town* Indonesia 81 F9

Sousse *Town* Tunisia 62 D7

South Africa *Country* 68

Southampton *Town* England, UK 41 I9

Southampton Island Nunavut, Canada 29 F10

South Australia *State* Australia 91

South Bend *Town* Indiana, USA 20 G6

South Carolina *State* USA 23

South China Sea 79 G8, 85 J12

South Dakota *State* USA 25

Southern Ocean 16, 90

South Georgia *Dep. territory* UK 37 J10

South Island New Zealand 92

South Korea *See* Korea, South

South Orkney Islands Antarctica 16 C1

South Ossetia *State* Georgia 59 I8

South Sudan *Country* 66

Soweto *Town* South Africa 69 I8

Spain *Country* 44

Spanish Town *Town* Jamaica 35 D8

Spartanburg *Town* S Carolina, USA 23 D10

Split *Town* Croatia 49 D8

Spokane *Town* Washington, USA 24 D5

Springfield *State capital* Illinois, USA 20 I5

Springfield *Town* Massachusetts, USA 21 E12

Springfield *Town* Missouri, USA 22 C4

Srebrenica *Town* Bosnia and Herz. 49 C9

Sri Lanka *Country* 77

Stamford *Town* Connecticut, USA 21 F12

Stara Zagora *Town* Bulgaria 55 I11

Stavanger *Town* Norway 42 G5

Stavropol *Town* Russia 59 I8

Stewart Island New Zealand 92 J6

Stockholm *Capital* Sweden 43 G8

Stockton *Town* California, USA 26 C4

Stockton Plateau Texas, USA 27 H10

Stoke-on-Trent *Town* England, UK 41 G9

Strasbourg *Town* France 47 D12

Stuttgart *Town* Germany 51 H8

Subotica *Town* Serbia 49 B10

Suceava *Town* Romania 55 C11

Sucre *Capital* Bolivia 36 E7

Sudan *Country* 66

Sudbury *Town* Ontario, Canada 29 I11

Suez, Gulf of 63 F13

Suez *Town* Egypt 63 F13

Sühbaatar *Town* Mongolia 85 C9

Sukkur *Town* Pakistan 76 C7

Sulu Archipelago Philippines 79 I10

Sulu Sea 79 H10

Sumatra *Island* Indonesia 80 F2

Sunderland *Town* England, UK 41 F9

Sundsvall *Town* Sweden 43 F8

Sunnyvale *Town* California, USA 26 D4

Superior, Lake USA 20 C5

Sur *Town* Oman 75 F11

Surabaya *Town* Indonesia 80 H4

Surakarta *Town* Indonesia 80 H4

Surat *Town* India 76 E7

Surgut *Town* Russia 86 G4

Suriname *Country* 35

Surt *Town* Libya 63 E9

Suwalki *Town* Poland 57 B11

Svalbard *Dep. territory* Norway 17 H12

Swansea *Town* Wales, UK 41 H8

Sweden *Country* 43

Swindon *Town* England, UK 41 H9

Switzerland *Country* 52

Sydney *Town* Australia 91 H12

Syktyvkar *Town* Russia 59 E9

Sylhet *Town* Bangladesh 77 E12

Syracuse *Town* New York, USA 21 E11

Syria *Country* 73

Syrian Desert Syria 73 G11, 74 C6

Szczecin *Town* Poland 56 C5

Szeged *Town* Hungary 54 D6

Székesfehérvár *Town* Hungary 54 D5

Szombathely *Town* Hungary 54 D4

Tabora *Town* Tanzania 67 H8

Tabriz *Town* Iran 74 B7

Tacoma *Town* Washington, USA 24 D3

Taegu *Town* South Korea 85 E13

Taejon *Town* South Korea 85 E13

Taguatinga *Town* Brazil 37 D9

Taipei *Capital* Taiwan 85 H13

Taiwan *Country* 85

Taiyuan *Town* China 85 E10

Ta'izz *Town* Yemen 74 I7

Tajikistan *Country* 86

Takasaki *Town* Japan 83 F9

Taklimakan Desert China 84 F5

Talcahuano *Town* Chile 36 G6

Taldyqorgan *Town* Kazakhstan 86 I4

Tallahassee *State capital* Florida, USA 23 G9

Tallinn *Capital* Estonia 58 E5

Tamale *Town* Ghana 64 H7

Tamanrasset *Town* Algeria 62 H6

Tampa *Town* Florida, USA 23 H10

Tampere *Town* Finland 43 F9

Tampico *Town* Mexico 31 G10

Tamworth *Town* Australia 91 G12

Tanami Desert Australia 91 D8

Tanga *Town* Tanzania 67 H9

Tanganyika, Lake DRC/Tanzania 66 I7, 69 E9

Tangier *Town* Morocco 62 D3

Tanzania *Country* 67

Taranto *Town* Italy 49 F8

Tarbes *Town* France 46 G7

Târgu Mures *Town* Romania 55 D10

Tarija *Town* Bolivia 36 E7

Tarim Basin China 84 E6

Tarnow *Town* Poland 57 G10

Tarragona *Town* Spain 45 D12

Tarsus *Town* Turkey 73 E9

Tartu *Town* Estonia 58 F6

Tartus *Town* Syria 73 G10

Tashkent *Capital* Uzbekistan 86 I3

Tasmania *State* Australia 91

Tasman Sea 91 I12, 92 F6

Tatra Mountains Slovakia 57 H9

Taupo, Lake New Zealand 93 D10

Tauranga *Town* New Zealand 93 C10

Taurus Mountains Turkey 73 E8

Tavoy *Town* Burma (Myanmar) 78 G3

Tbilisi *Capital* Georgia 59 I8

Tegucigalpa *Capital* Honduras 34 D5

Tehran *Capital* Iran 75 C9

Tehuantepec, Gulf of 31 I11

Tekirdag *Town* Turkey 72 B6

Tel Aviv *Town* Israel 73 H9

Temuco *Town* Chile 36 H6

Tennessee *River* Alabama/ Tennessee, USA 23 D8

Tennessee *State* USA 23

Tepic *Town* Mexico 30 G7

Teramo *Town* Italy 48 D7

Teresina *Town* Brazil 37 B10

Terni *Town* Italy 48 D6

Terrasa *Town* Spain 45 C12

Terre Haute *Town* Indiana, USA 20 H6

Teruel *Town* Spain 45 E10

Tete *Town* Mozambique 69 G10

Tétouan *Town* Morocco 62 D3

Texas *State* USA 27

Thailand, Gulf of 78 H4

Thailand *Country* 78

Thai Nguyen *Town* Vietnam 78 E5

Thames *River* England, UK 41 H10

Thanh Hoa *Town* Vietnam 78 E5

The Hague *Capital* Netherlands 50 D5

Thessaloníki *Town* Greece 49 F11

Thimphu *Capital* Bhutan 77 D11

Thiruvananthapuram (Trivandrum) *Town* India 77 I8

Thun *Town* Switzerland 52 G3

Thunder Bay *Town* Ontario, Canada 29 I10

Tianjin *Town* China 85 E11

Tibesti Mountains Chad 65 E13

Tibet China 84 G6

Tibet, Plateau of China 84 G7

Tigris *River* Iraq 74 C7

Tijuana *Town* Mexico 30 B3

Tilburg *Town* Netherlands 50 E6

Timaru *Town* New Zealand 92 H7

Timisoara *Town* Romania 54 E7

Tindouf *Town* Algeria 62 F2

Tiranë *Capital* Albania 49 F10

Tiraspol *Town* Moldova 58 H6

Tiruchchirappalli *Town* India 77 I8

Tisza *River* Central Europe 54 D7

Titicaca, Lake Peru 36 D6

Tocantins *River* Brazil 37 C10

Togo *Country* 65

Tokelau *Dep. territory* New Zealand 93 I13

Tokushima *Town* Japan 82 H7

Tokyo *Capital* Japan 83 G10

Toledo *Town* Ohio, USA 21 G8

Toledo *Town* Spain 45 E8

Toluca *Town* Mexico 31 H9

Tolyatti *Town* Russia 59 G9

Tomakomai *Town* Japan 83 C10

Tombouctou *Town* Mali 64 F7

Tomsk *Town* Russia 86 G5

Tonga *Country* 93 I13

Tonkin, Gulf of 78 E5, 85 J10

Tonopah *Town* Nevada, USA 26 D6

Toowoomba *Town* Australia 91 F13

Topeka *State capital* Kansas, USA 27 D13

Toronto *Province capital* Ontario, Canada 29 J11

Torun *Town* Poland 57 D8

Tottori *Town* Japan 82 G7

Touba *Town* Senegal 64 F3

Toubkal, Mount Morocco 63 E2

Toulon *Town* France 47 H10

Toulouse *Town* France 46 G7

Tournai *Town* Belgium 50 E4

Tours *Town* France 47 D8

Townsville *Town* Australia 91 D11

Toyama *Town* Japan 83 F8

Toyota *Town* Japan 83 G8

Trabzon *Town* Turkey 73 C12

Trans-Dniester *State* Moldova 58 H6

Transylvanian Alps Romania 55 E9

Trapani *Town* Sicily, Italy 48 H6

Trencin *Town* Slovakia 56 I7

Trent *River* England, UK 41 G10

Trento *Town* Italy 48 B6

Trenton *State capital* New Jersey, USA 21 G12

Treviso *Town* Italy 48 B6

Trier *Town* Germany 50 G6

Trieste *Town* Italy 48 B7

Trincomalee *Town* Sri Lanka 77 I9

Trinidad and Tobago *Country* 35

Tripoli *Capital* Libya 63 E8

Tripoli *Town* Lebanon 73 G10

Trivandrum *See* Thiruvananthapuram

Trnava *Town* Slovakia 56 I7

Trois-Rivières *Town* Quebec, Canada 29 I12

Troll (Norway) *RS* Antarctica 16 C4

Tromsø *Town* Norway 43 B8

Trondheim *Town* Norway 42 E6

Troy *Town* New York, USA 21 E12

Troyes *Town* France 47 C10

Trujillo *Town* Peru 36 C5

Tshikapa *Town* DRC 68 E7

Tubruq *Town* Libya 63 E11

Tucson *Town* Arizona, USA 27 G8

Tuguegarao *Town* Philippines 79 E10

Tula *Town* Russia 58 G7

Tulcea *Town* Romania 55 E13

Tulsa *Town* Oklahoma, USA 27 E13

Tunis *Capital* Tunisia 62 D7

Tunisia *Country* 62

Tunja *Town* Colombia 35 G8

Turin *Town* Italy 48 B4

Turkana, Lake Kenya 67 F9

Turkey *Country* 73

Turkmenabat *Town* Turkmenistan 86 J3

Turkmenistan *Country* 86

Turks and Caicos Islands *Dep. territory* UK 35 B9

Turku *Town* Finland 43 G9

Tuvalu *Country* 93 I12

Tuxtla Gutiérrez *Town* Mexico 31 I12

Tuz, Lake Turkey 73 D8

Tuzla *Town* Bosnia and Herz. 49 C9

Tver *Town* Russia 58 F7

Twin Falls *Town* Idaho, USA 24 H6

Tyler *Town* Texas, USA 27 G14

Tyrrhenian Sea 48 G6

Uberaba *Town* Brazil 37 E10

Uberlândia *Town* Brazil 37 D10

Ubon Ratchathani *Town* Thailand 78 G5

Uchiura Bay Japan 83 C10

Udaipur *Town* India 77 E8

Udine *Town* Italy 48 B7

Udon Thani *Town* Thailand 78 F4

Uele *River* DRC 69 C9

Ufa *Town* Russia 59 G10

Uganda *Country* 67

Ukhta *Town* Russia 59 D9

Ukraine *Country* 58

Ulaanbaatar *Capital* Mongolia 85 C9

Ulaangom *Town* Mongolia 84 C7

Ulan-Ude *Town* Russia 86 H7

Ulm *Town* Germany 51 I9

Umeå *Town* Sweden 43 E8

Umtata *Town* South Africa 69 J8

Ungava Peninsula Quebec, Canada 29 F11

United Arab Emirates (UAE) *Country* 75

Uppsala *Town* Sweden 43 G8

Ural Mountains Russia 59 F10, 86 G2

Uruguay *Country* 37

Urumqi *Town* China 84 D6

Usak *Town* Turkey 72 D6

Ushuaia *Town* Argentina 36 J7

Usol'ye-Sibirskoye *Town* Russia 86 H6

Ust'Ilimsk *Town* Russia 86 G6

Ústí nad Labem *Town* Czech Republic 56 G5

Ustyurt Plateau Uzbekistan 86 I2

Utah *State* USA 27

Utica *Town* New York, USA 21 E11

Utrecht *Town* Netherlands 50 D6

Utsunomiya *Town* Japan 83 F10

Uzbekistan *Country* 86

Vaal *River* South Africa 69 I9

Vaasa *Town* Finland 43 E9

Vadodara *Town* India 76 E7

Vadsø *Town* Norway 43 A10

Vaduz *Capital* Liechtenstein 52 F5

Valdivia *Town* Chile 36 H6

Valdosta *Town* Georgia, USA 23 F10

Valence *Town* France 47 G10

Valencia, Gulf of 45 F11

Valencia *Town* Spain 45 F11

Valencia *Town* Venezuela 35 F10

Valladolid *Town* Spain 45 D8

Valletta *Capital* Malta 48 I7

Valparaíso *Capital* Chile 36 G6

Van *Town* Turkey 73 D13

Vancouver *Town* British Columbia, Canada 28 I6

Vancouver Island British Columbia, Canada 28 H5

Vantaa *Town* Finland 43 G10

Vanuatu *Country* 93 I12

Varanasi *Town* India 77 E10

Varna *Town* Bulgaria 55 H13

Västerås *Town* Sweden 43 G8

Vatican City *Country* 48

Växjö *Town* Sweden 42 I7

Venezuela *Country* 35

Venice, Gulf of 48 C7

Venice *Town* Italy 48 C6

Veracruz *Town* Mexico 31 H10

Verkhoyanskiy Mountains Russia 87 F9

Vermont *State* USA 21

Verona *Town* Italy 48 B6

Versailles *Town* France 47 C9

Verviers *Town* Belgium 50 F6

Viareggio *Town* Italy 48 D5

Vicenza *Town* Italy 48 B6

Victoria, Lake Kenya/Tanzania/ Uganda 67 G8

Victoria *Province capital* British Columbia, Canada 28 I6

Victoria *State* Australia 91

Victoria *Capital* Seychelles 69 D14

Victoria Falls Zimbabwe 69 G8

Victoria Island Canada 17 E8, 29 E8

Vidin *Town* Bulgaria 55 G9

Vienna *Capital* Austria 40 E13

Vientiane *Capital* Laos 78 F4

Vietnam *Country* 78

Vigo *Town* Spain 44 C5

Vijayawada *Town* India 77 G9

Villach *Town* Austria 40 H10

Villahermosa *Town* Mexico 31 H12

Villavicencio *Town* Colombia 35 H8

Vilnius *Capital* Lithuania 58 G5

Vina del Mar *Town* Chile 36 G6

Vineland *Town* New Jersey, USA 21 G12

Vinh *Town* Vietnam 78 F5

Virginia *State* USA 23

Virginia Beach *Town* Virginia, USA 23 B12

Virgin Islands *Dep. territory* UK 35 D11

Virgin Islands *Dep. territory* USA 35 D11

Vishakhapatnam *Town* India 77 G10

Vitoria *Town* Brazil 37 E11

Vitória-Gasteiz *Town* Spain 45 B9

Vitsyebsk *Town* Belarus 58 F6

Vladikavkaz *Town* Russia 59 I8

Vladivostok *Town* Russia 87 I9

Vlissingen *Town* Netherlands 50 D5

Vlorë *Town* Albania 49 F10

Volga *River* Russia 59 F8

Volgograd *Town* Russia 59 H8

Vólos *Town* Greece 49 G11

Volta, Lake Ghana 64 I7

Vorkuta *Town* Russia 59 C11, 86 E3

Voronezh *Town* Russia 58 G7

Vosges Mountains France 47 D11

Voss *Town* Norway 42 F5

Vostok (Russian Federation) *RS* Antarctica 16 F5

Vratsa *Town* Bulgaria 55 H9

Vyborg *Town* Russia 58 E6

Waal *River* Netherlands 50 D6

Waco *Town* Texas, USA 27 H13

Waddenzee *Sea* Netherlands 50 B7

Wadi Halfa *Town* Sudan 66 A7

Wad Medani *Town* Sudan 67 C8

Wagga Wagga *Town* Australia 91 H11

Wakayama *Town* Japan 82 H7

Wakkanai *Town* Japan 83 A10

Walbrzych *Town* Poland 56 F6

Wales *Country* UK 41

Wallis and Futuna *Dep. territory* France 93 I13

Walvis Bay *Town* Namibia 68 H6

Wandel Sea 17 G11

Warren *Town* Michigan, USA 20 F8

Warsaw *Capital* Poland 57 E10

Washington, Mount USA 21 D12

Washington *State* USA 24

Washington D.C. *Capital* USA 21 H11

Waterford *Town* Republic of Ireland 40 H6

Waterloo *Town* Iowa, USA 20 G4

Watertown *Town* New York, USA 21 E10

Wau *Town* South Sudan 66 E7

Weddell Sea 16 D2

Weimar *Town* Germany 51 F10

Wellington *Capital* New Zealand 93 F9

Wels *Town* Austria 40 E10

Wenzhou *Town* China 85 G12

West Bank *Disputed region* Near East 73 H9

Western Australia *State* Australia 90

Western Ghats *Mountain range* India 76 F7

Western Sahara *Territory* 64

West Palm Beach *Town* Florida, USA 23 I12

West Virginia *State* USA 21

Whitehorse *Province capital* Yukon Territory, Canada 28 F5

White Nile *River* Sudan 67 D8

White Sea 58 D7

Whitney, Mount California, USA 26 D5

Wichita *Town* Kansas, USA 27 E13

Wichita Falls *Town* Texas, USA 27 F12

Wieliczka *Town* Poland 57 G9

Wiener Neustadt *Town* Austria 40 F13

Wiesbaden *Town* Germany 51 G8

Wilhelmshaven *Town* Germany 51 C8

Wilkes Land Antarctica 16 G6

Williston *Town* N Dakota, USA 25 E11

Wilmington *Town* Delaware, USA 21 G11

Wilmington *Town* N Carolina, USA 23 D12

Windhoek *Capital* Namibia 68 H7

Windsor *Town* Ontario, Canada 29 J11

Winnipeg *Province capital* Manitoba, Canada 29 I9

Winston-Salem *Town* N Carolina, USA 23 C10

Winterthur *Town* Switzerland 52 F4

Wisconsin *State* USA 20

Wloclawek *Town* Poland 57 D8

Wolfsberg *Town* Austria 40 H11

Wolfsburg *Town* Germany 51 D10

Wollongong *Town* Australia 91 H12

Wonsan *Town* North Korea 85 D13

Worcester *Town* Massachusetts, USA 21 E13

Worms *Town* Germany 51 G8

Wroclaw *Town* Poland 56 F7

Wuhan *Town* China 85 G11

Wuppertal *Town* Germany 50 E7

Würzburg *Town* Germany 51 G9

Wyoming *State* USA 25

Xiamen *Town* China 85 H12

Xi'an *Town* China 85 F10

Xining *Town* China 85 F8

Xuzhou *Town* China 85 F11

Yakima *Town* Washington, USA 24 E4

Yakutsk *Town* Russia 87 F9

Yambol *Town* Bulgaria 55 I12

Yamoussoukro *Capital* Côte d'Ivoire 64 I6

Yanbu *Town* Saudi Arabia 74 F5

Yangon (Rangoon) *Town* Burma (Myanmar) 78 G2

Yantai *Town* China 85 E12

Yaoundé *Capital* Cameroon 68 C5

Yaroslavl *Town* Russia 58 F7

Yazd *Town* Iran 75 D9

Yekaterinburg *Town* Russia 86 G3

Yellowknife *Province capital* Northwest Territories, Canada 28 F7

Yellow Sea 85 E12

Yemen *Country* 75

Yenisey *River* Russia 86 F5

Yerevan *Capital* Armenia 59 J8

Yinchuan *Town* China 85 E9

Yining *Town* China 84 D5

Yokohama *Town* Japan 83 G10

Yonago *Town* Japan 82 G7

York *Town* England, UK 41 F9

Youngstown *Town* Ohio, USA 21 G9

Yucatán Peninsula Mexico 31 G13

Yukon *River* Alaska, USA 25 B10

Yukon Territory *Province* Canada 28

Yuma *Town* Arizona, USA 26 G6

Yumen *Town* China 85 E8

Yuzhno-Sakhalinsk *Town* Russia 87 I10

Zadar *Town* Croatia 49 D8

Zagreb *Capital* Croatia 49 B8

Zagros Mountains Iran 75 C8

Zahedan *Town* Iran 75 D11

Zajecar *Town* Serbia 49 D11

Zambezi *River* Southern Africa 69 G8

Zambia *Country* 69

Zamboanga *Town* Philippines 79 H11

Zamora *Town* Spain 44 D7

Zanzibar *Town* Tanzania 67 I9

Zanzibar Island Tanzania 67 I10

Zaporizhzhya *Town* Ukraine 58 H7

Zaria *Town* Nigeria 65 H10

Zeebrugge *Town* Belgium 50 E4

Zenica *Town* Bosnia and Herz. 49 C9

Zhangjiakou *Town* China 85 E11

Zhanjiang *Town* China 85 I11

Zhengzhou *Town* China 85 F11

Zhezkazgan *Town* Kazakhstan 86 I3

Zhongshan (China) *RS* Antarctica 16 E7

Zibo *Town* China 85 E11

Zielona Gora *Town* Poland 56 E6

Zilina *Town* Slovakia 57 H8

Zimbabwe *Country* 69

Zinder *Town* Niger 65 G10

Zlin *Town* Czech Republic 56 H7

Zomba *Town* Malawi 69 F10

Zonguldak *Town* Turkey 73 B8

Zrenjanin *Town* Serbia 49 C10

Zug *Town* Switzerland 52 F4

Zürich *Town* Switzerland 52 F4

Zwettl Stadt *Town* Austria 40 D12

Zwickau *Town* Germany 51 F11

Zwolle *Town* Netherlands 50 C7

Index

Acknowledgements

Cover artwork by Collaborate

Map Artworker Julian Baker (J B Illustrations)

Mountain High Maps® Copyright © 1993 Digital Wisdom, Inc.

The publishers would like to thank Richard Burgess for his contribution to this book

All other artworks are from the Miles Kelly Artwork Bank

The publishers would like to thank the following source for the use of their photographs:

Cover © Globe Williams Noble/Dreamstime.com
Fotolia.com 10(b) Andrey Mirzoyants, Jean Luc Bohin, Giovanni Catalani, Kárpáti Gábor, Matt Ireland; 20 David Ruderman; 22 Daren Whitaker; 25 Sascha Burkard; 27 Tomasz Kawka; 28 Melissa Schalke; 29 Roman Krochuk; 30 Beatrice Preve; 31(t) Lein De Leon; 34 Françoise Bro; 35 pixphoto; 36(t) urbanhearts; 41(b) C J Photography; 43 Marco Regalia; 44 Hugues Argence; 48 Dubravko Grakalic; 50 Jarno Gonzalez/Fotolia.com; 51 Philip Lange; 52(t) Renato Francia; 54(b) Jozsef Szasz-fabian; 56(b) Bartlomiej Kwieciszewski; 57 Martin Džumela; 58(b) Salazkin Vladimir; 59 Jacek Malipan; 65(t) Natasha Owen; 74(t) Richard Connors, (b) MaxFX; 79(c) Dmitry Ersler; 80 Stuart Taylor; 81(b) TAOLMOR/; 83(t) Anna Cseresnjes; 87(b) NFive; 91 Flavia Bottazzini; 92(b) Rico Leffanta; 93 Adam Booth
Shutterstock.com 27 somchaij/Shutterstock; 29 Roman Krochuk/Shutterstock; 36(b) Mark Schwettmann; 41(t) ShaunWilkinson; 73(t) Nickolay Vinokurov; 74(b) Zurijeta; 75 S-S; 76(t) turtix; 83(b) SIHASAKPRACHUM; 84(b) ESB Professional; 90 totajla

All other photographs are from: Corel, digitalSTOCK, digitalvision, istock.com, John Foxx, PhotoAlto, PhotoDisc, PhotoEssentials, PhotoPro, Stockbyte

Every effort has been made to acknowledge the source and copyright holder of each picture.
Miles Kelly Publishing apologizes for any unintentional errors or omissions.